Tom Noble joined the *Age* in 1982 as a cadet reporter. He worked as chief police reporter until he left in 1987 to complete a degree.
In 1989 his first book, *Untold Violence: crime in Melbourne today*, a bestseller, was published. He now works as a freelance journalist.

WALSH STREET AND ENVIRONS

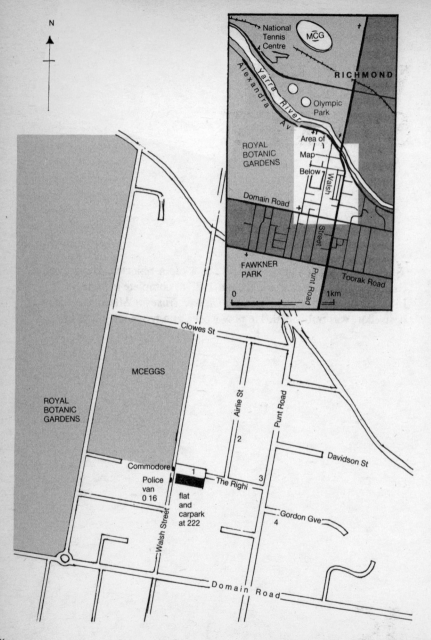

Key:

1 Residents hear footsteps running behind flats after shots are fired

2 Two men seen running to a sedan that drives off

3 Two men seen at corner after shooting, and a panel van picked up at least one moments later and headed north

4 The flat in Gordon Grove the Crown alleged was the headquarters for the executions

WALSH STREET

Tom Noble

JOHN KERR

First published 1991
by John Kerr Pty Ltd
117 Swan Street
Richmond 3121
Telephone (03) 427 1544
Facsimile (03) 427 9050

Distributed to bookshops and newsagents by Tower Books in Victoria, New South Wales, Western Australia and Tasmania; Herron Books in Queensland; Bookwise in South Australia; and David Bateman Ltd and Fiesta Products in New Zealand.
Cover photography Maria Foster
Typeset in 10/12 Plantin by Bookset Pty Ltd, Melbourne
Printed and bound by The Book Printer, Maryborough, Victoria

National Library of Australia cataloguing-in-publication data:

Noble, Tom, 1964– .
  Walsh Street.

  Includes index.
  ISBN 0 9588004 5 6.
  1. Police murders — murders — Victoria — Melbourne — Case studies.
  I. Title.

364.1523099451

Contents

The People

Abdallah, Gary: Walsh Street suspect, shot dead by police
Albanis, Theo: car thief
Alexandridis, Emmanuel: Walsh Street suspect
Allen, Dennis: son of Kath Pettingill, deceased
Angwin, Christine: a girlfriend of Abdallah
Bowles, Allen: police prosecutor
Brooks, Vicki, *nee* Ryan: Kath Pettingill's daughter, mother of Jason Ryan, protected Crown witness
Butts, Peter: armed robbery squad detective
Cameron, Bill: Kim's father
Cameron, Kim: Houghton's girlfriend
Cole, Brendon: homicide squad chief
Eyre, Damian: Walsh Street murder victim
Faure, Sandra: Jensen's girlfriend
Farrell, Anthony: acquitted of Walsh Street murders
Flannery, Chris: hitman, deceased
Flatman, Geoff: defence barrister
Fraser, Andrew: solicitor
Gouroff, Victor: deceased
Hall, Michael: burglar
Hefti, Dominik: Aramaguard security guard, deceased
Houghton, Jedd: Walsh Street suspect, shot dead by police
Jensen, Graeme: armed robber, shot dead by police
Kenny, Anton: deceased
McEvoy, Peter: acquitted of Walsh Street murders

McLaren, Col:	TyEyre detective
Martin, Harold:	protected Crown witness
Morrissey, Jim:	Crown prosecutor
Mullett, Paul:	armed robbery squad detective
Nikakis, Charlie:	solicitor
Noonan, John:	TyEyre detective
O'Brien, Jim:	TyEyre detective
Parkinson, Sue:	Farrell's mother
Pasche, Greg:	deceased
Peirce, Victor:	son of Kath Pettingill, acquitted of Walsh Street murders
Peirce, Wendy:	wife of Victor
Pettingill, Jamie:	son of Kath Pettingill, deceased
Pettingill, Kath:	Melbourne identity
Pettingill, Trevor:	son of Kath Pettingill, acquitted of Walsh Street murders
Rice, Belinda:	Farrell's girlfriend
Richards, Shane:	protected Crown witness
Rogerson, Roger:	former Sydney detective
Ross, David:	defence barrister
Rountree, Lindsay:	protected Crown witness
Ryan, Col:	TyEyre detective
Ryan, Jason:	son of Vicki Brooks, protected Crown witness
Saliba, Stephen:	car thief
'Smith':	*pseud.* suspected armed robber
Sprague, David:	TyEyre detective
Stanhope, Wayne:	deceased
Tynan, Steven:	Walsh Street murder victim
Valastro, Frank:	armed robber, shot dead by police
Warner, Michael:	protected Crown witness
Wagnegg, Helga:	deceased
Williams, Alan:	heroin dealer

Author's Note

Much of the material in this book is based on transcripts from the committal hearings and the trial of the Walsh Street accused, from material presented to Coroner Hal Hallenstein's police shootings inquiry and from transcripts of other court cases. I am grateful to those who agreed to interviews and who supplied material for this book.

1
Walsh Street

'For God's sake, get an ambulance'

Policeman over police radio on
finding two wounded colleagues

About 3.30 pm on Tuesday 11 October 1988, a man named Graeme
Jensen was cut down with a shotgun blast in Melbourne's outer eastern
suburbs. He died instantly.

Seven hours later, two young men arrived for work at the large and
modern Prahran police station, the district headquarters for most of
Melbourne's inner-city suburbs south of the city, covering suburbs
including Prahran, Toorak, South Yarra, Richmond and St Kilda. The
men, Steven Tynan and Damian Eyre, changed into their police uni-
forms, signed out their handguns from the desk sergeant, checked with
the district collator on what was happening in the area, then walked to a
police divisional van in the station's car park. It was 11.10 pm.

Their night began routinely enough; a call to an external alarm at a
furniture shop in Malvern Road — the building was secure despite the
blaring alarm. They patrolled the popular late-night haunts, bars and
discos in Chapel Street before their second call of the night to a flat in
Prahran, where a woman had sought refuge from her violent husband at
her mother's home. They advised her to see a solicitor about an inter-
vention order.

Steven Tynan, at 22, was the senior of the two police. He had joined
the police force three years earlier and spent 18 weeks at the Police
Academy in Glen Waverley, before passing through a number of training jobs and a year at the southern suburb of Cheltenham. In early 1988
he began at Prahran, known as a tough inner-city area with a wide
variety of work. It is the sort of station where a young policeman sees
more crime and criminals in a year than peaceful beats see in ten. And

Tynan had already learnt about policing at the sharp end.

On a Saturday evening shift only 10 days earlier, Tynan was working with another partner, Constable Rohan Bodsworth, when the two police were dispatched to investigate an armed robbery alarm at a TAB agency in Myrtle Street, South Yarra.

As the police arrived they saw two masked men inside the agency, one carrying a knife, the other with what was later discovered to be an imitation pistol. The men had demanded cash from the manageress, who told them they would have to wait 10 minutes before the safe could be opened. The bandits began their wait, unaware that the woman had set off an alarm. The two constables arrived within minutes and confronted the bandits, who grabbed the woman to use as a shield. But she dropped to the floor and Steven Tynan fired two shots, hitting one bandit in the neck, the other in the stomach.

The bandits were students from Asia who had fallen into debt and sought a quick way out of their financial problems. One of the men, Joshua Yap, 19, had amassed debts of $20,000 after gambling heavily at illegal gaming clubs in Little Bourke Street's Chinatown district. The bullet that hit him in the neck travelled down his spine and lodged in his shoulder blade. It left him a paraplegic. Yap died seven months later from a combination of paraplegia and pneumonia. The other bandit, Jimmy Tsen, 23, lost part of his bowel as a result of the shooting. He was later convicted of armed robbery and jailed.

Tynan was upset by the shootings and took several days off work. He had been back only three days as he drove the Prahran divisional van, with the radio code-name 'Prahran 311 (three-eleven)'. Tynan's partner that night was a relative rookie, Constable Damian Eyre.

Eyre had been in the force less than a year. He was 20. In his first attempt to join the police force he failed the admission test. But with a flatmate he crammed for a second attempt and got through.

His father had been a country cop in Shepparton, his brother was a detective and married to a former policewoman, and Eyre's sole career aim was to become a police officer. On his application form he wrote: 'As most of my family are in the Victoria Police force, I believe I have a good knowledge of the force as a whole and how it operates. This has been a life-long ambition and I respect the Victoria Police force very much.'

Their evening continued in a routine fashion: a noisy party; picking up a drunk in Fitzroy Street, St Kilda; an assault at a pub in Chapel Street, Prahran; a smashed window at a Prahran shop; two more security alarms. Then came their ninth call for the evening.

About midnight on 11 October, as Constables Tynan and Eyre were talking to a battered wife in Prahran, David Wilkinson, a customer service manager with Myer, arrived home from work. He parked his white Holden Commodore outside his flat in Walsh Street, locked the car doors then went inside.

About four hours later the driver's door of the Commodore was forced open and the engine started by pushing a screwdriver down the driving column. The car was turned around, driven about 20 metres along the road and left in the middle of Walsh Street. The engine was stopped, the screwdriver removed and the back quarter-panel window on the passenger's side smashed.

The first person to notice the car was a taxi driver, called to pick up a fare at a block of flats at 212 Walsh Street. 'I tooted the car horn and waited, and while doing so I noticed a car parked in the middle of Walsh Street about 20 yards ahead of me,' the driver later told police.

The cab driver took little notice of the car, but as he waited outside the flats, no one emerged. He got out and saw there were no lights on in the block. 'I then thought the car in the middle of the road had broken down and the owner had rung for a taxi. I walked towards the car in the middle of the road. On reaching it I looked in and then walked around it . . . On seeing nobody around I went back to my taxi and reported to my base that I had no job.'

With the Commodore sitting in the middle of the road, the cab driver reversed back to Domain Road. He did not report the car to police. This was about 4.05 am.

The next person to see the abandoned Commodore was Peter Ellis, the morning manager of a South Yarra newsagency. As he got up at 4.15 am he glanced out his bedroom window at what he thought was a figure at the front of a white car. The vehicle's bonnet was up, its lights off, its front door open and a back window smashed.

Ellis got dressed and about five minutes later wheeled a bicycle out of the front entrance of the flat. The car was still there, but there was no one near it. He later told police: 'I pretty much believed then that it had been stolen, and had run out of petrol, or something like that.' He made a mental note of the registration number and set off for work.

On the five-minute ride Ellis ate an orange, arriving at the agency around 4.25 am. Soon afterwards he telephoned Prahran police station and reported the car. The constable who took the message rang the police communications centre D-24, which is still named after the original room number (D-24) that housed the Victoria Police's first wireless sets. The message was taken at 4.36 am.

It was, in police parlance, a call to a 'suspect vehicle': a routine job. The radio operator at D-24 called up the van codenamed Prahran 311 containing Constables Tynan and Eyre and said: 'If you can slip down to Walsh Street, South Yarra. Mr Ellis of 222 Walsh Street states there's a white Holden sedan. Not known what the rego is. It's got the lights on and smashed windows in the middle of the road.' Damian Eyre, sitting in the passenger seat, acknowledged the call. It was 4.39 am.

But for a change in rosters at nearby St Kilda Road police station and a suicide in St Kilda, Damian Eyre and Steven Tynan may not have been dispatched to Walsh Street. The street is not strictly in the Prahran 'patch' and should have been allocated to a St Kilda Road unit. But that week, starting on the Sunday, staff levels at St Kilda Road had dropped to a point where, for the first time in months, there was not enough police to send out a divisional van. In turn, the Walsh Street area should have then been covered by South Melbourne police — but their divisional van was in St Kilda, where a man had committed suicide after jumping from a third-floor window.

The South Melbourne police van contained a policewoman and a policeman. Had they arrived first in South Yarra, detectives have no doubt they would have been murdered instead. Whether the public reaction to the killing of a young policewoman would have been any different is hard to know. What the set of circumstances does illustrate is how calls to police bring up the nearest and least busy unit. And for this call, it was Prahran 311.

What happened over the following minutes is known only to the killers. It appears certain that the two police were lured to the scene by the car and ambushed in cold blood. It is unlikely that any car thief would spend 40 minutes trying to steal a Commodore. Likewise, there is no evidence that any other crime was committed in the Walsh Street area that night which would have required a criminal to carry a shotgun. There is also no evidence that Tynan or Eyre had anything in their professional or personal lives that warranted retribution, and the random nature of which car attended the call makes any such theory highly dubious to start with.

The ambush and execution of two police — *because* they were police — is the only plausible theory for the killings. The fact that Tynan and Eyre were relatively inexperienced played no part in their deaths — the ambush was well plotted and executed, and no amount of policing experience would have foiled the plan.

What can be established is the two police drove into Walsh Street from Domain Road and parked their car only metres behind the white Commodore. They got out and walked to the Commodore, where Tynan, the senior partner, climbed into the driver's seat, while Erye squatted on the road next to him. They were probably looking at the broken ignition when the killers struck and, by the way they were killed, it is certain that at least two people were involved.

Tynan, sitting in the car, had his head turned towards the driver's door, possibly looking at his killer, when he was hit once in the head with a shotgun blast fired from just over one metre away. The heavy calibre SG shot devastated his skull and he collapsed inside the car.

A shotgun blast hit Eyre across his back as he rose from the squatting position. He turned and, incredibly considering his injuries, grappled with the gunman, who fired two more shotgun blasts into the air, one crashing into the wall of a nearby house. But as Damian Eyre turned, a second man grabbed the police-issue .38 revolver from Eyre's holster, put it to the policeman's head and fired. Eyre fell to the ground, bleeding profusely. The gunman fired a second shot with the .38 into Eyre's back as he lay on the ground. The killers then fled.

The number of killers was to be a point of contention at the trial. The Crown maintained there were five: Jedd Houghton, Victor Peirce, Peter McEvoy, Trevor Pettingill and Anthony Farrell. The defence argued, quite correctly, that the ambush needed only two men to complete, and that witnesses who saw the killers flee only ever saw two men at the one time.

While numerous witnesses were woken by the gunshots — four loud blasts (from the shotgun) followed by a pause, then two softer reports (the police revolver) — only a handful of people saw running figures. More certainly heard footsteps, but they were generally described as the heavy steps of one or two people, never four or five.

Jean Borg, who lived in Walsh Street, was woken by the shotgun blasts. She got out of bed and looked out of her kitchen window into a laneway metres from the scene of the ambush, a laneway that runs between Walsh Street and The Righi. She later told police: 'I saw a medium-size, what I call bandit-looking person. This person appeared to be wearing something over his head. It was semi-dark at the time and I couldn't see any hair. He was running along the lane towards Punt Road at a very fast speed. As I was watching this person I heard further gunshots, I think one or two. It came from the same direction as the first set of gunshots had come from . . .

'I then saw the person who I'd previously seen ... running very fast towards Punt Road. I then looked back at the laneway towards Walsh Street and saw a second person running down the lane in the same direction as the first person. The second person was very much like the first person. It was as if they were dressed identically. I then lost sight of this person, and again saw him on the other side of the rear fence running at a very fast speed in the direction of Punt Road.' Borg phoned the police.

There were two key witnesses for police, and each saw two men within minutes of the shooting. They were seen at different locations and, in each case, the men appeared to get into different cars that then sped off.

Around the corner from Jean Borg, 18-year-old student John Rose was also woken by the shotgun blasts. He went to the window of his Airlie Street home and then heard the shots fired from Constable Eyre's revolver.

'It was only a few seconds after this that I heard the sound of running footsteps coming from the direction of The Righi into Airlie Street. I then saw the figure of a man run up Airlie street to a car that was parked ... [in] Airlie Street facing north ...

'This car was very light in color, possibly white. The man was breathing very heavily and loudly. He was obviously in a big hurry. I saw him open the driver's side door and get in. He then started the car and started to slowly drive off, then I heard the sound of a second guy running up Airlie Street from the same direction. He also was breathing very heavily and loudly and moved very quickly. I saw the second guy open the passenger door and get in, closing the door after him.' Rose watched as the car sped up Airlie Street, without its lights on. He heard the squeal of tyres at the end of the street and the car was gone. Other Airlie Street residents also saw the small white car that night and heard it speed off within minutes of the shots being fired — but Rose was the only one who saw two men get in the car.

The idea that at least another two men were involved came from the testimony of another witness, Serina Coates, who watched from a flat in Punt Road that overlooked the entrance to The Righi. After hearing the shots, she went to a window and looked up and down Punt Road and saw nothing. She looked again and saw two men running along The Righi towards Punt Road.

'When they both got to the corner they stopped, crossed to the northern side of the road, and one jumped the fence into the garden of the house on the corner,' she told police soon after the shootings. 'The second then walked into the entrance of the house at 923 Punt Road and stood beside the tree just inside the entrance. The person that jumped the fence into the garden was carrying something in his left hand and holding it against his left side. I couldn't make out what he was holding. I didn't see that person again.

'The person I saw go into 923 Punt Road stood beside the tree for a short time, then walked out into Punt Road and appeared to be looking up towards Domain Road. Then he went back to the entrance of the house and within a minute I saw a dark-colored panel van travelling at a fast rate of speed down Punt Road towards Alexandra Avenue. It skidded and stopped outside 923 Punt Road. I could only see the driver in this panel van. As the van stopped the second person rushed from 923 Punt Road, opened the front door of the panel van ... The panel van then took off towards Alexandra Avenue and out of sight.'

Witnesses had seen two men running to two cars: a light-colored sedan and a panel van. And the fact that Serina Coates appeared to see only one person getting into the panel van before it sped off, the other having disappeared in bushes, fitted with the Crown's assertion at the trial that one of the alleged killers, Anthony Farrell, did not flee the scene, instead running back to his girlfriend's flat in nearby Gordon Grove. So the Crown theory divided thus: two men ran to the white car and disappeared; one was picked up by the panel van, driven by a fourth person; and the fifth ran back to Gordon Grove, where Jason Ryan was waiting.

The shooting took place at about 4.47 am. Dozens of residents were woken by the shotgun blasts and many rang police. As these calls began arriving at D-24, the police radio operator, Sergeant Ron Beaton, began calling without success for Constables Tynan and Eyre to respond. Beaton's tone of voice became more urgent as more reports of the shootings came through.

At 4.51 am, 13 minutes after dispatching Prahran 311 to Walsh Street, he first tried to get through.

D-24 (Sergeant Beaton):   VKC to Prahran 311. [pause] VKC to Prahran 311. [pause] VKC to Prahran 250. [pause] VKC to South Melbourne 250, any unit clear near Walsh Street, South Yarra. [pause] VKC to Prahran 311, South Melbourne 250, any unit clear near Walsh Street, South Yarra.
Police car: South Melbourne 150. [The duty inspector, using a radio at South Melbourne police station].
D-24:   South Melbourne 150.

Police car: South 150, I'm in the area near South Yarra.

D-24:   South Melbourne 150. I sent Prahran 311 down to Walsh Street. There's a car, a white Holden sedan parked in the middle of the road with lights on and smashed windows. Since then I've had about three or four cards [information given by callers to the police emergency number] come down saying that they've heard shots fired in that street and I can't get Prahran 311 at this stage.

Police car: South Melbourne 150. On my way.

D-24:   Roger. Is there any other unit?

Police car: Russell Street 621, [we] can head that way.

D-24:   621 roger.

Police car: St Kilda 311. Do you want us to go down?

D-24:   Affirmative.

Police car: 650. Would you like us to assist?

D-24:   650. You can if you want.

Police cars: [Unintelligible]

D-24:   Unit calling?

Police car: 650. What was the location of the last?

D-24:   Walsh Street in South Yarra.

Police car: Roger that.

Police car: South Melbourne 250. We're clear of South [Melbourne police station] heading to that one in Prahran.

D-24:   Roger. And the first unit down there give us a sit-rep [*sit-rep*: situation report] thanks, and take care. I sent Prahran 311 down there and haven't heard from him since. [pause] South Melbourne 250. There's one complainant, a Mrs Borg from Walsh Street. Says she heard approximately three or four shots. She saw a male run into a lane behind the flats there and into Airlie Street and then into Punt Road. She also saw a white car in the street and another man chasing after him.

D-24:   Russell Street 650.

Police car: 650.

D-24:   Can you come down Punt Road and have a look around there?

Police car: 650. Roger that.

Police car: St Kilda 350.

D-24:   St Kilda 350.

Police car: En route to your last. What's the address again thanks?

D-24:   It's 220 Walsh Street in South Yarra and the last we've heard was a person running up into Punt Road with another man chasing after him.

Police car: South 250, urgent. South 250, urgent.

D-24:   Unit calling?

Police car: South Melbourne 250. Two members down, urgent.

D-24:   Roger. Need an ambulance?

Police car: 250 urgent. Yes, an ambulance please. Two members down.

Police car: City West 250, do you need any assistance?

D-24:   City West 250, affirmative.
Police car: South Melbourne 250, for God's sake get an ambulance.
D-24:   Yeah, we're getting one now.
Police car: South Melbourne 250. We need an ambulance. We've got two members down with gunshot wounds outside 222 Walsh Street, 222 Walsh Street.
D-24:   All members take care.
Police cars: [unintelligible transmissions]
D-24:   Unit calling?
Police car: South Melbourne 250. Hurry up. We'll need a Mica ambulance [Mobile Intensive Care Ambulance] for these two ...

The first police on the scene, 250 from South Melbourne, had been confronted by the sight of Damian Eyre lying by the back wheel of the Commodore, blood gushing from his head. Slumped across the blood-spattered front seat of the Commodore was Steven Tynan. Both were unconscious but, amazingly enough, breathing. As one of the police made frantic calls to D-24 he was confronted by a man who walked out of bushes carrying something in his hand. The policeman ordered him to get back and put down what he was holding. Bill Wesson, a resident of the flats overlooking the ambush scene, put his torch on the ground. He had been woken by the gunfire, heard moans in the street and come out to see what he could do: he also wanted to know if his girlfriend, Jillian Ball, could help — she was a nurse. After a pause, the policeman said 'Yes'.

Jillian Ball found there was little she could do. Eyre was slumped on his left side, his headwound bleeding profusely. Tynan was slumped backwards inside the car, his head tilted backwards. Ball asked the two police to move Tynan from the car on to the road, which they did, where he was put into the coma position. Jillian Ball found both men had faint pulses and were breathing intermittently. But both had severe headwounds and Tynan's condition deteriorated as they waited for an ambulance.

In the meantime police converged on the scene. Roads around the area were blocked as police looked for suspects: but the problem was they didn't know what to look for. At that time police had no informa-tion on getaway cars. The only sighting was of two men running near the flats and they were long gone. Patrols were sent along the Yarra River and into the Royal Botanic Gardens. The police helicopter was airborne from its Essendon Airport base within minutes — even before the ambulances arrived — and helped scour the Gardens and river bank from above. But nothing was found.

At the scene, two ambulances, one a Mica, the other a normal ambulance, arrived simultaneously. The Mica crew, more highly trained in trauma work, split, with one officer going to each patient. The four ambulance officers spent 19 minutes attempting to stabilise the two police, both of whom had devastating injuries.

One ambulance officer's examination of Steven Tynan showed the brutality of the killing. He later told police: 'My examination of the patient showed a large 15 by 10 centimetre wound to the top rear left of the head with large blood loss and brain matter and bone fragments around the head. His pupils were fixed and dilated. He had no pulses but he was having periodic breaths, about two per minute. He appeared to have no other injuries. At this point in time, my judgement was that he had a non-survivable head injury . . .'

Eyre's prognosis was little better. He had a severe headwound, no pulse and sporadic breaths. He was connected to a monitor and oxygen and, like Tynan, rushed to hospital. Both were pronounced dead on arrival.

2
Fear and Loathing

Mr Death is Dead

Wall graffiti, Richmond 1987

The one-eyed former prostitute punched the air joyfully; for days Kath Pettingill had waited in the corridors of Victoria's Supreme Court for a jury to give its verdict on two of her sons and now, one day before her fifty-sixth birthday, she was no longer sitting anxiously on the wooden benches that line the court's corridor; she was relaxed on a lounge in a rental suite in South Yarra, unable to suppress a big grin.

'Three cheers for the boys,' she cried, as television cameras filmed the scene. On the other side of the room sat Trevor, the youngest of her seven children, acquitted only hours earlier of the murders of two policemen. Next to him was Anthony Farrell, also cleared of the killings. The youngest of the accused, Farrell had celebrated his twenty-first birthday in Pentridge.

The mood was elevated, although two of the acquitted men, another of Kath's sons, Victor Peirce, and his friend Peter McEvoy, were still in jail. They were awaiting bail on other charges, but would soon be out. What dampened the mood were questions from a journalist about her eldest child.

On 7 November 1951, Kath Pettingill gave birth to her first child, a baby boy she named Dennis Bruce Allen. She was 16. Before her twentieth birthday she bore two more children, Peter and Vicki. Three more sons followed, Victor, Lex and Jamie, until February 1965, only weeks before her thirtieth birthday, when Kath Pettingill bore her seventh and last child, Trevor.

Dennis, the eldest, was the man who brought 'the family' to prominence, building a substantial heroin trafficking empire in the mid-1980s. His mother, brothers, nephew and various hangers-on all had roles in defending a business that had links to corrupt police, gun dealing and murders. And although Allen died 18 months before the Walsh Street shootings, his family would blame him for the police action that followed the murders. To understand the story of the Walsh Street killings, one has to look at Dennis's role in the family and in Melbourne's underworld.

Dennis was always the leader among Kath's children and by the mid-1980s he was one of the most feared members of Melbourne's underworld. He not only threatened to kill people, he carried out the threat personally on a number of occasions. In protecting his drug business, bashings and torture, like threats with guns, were common. And Allen's success was shored up by being a police informer, which allowed him to trade his freedom and safety for information. He also knew corrupt Victorian police and paid bribes for information. With quality legal advice, Allen remained free for most of his reign as one of Melbourne's biggest drug dealers — and literally got away with murder.

When he died aged 35 of a rare wasting heart disease in April 1987, Dennis Allen was facing dozens of drug and firearm charges, having — remarkably in some cases — been granted bail at numerous court appearances. Seven weeks before his death, he was charged with murder and was finally refused bail. But it meant little. Allen was too sick to run his drug organisation, which by then was crumbling. He spent the last weeks of his life in St Vincent's Hospital, emaciated, shrunken in stature and barely able to move his limbs.

In his prime, however, Allen drew his fair share of police attention, especially during his drug dealing days, which centred around his 'patch' in Richmond. Some investigations were 'sold out' by other officers which, as the term suggests, implies money changing hands for details of the inquiries. Many police hated Allen — what he stood for, and what he got away with. Some saw him as a brutal criminal who seemed to have a free rein. And it was these themes that Kath Pettingill pushed when journalist Martin King from *A Current Affair* asked why her sons had been charged with the Walsh Street murders.

The charges were Dennis's fault, she said. 'We're still paying for his sins. We all are. He died before he could be punished,' she said. 'Dennis is Dennis and we're the rest of the family. We can't be blamed for Dennis's sins.'

Trevor Pettingill, acquitted hours earlier of the police murders, agreed with his mother's sentiments. 'We are getting punished for what the police think he got away with.'

Allen's rise to power and prominence was quick, and illustrates the massive profits available in the drug trade. But before he made 'good', he learnt the hard way, serving a long stretch in jail for rape.

With his brothers and sister, Allen grew up in West Heidelberg in what was known as the Olympic Village. These now decaying structures were built to house athletes for Melbourne's Olympic Games in 1956. Life was tough, and there was little money for the children. 'I brought them up mostly on my own and it was a very rough area and you had to be able to look after yourself. My kids were, fortunately, able to look after themselves,' Kath Pettingill recalled.

After a while, the family moved to Northcote, but life was still hard. Lex Peirce, in a statement to police, remembered living with the man who was the father of Trevor and Jamie Pettingill: 'He was a real mongrel. I met him when I was young and seen the end of him when I was about eight. He used to torture me when I was a kid. He broke my arm twice. One day I came home with bad sunburn blisters on my back, I was about seven I think. He stuck sticky tape on my back and left it overnight and then the next day ripped it off. That's the sort of bloke he was.'

It was while Dennis Allen was a teenager, living in the bayside suburb of Carrum, that he first got into trouble with police. It began with assaults and progressed through several drink-driving charges. Allen developed a reputation among local police for violence, especially when drunk, which was often and was to be so all his life, staggeringly so towards the end of it. He was sentenced to several short jail terms and once police caught him with a gun. In October 1973 Allen, with two friends and his brother Peter, went to a flat in Bluff Road, Sandringham. Dennis Allen raped a woman and indecently assaulted her 16-year-old sister. His brother fired a shot inside the flat and bashed a man in the head with a pistol. Dennis Allen was found guilty of rape and, at 23 years of age, was sentenced to 10 years jail, and ordered to serve a minimum of five.

Out in four years, Dennis Allen was immediately in trouble, caught for harboring an escapee (his younger brother, Jamie Pettingill), carrying guns and driving offences. He returned to Pentridge to serve out his remaining time on the rape charge.

His release, on 2 July 1982, marked the start of his rise to notoriety. He chose to live in the industrial area of Richmond sandwiched between the railway line and the South-Eastern Freeway: then run-down working-class homes scattered between factories and warehouses where property was cheap and there were few troublesome neighbors. He went to Stephenson Street, where his mother, Kath Pettingill, ran an illegal brothel. Next door was her home.

At first, Allen stayed with his mother but, six months out of jail, he paid $35,000 cash for a house around the corner at 86 Chestnut Street, an address that six years later would become important to the Walsh Street murder inquiry. For an unemployed man with a wife who was a heroin addict and two children to support, his source of income appeared dubious. And it was. Dennis Allen was now a heroin dealer.

Business was brisk. At a retail level, heroin was sold mainly through the brothel, a trade that continued for several years, despite numerous police attempts to shut it down. Allen also traded heroin at a wholesale level — usually in ounces, rather than the adulterated half grams sold to addicts.

One of his suppliers was Alan 'Big Al' Williams, a five foot eleven, 16-stone man who wore glasses. Allen first met 'Big Al' in Pentridge in about 1974. On his release, Allen again contacted his old friend. But Williams was in trouble. In early March 1982, Williams was at a drug deal where $110,000 was to be swapped for a package of heroin in a motel carpark. Unbeknown to Williams, the buyer was an undercover NSW policeman, Michael Drury, who was working on a joint NSW-Victoria Police drug operation. As the moment for the exchange approached, Williams sat in a car with the drugs. The undercover cop approached with the money, which had already been checked as authentic by another man. As the undercover man walked up, he gave a signal for other police to move in. Williams realised it was a bust and drove off, eluding police in the chase that followed. He dumped the car, with the heroin still inside.

But police knew his identity; it was not long before Williams was arrested and charged with drug trafficking. Williams realised that because he hadn't been caught red-handed with the heroin, when the case came to court, evidence given by the undercover buyer, Detective Drury, would be crucial to the police case. In the meantime he was released on bail. The charge, however, did little to discourage him from dealing in drugs.

Not long after Dennis Allen emerged from jail, Williams was still selling heroin, and Allen became one of his best customers. Williams later told detectives: 'It was good quality heroin — not garbage.' Although Allen 'ran hot and cold and some weeks he wouldn't want any', Allen usually bought between four and eight ounces a week — at around $5500 an ounce. Dennis Allen had at least three other drug suppliers, but Alan Williams was special; he supplied heroin on credit. Others demanded cash on delivery.

Their business relationship remained steady as Allen built his fledgling drug empire which, by 1984, was steadily growing in power. And that power was established by flexing muscles.

On the streets of Richmond, Allen cut a strange sight. He often wore bib-and-brace overalls, or a singlet and jeans. But what marked him out was the gold chains around his neck and wrists. Added to expensive rings on his fingers, Allen's jewellery was valued at $250,000. The mass of chains around his neck led to him being dubbed 'Mr T', after the wrestler and television star who also had a penchant for gold chains. On seeing Allen in his local hotel, hearing his gruff voice and seeing a zoo of animals tattooed on to his body, one could have been forgiven for thinking he was a working class boy made good. In a way, this was right: by 1984 he was amassing great wealth, and wielding the power of life and death.

Twice, murder had been used to solve a problem. In May 1983 one of Dennis's quasi-brothers arrived back in Melbourne after a long absence. Greg Pasche, a man with a history of crimes of violence and dishonesty, had wandered into the care of Kath Pettingill some ten years earlier when Pasche was 13. Pettingill became, she later said, 'his unofficial stepmother'. Pasche had befriended her son, Lex Peirce, who was living in a boys' home. Pasche had lost touch with his own parents so the two boys would spend weekend leave together staying with Kath Pettingill.

When Kath went to Sydney to visit her son Peter in Long Bay Jail in 1983, Peter told his mother that Pasche was in jail and needed $500 to be bailed. She paid up and took Pasche back to Melbourne, where he stayed with her at Stephenson Street. Back in Melbourne for just nine days, Pasche disappeared. His body was found ten weeks later under bushes off a forest track on Mount Dandenong. Pasche had multiple stab wounds to the body and his skull was fractured, probably as a result of stab wounds.

No charges were ever laid for the murder. An inquest found that the 23-year-old was killed by person or persons unknown.

There is no clear motive for Pasche's murder. It could have been drug related — or simply the fact Dennis didn't like him. According to information that came to light in 1989, Pasche was slashed across the throat by a friend of Allen's then, still alive, taken into the rear yard of a house. Dennis Allen then stabbed him in the head, before the body was wrapped in blankets, driven to Mount Dandenong and dumped.

The disposal of another 'problem' came with the disappearance of Victor Gouroff, a short, strong man who was born in post-war Germany. As a teenager Gouroff grew up around Carlton and drifted into crime, progressing from serious assaults, to guns, to armed robbery. By the early 1980s he had developed a bad drug habit. On 20 November 1983 he disappeared. No one reported him missing for three months, by which time he was undoubtedly dead and buried.

There were dozens of rumors about his death, some inventive, some unlikely. The common thread was that Dennis Allen was in some way involved. But without witnesses, evidence or a body, there was little detectives could do. Police were recently told by a person claiming to have seen Gouroff's body after he was killed, that he was a victim of Dennis Allen, killed with a 'hot-shot', or deliberate lethal overdose of drugs. His body was buried at an unknown location, possibly in the concrete slab of a building. Police regard the information as good. The motive, however, is open to speculation: Gouroff may have stolen drugs or money, reneged on a debt, talked to police — or it may be Allen decided he didn't like his friend any longer.

Whatever the reason, the deaths of Pasche and Gouroff stamped a climate of fear around Allen's drug operation. The talk this elicited among drug users, combined with the increase in crime around the Richmond area as dozens of drug addicts drifted in looking for a fix, brought police attention to the Stephenson Street brothel.

At first the raids were infrequent, but nevertheless productive. A federal police raid on Allen's Chestnut Street home in May 1983 turned up packages of heroin and amphetamines. The treasures were buried in the backyard: a steel box containing three well-oiled revolvers; a thermos flask holding almost 30 grams of heroin; a sawn-off .22 calibre rifle wrapped in plastic; and four sticks of Dupont Tovex plastic explosive. The detective with the spade was considered lucky not to have blown himself up during the digging. Allen was charged and bailed. (In another federal police raid on Dennis Allen, several hundred dollars of drug money went missing, prompting an internal police inquiry that left the federal police embarrassed about its dealings with Allen and his family.)

Allen's caution grew, beginning with a phone scrambler. So did his business. He bought two more houses, in Stephenson Street, where he spent thousands on renovations and security, including features like high walls, lighting and reinforced steel fencing. Once complete, he moved into number 37, while his mother and her youngest son, Trevor, moved in next door. This left the brothel at 108 Stephenson Street and Kath Pettingill's former house at 106, as the centre of the retail drug operation.

Throughout this time, Alan 'Big Al' Williams proved a reliable drug supplier. He usually delivered packages of heroin to Allen's house, to the Cherry Tree Hotel, or to a tropical fish shop in Preston. The shop was a favorite haunt of Dennis Allen, whose renovations to his new home at 37 Stephenson Street included a 3.5-metre fishtank that took up the length of one wall. At the shop Allen could find new fish for the tank.

Williams, however, had his mind on other things — trying to beat the drug trafficking charges laid after the 1982 bust by undercover policeman Michael Drury. Williams put a lot of effort into avoiding jail: he knew the undercover cop's testimony, putting him at the motel carpark with the heroin, was crucial to the defence case. Williams needed to prevent that damaging evidence being given. The irony was that despite his failing to stop the testimony being given, when it came to court Williams was acquitted.

His first attempt to solve the problem relied on the age-old method of bribery.

In September 1983, according to evidence given in court, a disgraced former NSW detective sergeant, Roger Rogerson, offered Drury money if he changed his evidence against Williams. But Drury refused. The Crown alleged in a later trial that Williams had contacted his long-time friend, Melbourne hit-man Christopher Dale Flannery, and arranged for Flannery to offer the bribe — and Flannery had used Roger Rogerson to extend the offer to Drury. (Williams later pleaded guilty to attempting to bribe Drury. Rogerson, charged with the same offence, was found not guilty by a jury.)

In March 1984 Williams, and one of his co-accused, Jack Richardson, failed to appear at the Melbourne County Court to face trial on the drug charges. The third man charged — who checked the money on the night of the ill-fated deal — was the only one who turned up. Williams and Richardson were put on the Victoria Police's Top Ten Most Wanted List and warrants were issued for their arrest. Within days of the list being compiled, Richardson's decomposed body was found in a ditch near Yea, 100 kilometres north-east of Melbourne. He had been shot once in the back of the head. It appears Richardson was killed the night before his scheduled court appearance. His murder remains unsolved.

Only days after Richardson's body was discovered, Williams surrendered to police. He was granted $50,000 bail and released.

In evidence later given in court, Williams said he became increasingly worried about the approaching court case and what to do about Drury, the bribe offer having failed.

On 23 May 1984 he travelled to Sydney where he met Rogerson and Flannery at a Sydney restaurant. There, while Rogerson was in the toilet, Flannery and Williams discussed the possibility of killing Drury. (Flannery, a Melbourne enforcer and hit-man who had moved to Sydney, was killed in May 1985. His body was never found and no charges have been laid.) Williams told a court that when Rogerson returned, Flannery told the NSW detective that Williams wanted Drury killed. Rogerson replied: 'All right.' According to Williams, Rogerson said a little later: 'I think everything will be sweet as long as everybody keeps their mouths shut.' Williams told the court that Flannery's fee for the killing was $100,000. Flannery told him most of the $50,000 deposit went to Rogerson.

Two weeks later, on 6 June 1984, the former undercover cop was standing in the kitchen of his Chatswood home when two bullets ripped through the window, hitting him in the back and side. Drury was critically wounded and his chances of survival were not regarded as good. But he pulled through. Six weeks later police colleagues interviewed him about the assassination attempt, and Drury told them Rogerson had twice tried to bribe him, offering $25,000 to $35,000, to give evidence that would assist Alan Williams.

This testimony led to a major internal police inquiry into Rogerson's activities and several criminal charges being laid. Rogerson was acquitted on those charges — including attempting to bribe Drury and conspiring to kill Drury — but was convicted by a jury on a charge of having perverted the course of justice and sentenced to a minimum of six years jail. This conviction was quashed in December 1990 after Rogerson had spent nine months inside.

The case centred on allegations that Rogerson conspired with three other men to pervert the course of justice by seeking to hide two bank accounts containing $110,000 opened by Rogerson in false names.

The Crown alleged the money came from a cash-for-drugs swap made at Sydney airport in May 1985. A Crown witness known only as 'Miss Jones' said she flew to Sydney where she delivered a bag containing cash to Rogerson which she swapped for a bag containing around one kilogram of heroin. 'Miss Jones' said Dennis Allen gave her the cash and told her to meet Rogerson. The three judges on the NSW Court of Criminal Appeal said the Crown could only show that the money put into false bank accounts 'had probably come from some unspecified unlawful activity and this was insufficient' for the conviction.

The link between Dennis Allen and Roger Rogerson was again raised during a Melbourne court case in 1990, this time in relation to a killing known as the 'mistaken identity murder'. It was a hit that went wrong, a hit organised by Dennis Allen. And the central question raised: why *did* Allen organise the murder?

On a cold, rainy Melbourne evening in September 1984 — three months after the assassination of Michael Drury had failed — Lindsay Simpson, a 32-year-old council worker, pulled up outside his brother-in-law's house in Lower Plenty, in Melbourne's outer north-east. Leaving his wife and eight-month-old daughter in the car, he walked up the driveway to the house to see if anyone was home. In the driveway, he was confronted by a man with a gun who ordered him to kneel down. Simpson was then shot in the back of the head. The dead man's brother-in-law, and the owner of the house, was Alan Williams.

The story behind the bungled hit began some months earlier with a man named Roy Pollitt. Pollitt had escaped from a NSW jail and made his way to Melbourne where he went to see Dennis Allen, whom he knew from a previous term in jail.

Allen was good to Pollitt. He helped the escapee cut and dye the flaming red hair that had earnt Pollitt the nickname 'Red Rat'. He organised accommodation, helped obtain a car and supplied Pollitt with a sawn-off shotgun, which Pollit used to rob a bank in Altona. The escapee became a regular visitor to Allen's house, although he would always telephone first, fearful that police may grab him in a raid.

In about September 1984, Allen asked Pollitt to do a job for him: kill Alan Williams. According to evidence given by Allen's former girl-friend, whose name cannot be used for legal reasons, Allen arranged for Williams to visit Stephenson Street while Pollitt was there, to allow the escapee to have a good look at his target. Allen supplied Pollitt with a gun and paid a $5000 deposit on the hit.

The motive for the hit is not clear. Allen certainly owned Williams money — around $17,000 — for heroin he had bought on credit. But in terms of Allen's turnover, this was a small amount.

When Pollitt was put on trial for the murder, the court was told that a

Tasmanian named Gary Jones, who helped rob the Altona bank, drove Pollitt to Lower Plenty where they waited for Williams to arrive home. Pollitt hid in bushes beside the driveway and, when a car pulled up and a man walked towards the house, Pollitt confronted him. Lindsay Simpson's wife later told police that she heard snatches of conversation — a man saying, 'Get down, sucker' and her husband protesting, 'But my name is Simpson' — then a gunshot.

According to Allen's girlfriend, Pollitt telephoned Allen's house on the night of the murder. She answered the phone and Pollitt told her: 'Tell Dennis the job's done.' Then he hung up. But the next day, 'Dennis was going off his head, saying things like "He's got the wrong man".' Later, she said, Pollitt came around and said to Dennis: 'I had to shoot the guy because he saw my face.'

Allen, unhappy about Pollitt's fatal error, refused to pay the outstanding $5000 on the hit. This angered Pollitt, who began demanding the outstanding money. To counter any threat, Allen ordered associates to ensure doors were locked in case Pollitt turned violent. But he also had another card up his sleeve and played it.

Allen, who used the code-name 'Gus', put on his police-informer's hat to solve the problem of the 'Red Rat'. He called a detective in the armed robbery squad and tipped him off about Pollitt's involvement in the Altona bank hold-up. For police, the evidence was excellent: in the excitement of the robbery, Jones and Pollitt both forgot to pull down their balaclavas and their faces were captured by bank security cameras. Allen told police where Pollitt was living and he was quickly arrested.

At the Simpson murder trial, Pollitt denied any involvement in the killing, but was found guilty by a Melbourne jury in 1990 and sentenced to a minimum of 18 years in jail.

Allen also won in another way. Pollitt's $5000 down-payment had been in counterfeit $20 notes. The source of the notes is unclear, although after newspaper reports of counterfeit money being passed at the Royal Melbourne Show, Allen quickly disposed of what was left — one associate remembers him burning about $20,000 in fake notes in a fireplace. And it appears one of those at the Show with fake notes was a man who would play a pivotal role in the Walsh Street story — Allen's young nephew, Jason Ryan. Allen gave Ryan $200 to go to the Show. After the publicity on the fake notes, Allen retrieved what the 13-year-old boy had not spent and that too was burnt.

Allen was now a multiple killer: Greg Pasche, Victor Gouroff and the mistaken execution of Lindsay Simpson. It was enough to earn him the nickname 'Mr Death', or the abbreviated version, 'Mr D'.

But his killings, like his drug and gun dealing, were far from finished. The legacy he left behind when he died in April 1987 was enormous. His relationship with corrupt detectives left many police angry. His activities brought all his family members to the attention of police. He died still facing more than 60 charges, some almost four years old. And he gave his nephew, Jason Ryan, a remarkable insight into the underworld.

For his mother, Kath Pettingill, it was enough to blame her son for what followed the Walsh Street murders. She was asked: 'If you could change something in your life, what would you change?' Pettingill thought for a moment, then replied: 'Probably not having Dennis.'

3
Travels with my Uncles

'She certainly wasn't the kind of nanna who'd sit around and do the knitting.'

Jason Ryan on Kath Pettingill

For Jason Ryan, the offer was too good to refuse: money, guns, drugs, women and alcohol. Having just turned 13, it seemed the door to excitement had just opened. His Uncle Dennis had offered him a room at the newly renovated house in Stephenson Street in Richmond. Ryan grabbed the chance. 'I'd been to visit Uncle Dennis earlier and he gave me all this money and I thought it was pretty terrific,' Ryan recalled. 'So I ran away from home and went to stay with him.' Ryan's home life had not been good as he had begun arguing frequently with his mother, Dennis's sister, Vicki Brooks. Besides, Dennis had also said Ryan didn't have to go to school any more.

At first, Ryan's new home was exciting: Dennis gave him cash, let him carry guns and handle drugs. Visitors were frequent and Dennis was obviously a popular man. Ryan often visited the brothel at the end of the street, the base for Dennis's drug business, and went with his uncle to the nearby Cherry Tree Hotel. He could chat with his grand-mother, Kath, and her sons Jamie and Trevor, who were not much older than Jason.

But Ryan soon found that this new grown-up world had its dark moments. He discovered how his uncle enforced his will.

Ryan had been living with his uncle only a matter of weeks when, one Saturday afternoon, a drinking binge began. Not that drinking sessions were uncommon: it was what came after this one that made it different.

For most of the afternoon Dennis drank with a few friends, mostly at home but with the occasional visit to the nearby Cherry Tree Hotel. Ryan joined Uncle Dennis and the visitors, but as the evening wore on he retreated to his room. By 11 pm, there were five people in the loungeroom — Allen, his girlfriend, a builder and his wife, and a friend of Allen's, Wayne Stanhope. All were drunk, but Allen especially so. He and Stanhope were also 'speeding', having twice injected amphetamines.

Ryan had fallen asleep in his room when a shot rang out. Moments later more gunshots. There was a pause, then a knock on his bedroom door. His Uncle Dennis told him to pass out a gun. Ryan knew what to do. Staying with his uncle involved carrying guns of many different calibres, especially when Allen was out and about. If Allen was caught with a gun he faced charges and, because of his criminal record, probably jail. Ryan, however, at 13, had no criminal record. (When, some months later, he was caught with a pistol belonging to his Uncle Dennis, Ryan was charged. In court, no conviction was recorded and the case was adjourned indefinitely.)

Ryan passed his uncle a pistol and followed him into the loungeroom. On the floor was Wayne Stanhope, blood gushing from his head.

Dennis Allen had pulled a pistol from his pants and shot him as Stanhope changed a record on the stereo. Then he had walked across the room and shot Stanhope several times in the head before he went to Jason's bedroom.

With the gun his nephew gave him, Allen walked up to the body and emptied the magazine's contents — seven bullets — into Stanhope's head. Allen was in a rage. He screamed at his girlfriend to give him a knife. Then he cut the dead man's throat.

Allen ordered those present to clean up. Stanhope's body was dragged on to the kitchen tiles to stop blood soaking into the carpet. With the others in the house, Jason Ryan took a hot soapy towel and began mopping blood from the floor. Ryan was then told to take the two guns used on Stanhope and hide them in the railway embankment behind the house. Bloody clothing was removed and burnt in the backyard. After a while, three of Dennis's brothers arrived and removed Stanhope's body. It was never found.

Why Allen killed Stanhope — only a month before Lindsay Simpson was mistakenly executed — is unclear. It may have been over a debt, something Stanhope said, or just a fit of blind rage. Jason Ryan later said that only hours before the shooting, Allen said he feared Stanhope planned to steal his jewellery. For Ryan, the killing was a quick, brutal lesson in what life with Uncle Dennis was like.

Six years later, barristers at the Walsh Street hearings would closely examine Jason Ryan's life. The defence counsel would say he was not a credible witness: he was a criminal, untrustworthy and a liar. While police concede Ryan is no angel, they argue that to understand him — especially the events that followed the Walsh Street murders — one needs to realise where he came from.

Ryan's early childhood was not easy. His mother, Vicki Brooks, like her mother Kath Pettingill, had her first child, Jason, at 16. A second son followed before she was 20, by which time she was separated from the boys' father. When Jason ran away from home at 13, it was, in effect, the end of a 'stable' childhood. Over the years that followed, he would move frequently, staying with different friends and relatives.

When Ryan moved in with his Uncle Dennis, Allen's empire was at its peak. Dennis's enormous income from the dozens of heroin addicts who daily bought their supplies from the brothel, allowed him to buy five more houses, taking his holding to nine Richmond properties.

There are two key reasons why Allen's empire rose so quickly and became so powerful: family and police support.

His family members supported his endeavors one way or another. His brother Victor Peirce lived around the corner in Dennis's former home, 86 Chestnut Street, which was still one of Dennis's properties. Although Peirce played little part in his brother's activities, he was there if needed. More active were his neighbours: his mother Kath, and his brothers Trevor and Jamie. Trevor was charged several times in relation to Allen's operation, eventually being sentenced to seven months jail for the possession of heroin. Kath Pettingill received an eight-month sentence for the same offence.

Jamie Pettingill, caught for burglary aged 11 and armed robbery at 15, acted as an enforcer in Allen's street dealings, bashing unwanted customers. He often carried a gun and knew how to use it — during one armed robbery he shot a bottle shop attendant in the leg. Jamie died in May 1985 after a mysterious heroin overdose that led the coroner to record an 'open finding': in other words, the coroner was not prepared to say whether it was an accidental overdose, a suicide or a murder. Jamie was 21. Rumors circulated that Dennis may have killed his brother because he was 'too big for his boots'. Certainly, Kath Pettingill expressed a fear that her son was deliberately killed.

Jason Ryan, although young, provided further support for Allen's empire, especially as a messenger carrying drugs and guns. And beside the family were loyal friends, who provided muscle or favors where necessary.

Peter Allen, another of Dennis's brothers, explained the power in a conversation secretly taped by police: 'The protection is created by the fucking psychological wall brought by the fucking family's actions, right? People won't dare go against . . . the family. Won't move against me — oh, repercussions from the other brothers. Won't move against them for repercussions from the other brothers. Then, so, all the murders, the fucking bashings, the shootings, and the victories . . .'

The other key element in Dennis Allen's success was his involvement with corrupt police. For legal reasons this aspect remains hard to explore. However, for Jason Ryan, growing up in his uncle's house, it was not uncommon for police to drop in for a drink or a chat. Phone calls were sometimes made to the house, according to Allen's former girlfriend, giving blunt tip-offs: 'Get out of the house, you're about to be raided.'

At the height of Allen's business success, a team of police mounted an operation to close down the drug dealing empire, in part because it caused a big rise in the crime rate around Richmond as dozens of heroin addicts came down for their daily fix. Police dubbed the investigation Operation Cyclops, after the one-eyed mythological giant, a police-humor reference to the fact Kath Pettingill had only one eye, the other having been lost in an argument with a woman that ended in a drunken shooting incident. Allen was given details of what investigators were doing by other police, making the inquiries useless. Allen paid $40,000 for the information.

After several weeks the inquiry began again in secret and, over the following months, raid after raid took place on Allen's houses. Jason Ryan was caught up in many of them, including one raid in which he was caught with a pistol hidden under his pillow. Some of the raids were lucrative. One raid alone on Allen's house turned up seven pistols, two shotguns and a silencer. Part of this small arsenal was hidden on a ledge above and inside a fireplace.

Other raids also produced handguns, shotguns and bullet-proof vests. The variety and quantities of this magnitude point to Allen's other line of business — selling guns to members of the underworld. There were also large amounts of drugs and the raids began to damage the heroin retailing operation. Allen countered the police action by beefing up security at his home and at the brothel. There was also direct action.

When family members discovered police were spying on them from a disused factory — who passed on that information is unclear — the observation post was riddled with bullets. No one was there at the time.

One officer involved in Operation Cyclops was almost killed at the Prahran police station when a bullet, fired from outside the building, smashed through a window and whizzed past centimetres behind his head. He had just moved forward to answer the phone when the shot was fired. Police suspected they knew who the marksman was, but no charges were laid because of lack of proof.

Family members were also responsible for a bombing at the Melbourne Coroner's Court in May 1985, when a device exploded harmlessly on the front steps in the early hours of the morning. One inquest scheduled that day was on Helga Wagnegg, a prostitute whose body was found floating in the Yarra River.

Again, 13-year-old Jason Ryan knew how she met her death. She was killed in November 1984, a time when the police raids began putting heavy pressure on Allen's empire. It appears Allen suspected her of being a police informer — and there was only one way to deal with informers.

Wagnegg, a heroin addict who had been out of jail only two weeks, went to the Stephenson Street brothel to buy some heroin. She injected herself, promptly collapsed and was taken into the backyard.

A male nurse and heroin addict, who dropped into the brothel to buy a fix, attended to Wagnegg. She came around. But Dennis Allen had different ideas — he walked to the backyard and injected Wagnegg with what he said were amphetamines. Minutes later the nurse again checked Wagnegg, who was blue in the face. He tried to bring her around but Allen walked into the backyard again and ordered him to leave.

At this time Jason Ryan arrived carrying a small silver package containing drugs. It was mixed into a solution, put into a syringe, and again Allen injected Wagnegg. Again the nurse tried to revive Wagnegg, but thought she was dead. Allen arrived once more with a syringe, injecting Wagnegg for the fourth time, this one in the neck, just to make sure.

Jason Ryan was dispatched to the nearby Yarra River with instructions to bring back some water. Attempts were made to pour this down the dead prostitute's throat and into her lungs to give the impression she drowned. Her body was then dumped in the Yarra. Allen, using his skills as a police informer, tipped off detectives, saying he 'had heard' of her death and that she may be in the river. The water police found the body a few days later.

Allen was to kill again a year later, shooting Anton Kenny, a former vice-president of the Nomads Motorcycle Club — sister chapter of the

Hell's Angels — before cutting off Kenny's legs with a chainsaw and a meat cleaver. The mutilated body was put into a 44-gallon drum, filled with concrete and rolled into the Yarra. Allen probably shot Kenny over a drug debt, a killing that received widespread publicity and became known as the 'body-in-the-barrel case'. After the body was ditched Allen set in train a series of events, including intimidating 'witnesses' to give false 'evidence', that led police to charge convicted killer Peter Ian Robertson with Kenny's murder. Robertson was later acquitted of the charge.

There are rumors that Allen killed other people, or commissioned their murders, among them a 30-year-old woman who went missing in 1984 and has not been seen since. There are other rumors: that Allen killed a Maori man and chopped off his hand after he stole Dennis's watch; and testimony in a NSW court by a woman who said she saw Allen, in company with a Victorian policeman, shoot a man dead.

During his time with his Uncle Dennis, Ryan witnessed many bizarre sights. One was when a woman was held captive for four days and beaten regularly. Why she was held captive is not known. However, during her detention, Allen told his nephew to hit her. Using a pick handle, Ryan swung a blow, hitting the woman in the neck and drawing blood.

Allen also chained up and bashed the girlfriend who witnessed the murder of Wayne Stanhope.

He also had a row with another girlfriend, heroin dealer Vicki Ward, that was witnessed by a police surveillance team. Ward, who was later murdered, ran from Allen's house to her car and locked herself in. Police watched as Allen emerged from the house with a hammer and smashed every window and light on the car as Ward sat in the front seat screaming. Allen stopped when family members restrained him.

Even Allen's mother concedes that her eldest son had what she called 'a dark side' to his character. 'He had periods of being above the law. He thought he was invisible, he could do anything he wanted and nobody could challenge him. Then some days he'd be back to reality and ask what he'd done.'

Ryan looked up to his uncle. He also found the trappings good. He was given a lot of money for a 13-year-old boy. The lifestyle was also exciting: guns, drugs, women. And a camaraderie that extended to wearing the same style of Japanese head band that his Uncle Dennis sometimes wore.

Ryan took custody of Allen's personal handgun as well as the one

Ryan usually carried himself. At night, in case of police raids, Ryan would hide guns on the railway embankment at the rear of the house: thus if they were found, it would be hard to prove possession. This was a popular spot, and police found several weapons in this area during raids. In one search they used a backhoe to excavate the ground behind the house. Said Ryan of the concealed guns: 'When I got told to go and get the guns I did ... [I would] go and get the guns and bring them back, and put them away overnight.'

Because of Jason Ryan's presence amid the drug dealing and murder, police applied to put him into care. A court ordered he stay with Fred Cook, the former champion footballer, who was a close friend of Dennis Allen. Cook ran the Station Hotel in Port Melbourne. But things did not go well. With a friend, Ryan stole some of the hotel's takings. After an argument with Cook's wife he slashed the tyres of her car. Ryan was also present when Dennis Allen decided to use the Cooks' bed with a girlfriend. Cook's wife walked into the room and turned on the light, prompting Allen to produce a gun and shoot out the globe. After only weeks with Cook, Ryan went back to stay with his Uncle Dennis.

Eventually, Dennis Allen became sick of his nephew and kicked him out. Over the following years, Ryan spent time with a number of relatives, among them his Uncle Peter.

Peter Allen was released from prison in August 1985. He quickly set himself up as a heroin middle-man, establishing a network of street-level dealers whom he supplied. Peter Allen did not trust his brother Dennis, or some other members of the family. He didn't want to be part of Dennis's empire — he wanted his own slice of the action.

Peter Allen was streetwise and, with good connections in the under-world, the money soon rolled in, enough for him to buy a house in outer-suburban Templestowe within five months of his release. His sister, Vicki Brooks, also moved in. And her son, Jason Ryan, spent time at the house. The problem was that a group of police, including a detective named John Noonan, had bugged Allen's house, gleaning enough to sink Allen and others when they were tried on drugs charges. (This police operation led to a massive reassessment of security by many criminals in Melbourne's underworld, who suddenly became aware of how damaging bugs could be. As a consequence of Peter Allen's experience, many criminals no longer held important conversations inside houses, let alone on the phone, as detectives investigating the police murders in Walsh Street were to discover.)

Jason Ryan was taped several times in the secret bugging operation. Also taped was his mother, Vicki Brooks, who said of her son: 'He needs to be educated ... He's got a big advantage on everyone else knowing what he knows. He can put his head down and learn ... What he's been taught criminal-wise, if he puts his brains to it, he could be a millionaire by the time he's thirty ... [but] he's the next generation of our family and he's a dill.'

Brooks was later jailed for two years for trafficking in marijuana as a result of the police investigation into her brother Peter. Peter Allen was sentenced to a minimum of eight years for heroin trafficking.

Once Peter Allen was arrested, Jason Ryan continued to move house. He spent almost a year at 86 Chestnut Street living with his Uncle Victor and Victor's wife Wendy, and the couple's children. The easy income that came his way when Dennis was making big money had dried up. And after Allen's death in April 1987, Ryan needed to earn a living.

One answer was burglaries, and Ryan did some of these with friends. Popular targets were warehouses and shops containing clothes. Premises used by companies including Dunlop and Opal Menswear were hit, as were companies dealing with furs, leather jackets, footwear and electrical goods.

In one robbery, Ryan said his Uncle Trevor used a car to smash the roller door of a warehouse in Balmain Street, Richmond. Ryan helped load jeans into the car before fleeing. Ryan was later arrested for the robbery and, it is believed, was told his Uncle Trevor had confessed and implicated him. Pettingill had done no such thing. But Ryan, believing he had been 'given up' by his uncle, subsequently gave police a statement implicating Trevor.

A phone call was made and Trevor Pettingill arrived at Richmond police station to bail his nephew on the burglary charges. He put up a small amount of money and Ryan was released. Police immediately arrested Trevor on the burglary charges, with Jason Ryan's statement ample evidence to lay the charges. Having no money left for his own bail, Trevor spent the night in the cells.

Ryan also took to helping his Uncle Trevor's drug-dealing ventures. In early 1988 police installed a video camera, behind one-way glass, in a factory overlooking Dennis Allen's former home at 37 Stephenson Street. Drugs and people were recorded coming and going and, after amassing evidence, the house, and number 35 next door, were raided. Pettingill was later jailed for trafficking in marijuana and Ryan, who admitted to running drugs for his uncle, was also charged.

In late 1987 Ryan, then aged 16, produced a knife from his pants and stabbed a man in the stomach at the Newmarket Hotel in Flemington. Ryan was charged and later given a bond. In a separate incident he pointed a crossbow pistol at a truck driver who parked illegally outside the house Ryan was staying in. The truck driver got the message and didn't park there again.

Although scrawny and not very tall, Ryan was proving that he had learned the power of violence from his late Uncle Dennis. And that influence marked him in another way. Ryan did not trust police. He later said his Uncle Dennis did not trust police either, except 'the ones he was paying'.

'There were some police that my uncle knew that were corrupt, and I knew of it. And I thought most of the police were like that.' This was the distrust and suspicion Jason Ryan was about to take into the most important series of events in his short life.

4
Death in Brunswick

Falsehood is the jockey of misfortune

Jean Giraudoux, 1928

For Dominik Hefti and his partner the cash pick-up from the Coles New World supermarket in Brunswick was a regular part of Monday's schedule at Armaguard. Armaguard, like all security companies, likes to vary the times its trucks deliver and pick up cash, but this can be difficult: the customers, who like routines, are sometimes their own worst enemies because adopting a routine makes it easier for thieves. For a criminal with time to invest in surveillance, a pattern can be readily traced.

As the heavily fortified Armaguard truck eased into the supermarket's loading bay, Dominik Hefti found the scene pleasantly familiar. Before joining Armaguard in mid-1987, Hefti had worked as a security guard at the shopping centre that included the supermarket. He knew many of the traders and had enjoyed his work there, but when the chance to join Armaguard came, he took it. He knew his new job presented higher risks: he would carry a gun and escort large amounts of cash, but then Hefti had always wanted to work as a security guard. A Swiss citizen who migrated in 1980, Hefti had discussed the risks with his wife Michelle, a German immigrant whom he met soon after his arrival. She said later that it was a job her husband always wanted to do, so she accepted that.

It was soon after 3 pm on 11 July 1988 when the van came to a halt. Hefti and the other guard, both armed with .38 revolvers, jumped out and walked through the loading bay and stockroom to the cash office, where they picked up a metal cash box containing the weekend's takings — $33,000. A third man remained in the van.

As Hefti and his partner returned to the truck through the stockroom their routine was shattered. A lone gunman emerged from behind a pallet of food and demanded the cash box. He attempted to grab the tin from Hefti's hands, but the fit 35-year-old guard refused to surrender it. For a brief moment the men struggled, face to face, chest to chest, over the supermarket's takings. Each man held a gun and each fired twice. Hefti slumped to the floor, shot in the chest and thigh. The bandit, now clutching the cashbox, fled through the stockroom leaving a trail of blood. Hefti's partner, stunned by the shooting, tried to help his wounded colleague.

The bandit, meanwhile, pushed his way through plastic doors at the end of the stockroom and emerged at the end of one of the supermarket's aisles. Shoppers watched stunned as the gunman ran down an aisle, through the checkout and into a car park. A woman driving slowly into the car park was stopped at gunpoint and forced from her car. The bandit, still bleeding, climbed in and drove off. The ambush was over in minutes.

Although the robbery was quick and simple, the hold-up plan had gone horribly wrong. Police now believe a second gunman was also meant to have ambushed the guards, but was not in position when the shooting began. They later found a stolen panel van parked near the scene that was probably used for surveillance, but it may also have been a getaway car. Either way, it was clear the bandits' plan did not involve one of them being shot: stealing a car at gunpoint appeared desperate improvisation.

Hefti was rushed to the Royal Melbourne Hospital in a critical condition. He died less than 48 hours later without regaining consciousness. He left a 27-year-old widow and two-year-old son.

The panel van, like the blood the bandit left on the supermarket floor and the bullets fired at Hefti, were the only physical clues police had. But, like most major criminal cases, there was no short supply of verbal information, material from informers and anonymous callers. And, like many major criminal cases, the pursuit of Hefti's killer over the following three months relied, to a great extent, on the word of informers. In the Hefti case, most of it proved to be wrong.

There are numerous reasons why those within the underworld offer information: some seek the money paid from police slush funds; others believe it a form of prestige; many are effectively forced to provide information by police, who may hold the threat of criminal charges over their heads; some inform out of spite, revenge, or simply use the police to remove the opposition by giving details of a rival's activities. The information is usually anonymous — the informer, if known, won't appear in court — and it ranges from excellent to useless.

Less than four hours after Hefti's shooting, as police continued to search for a white Nissan Pulsar with a red-and-black stripe, the car stolen at gunpoint in the shopping centre, information arrived that may well fit into another category — putting police on the wrong track. It came from a caller to the police communications centre, D-24.

D-24:   Police D-24.

Caller: Ah, I was out jogging before, in Brunswick . . .

D-24:   Yeah.

Caller: And I was in Evans Street. A little white car tried to run me over and the bloke got out of it and he got in a car with a girl. I got the number of it. It was [number supplied].

D-24:   What did the bloke look like?

Caller: About five eight, five ten, brown hair.

D-24:   Yeah.

Caller: Brown hair. I didn't take much notice of him, I just looked at the other car then.

D-24:   Right. And what kind of car was the other one?

Caller: Camira.

D-24:   Camira. And what did they get out of?

Caller: What's that?

D-24:   What car did they get out of?

Caller: He got out of the white car and got in the blue car.

D-24:   Right. Did that have any stripes, or anything down the side of the white car?

Caller: I'm not really . . . can't really tell.

D-24:   Right. Can I just get your name.

Caller: Mr [short pause] Clark.

D-24:   Clark. And whereabouts do you live Mr Clark?

Caller: Er, [number supplied] Victoria Street, Brunswick.

D-24:   And your phone number there?

Caller: Nah, haven't got the phone on. I had to go down the phone box. That's why it took me a while to ring. It was about an hour ago.

D-24:   So about an hour ago it happened?

Caller: Yeah.

D-24:   OK, we'll follow that up.

Caller: Yeah, he got in another car [repeats registration number].

D-24:   All right, I'll follow that one up.

Caller: OK.

D-24:   Great, thanks a lot.

Caller: Thanks a lot mate. Bye.

The caller was never traced. The address in Victoria Street, Brunswick, was a clothing factory where no one had heard of Mr Clark. However, the white Pulsar used in the robbery was found in Evans Street — where 'Mr Clark' said it had been dumped — with the bandit's bloodstains on the inside of the driver's door.

Armed robbery squad detectives traced the registration number of the Camira to a woman from Melbourne's bayside suburbs. She had links with two armed robbers — one had been arrested four months earlier for a bank hold-up and was in jail; the other was Graeme Jensen, released a year earlier from jail after a six-year stretch for armed robbery.

Detectives, however, quickly established that the Camira could not have been used as a changeover car for the wounded bandit. The owner had lent it to a friend and the car was in Sydney. The motive for Mr Clark's call for D-24 was most likely was an attempt to steer police away from the real robbers, although it could have been a deliberate attempt to steer the inquiry towards the car's owner — or Jensen's way.

Hefti's partner and shoppers from the supermarket compiled photofits of the bandit for police that added to the possibility of Jensen's involvement. The description of the bandit and the photofit were similar to Jensen. But police were also given the names of other men, whom informers and anonymous phone calls suggested were responsible for the Hefti shooting. It was the start of a long investigation in which detectives tried to sort fact from fiction. And the three-month Hefti investigation was to be strongly influenced by the inquiries of another team of armed robbery squad detectives, led by Detective Sergeant Paul Mullett.

Operation No Name began in April 1988, about three months before Hefti's murder. At the start, Mullett was given two pieces of information.

First, he was told the names of four men who had robbed a bank at the start of the year. For legal reasons, details of this robbery cannot be published, so we will call it The Summer Hold-Up. One of those named as a bandit is incidental to the Walsh Street story and another cannot be named for legal reasons, so we will call him 'Mr Smith'. The two others would be central characters in the Walsh Street case: Lindsay Rountree, a convicted armed robber who would become a protected Crown witness in the police shootings trial, and Victor Peirce, charged with the Walsh Street murders.

Mullett's second piece of information was that 'Smith' and Peirce were planning a robbery with other men — it was not known who they were.

As is so often the case in major criminal investigations, it was surveil-lance that provided crucial information. Over the following months 'Smith' and Peirce were sporadically followed by specialist surveillance teams from the bureau of criminal intelligence and gradually a picture began to form. The men met several times at Boronia Shopping Centre, always on the same day of the week, where they appeared to watch banks — first the National Australia, then the Commonwealth, then the ANZ — and the cash deliveries of security vans.

The police surveillance was not constant, because of a big shortage of surveillance police and heavy demand for their time. On the day of the Hefti shooting, for example, the men were not being watched.

During the surveillance at Boronia, however, two more faces appeared with 'Smith' and Peirce, the faces of two men whose fates are intimately tied up with the Walsh Street case. On 19 September 1988 — more than two months after Hefti's murder — police snapped pictures of Graeme Jensen and Jedd Houghton meeting 'Smith' and Victor Peirce.

About two weeks later, Operation No Name came to an end. The reason: the key informer, who had supplied a great deal of accurate information, told Mullett that any prospective armed robbery at Boronia had been cancelled because it was considered there was not enough money being delivered to any of the banks to warrant the risks. In other words, the job was off.

Mullett's crew had spent the best part of six months investigating the four men seen at Boronia, waiting for them to make their move. But with the four men having 'cancelled' their job, Detective Mullett could no longer justify the use of surveillance police: with his informer saying no alternative robberies were planned, Mullett decided to arrest 'Smith' and Peirce, suspects for The Summer Hold-Up, one of the starting points for Operation No Name.

For the armed robbery squad crew investigating the Hefti murder, led by Detective Sergeant Peter Butts, the developments in Operation No Name were intriguing, especially the photographs taken at Boronia Shopping Centre that featured Victor Peirce and Graeme Jensen. From the first day of the Hefti murder inquiry, Jensen was regarded as a suspect: his name was loosely connected to the stolen car, his appear-ance was not dissimilar to photofits compiled by witnesses, and police informers suggested he was involved. As well, the Boronia surveillance showed Jensen following security guards into banks as Armaguard trucks made cash deliveries, making Armaguard a common denominator in both cases.

Detective Butts also received information suggesting Victor Peirce was involved in the Hefti murder. One informer, regarded by detectives as reliable, stated categorically that Peirce was involved: the informer said it was Peirce's accomplice who was wounded in the shoot-out with Hefti. So with this informer's finger pointing at Peirce, there was the question of who else might have been involved: and Graeme Jensen seemed to fit the bill.

So, as Detective Mullett prepared to arrest 'Smith' and Peirce for The Summer Hold-Up, Detective Butts felt justified in questioning Jensen and Peirce about the Hefti shooting. The evidence was certainly circumstantial, but when additional information arrived on 11 October, again pointing at Peirce's involvement, detectives were reassured that they were heading in the right direction. DNA analysis of blood would settle the issue of whether Peirce or Jensen were involved. DNA in a human body is like a fingerprint: each is unique to the individual. For police, a comparison of the suspects' blood with that lost by the wounded bandit at Brunswick would resolve whether Jensen or Peirce had a role in the murder. Witnesses would also be called to try and identify Peirce and Jensen from a line-up, if either man agreed.

At the time, police were confident the Hefti murder case was coming to a close. But they were wrong. What soon became apparent was that the information detectives had received from informers about the Hefti murder was woefully inaccurate: neither Peirce nor Jensen was involved. Worse still, the arrest of Jensen would go wrong. For police, a nightmare was about to begin.

5
Graeme

'Look, it's OK for you. You know what it [a non-criminal life] is like. I don't, never have. I just can't picture it.'

Graeme Jensen to cell-mate, Bendigo Prison, 1984

To the disappointment of police, the surveillance at Boronia failed to produce enough evidence to lay any charges, leaving detectives where they began almost six months earlier: with the names of the four men allegedly involved in The Summer Hold-Up. Thus, in early October 1988, the final phase of Operation No Name began with plans to find and arrest those suspects. Of the four men named by the No Name informer, one was already in jail awaiting a hearing on other offences (he was later charged with The Summer Hold-Up). This left 'Smith', Lindsay Rountree and Victor Peirce.

The first arrest was at dawn on 6 October 1988 at a farmhouse near Euroa, a country town on the Hume Highway about 140 kilometres out of Melbourne. The property had a long, open driveway to the farm-house, which presented detectives with an immediate problem: how to approach the building without warning the occupants that the police were coming. The answer was a borrowed fruit truck, driven by Detective Mullett, with half a dozen other detectives concealed in the back.

But according to the police version of events, the covert approach was not entirely successful. As the truck approached the house, police spotted 37-year-old Lindsay Rountree move from one outbuilding towards another. The truck pulled up and detectives leapt from the back: Rountree was seen to be carrying a sawn-off shotgun. One detective raised a shotgun and fired two blasts over the wanted man's head. Rountree dropped to the ground and was pounced on by police and handcuffed. Rountree's version of his arrest was quite different. He claimed there was no sawn-off shotgun, he was bashed by detectives and police fired two shotgun blasts centimetres over his head after he was handcuffed.

But more significant than the differences in the accounts and the firing of shots by police, was something that Rountree claimed was said to him by the arresting police. Rountree said detectives told him that Victor Peirce was 'off', meaning Peirce was going to be killed. Police have denied saying any such thing to Rountree.

Whatever was, or was not said, Rountree was left with the impression that police would kill Peirce if they had a chance, a belief enforced by the firing of shots during the arrest at Euroa. As a friend of Peirce, Rountree felt it was his duty to warn him.

The conduit for the warning was Rountree's wife, Penny, who visited Rountree in Pentridge, where he was remanded, without bail, charged with The Summer Hold-Up. Rountree told his wife to get a message to Peirce that the police were out to kill him. She agreed to pass this on.

On the afternoon of Sunday 9 October, Penny Rountree rang Peirce at his Richmond home and arranged a meeting that night at the Mountain Gate Shopping Centre in Melbourne's outer eastern suburbs. The meeting was brief: Peirce got into Penny Rountree's car and was given the message; he was also told that Lindsay Rountree had been charged with The Summer Hold-Up. From evidence later given in court, it is clear that Peirce considered himself on the run and marked for an arranged death at the hands of police.

The following day, Detective Butts, who had begun leave two weeks earlier, returned to work only half way through his holiday: with the surveillance component of Operation No Name finished, Butts needed to be around for the arrest of Jensen and Peirce. While Mullett wanted to interview both men, Peirce especially for his alleged involvement in The Summer Hold-Up, Butts's inquiry into the Hefti murder took precedence because it was a more serious crime.

On Butts's first day back, Monday 10 October, another informer told the detective that Peirce and Jensen were involved in the Hefti robbery, and that Jensen 'was the shooter'. On the same day, Detective Mullett's crew arrested 'Smith', the second of the four men wanted for The Summer Hold-Up.

Meanwhile, surveillance was put on Victor Peirce's home and he was spotted. Police followed him to a hotel in Kensington, hoping he would meet up with Jensen (working on the premise that 'Smith's' arrest would quickly spread through the grapevine and the two men would rendezvous to discuss what to do next). But Peirce may have been aware of the surveillance. He walked into the hotel, out of the back door, and disappeared, leaving his car behind for someone else to collect. Peirce later said he was scared police were about to kill him so, instead of going back to his Richmond home, he went to Keilor where he stayed with friends. Police were unable to find him.

Meanwhile, armed robbery squad detective Col Ryan followed up a lead that came early in the Hefti investigation. Ten days after the security guard's murder, a man came forward saying a friend of his, whom we will call 'Bob', had seen Victor Peirce on the night of the Hefti killing and 'Bob' seemed aware that Peirce was involved. Detectives tracked 'Bob' down and on the morning of Tuesday 11 October interviewed him.

'Bob' claimed that about 10 days before Hefti's shooting, Peirce had said to him: 'Watch the news. I am going to Brunswick, I need some money. Watch the news.' Days later, after viewing a television bulletin on the Hefti shooting, 'Bob' rang Peirce and invited him over. He told police: 'When he [Victor Peirce] came in I noticed he was a bit jumpy and agitated. He sat down in the kitchen and had a smoke ... After we had had the smoke he said to me: "Did you see what happened?" I said yes. And then he said: "We fucked up bad, we fucked up." By him saying this I took it immediately that he was talking about what had occured that day in Brunswick ... While we sat there another item came on Channel Nine in relation to the Brunswick robbery. Victor drew my attention to it by saying: "See." At the same time as saying "See" he pointed to the television to draw my attention to it.'

Quite why 'Bob' made this statement is unclear. Bearing in mind that Victor Peirce played no part in the Hefti murder, the statement's accuracy is obviously open to question. 'Bob' later fled Australia for his native Greece and has not returned. At the time, however, it was another piece of 'evidence' against Peirce for the Hefti murder.

But police were having trouble finding Peirce. He did not return to 86 Chestnut Street on Monday night after surveillance police lost him at the Kensington Hotel. So on Tuesday 11 October, police surveillance switched to a house in Moray Court, Narre Warren.

During the surveillance at Boronia Shopping Centre several weeks earlier, a police car had discreetly followed Jensen back to a house in Moray Court. He was followed there again on a separate occasion after a meeting at Victor Peirce's Richmond house. On both occasions, Jensen was driving a blue Commodore owned by Sandra Faure, the wife of Keith Faure, a notorious Melbourne criminal.

Nine months earlier, Keith Faure had been arrested and jailed for his role in an armed robbery on 29 December 1987 in which a Thornbury jeweller, Mario Sassano, 56, was shot dead in front of his wife and son. Keith Faure was one of four men who took part in the raid, only weeks after he had been released from jail after serving more than 10 years for two counts of manslaughter and one count of attempted murder, which related to the shooting of a policeman in the back while escaping from a bank robbery.

When he was arrested in early 1988 for the jewellery robbery he was refused bail. He was lated convicted of the hold-up and sentenced to a minimum 11-year term.

Soon after his arrest, Sandra and Keith Faure decided to end their marriage. Sandra had met Graeme Jensen some eight years earlier through her husband and, although they saw little of each other for the next few years, in May of 1988 they began a relationship. Jensen began staying about three nights a week at Moray Court: at the end of June he moved in.

Jensen was born in Carlton in 1955. His parents separated when he was seven and he moved with his mother to the country. After two years he returned to Melbourne and stayed with his eldest sister, then moved in with his mother again. Soon after he turned 12 he was convicted for the second time for stealing a car, was made a ward of the state and sent to Melbourne's Tally Ho Boys' Home. He continued to get into trouble and with two friends in mid-1970 Jensen robbed the National Bank of Australasia in Queens Parade, Fitzroy. Jensen and a friend went into the bank armed with rifles and escaped with $3000 in a stolen car, which Jensen drove. On conviction, Jensen was sent to a youth training centre.

Jensen continued to be in trouble, mainly for housebreaking and theft. At 18 he was given his first stretch in jail, a minimum of 18 months for housebreaking.

He was involved in an assault in which a man was smashed in the face with a full bottle of beer. Jensen pleaded guilty and was sentenced to 14 days. At the time, a policeman noted on an official report: 'If a prediction is to be made about him, then one day he will kill someone or finish up being killed. He will also be in trouble for violence. He is an arrogant bash merchant after a bout of drinking. Will always come under notice.'

Three weeks after his arrest for the assault, Jensen came under notice after the infamous Carlton hotel bombing. On a Saturday night in late September 1973, an argument started at the Kent Hotel in Curtain

Street. Several men left and returned a short time later. Outside the hotel were members of a motorcycle gang known as the Donald Duck Motorcycle Club. An M-36 Australian Army-type hand grenade was rolled across the street towards the bikes and exploded, putting three gang members in hospital. Jensen was a key suspect for the bombing and was extradited from NSW to face charges. After a County Court trial he was found guilty and sentenced to seven years jail. The sentence was quashed on appeal.

Despite the successful appeal, Jensen was set to begin a long stretch behind bars. In October 1978 he was sentenced to a minimum of eight years jail after being convicted of three armed robberies. Between robberies Jensen travelled to New South Wales and Queensland: he was finally arrested in Canberra. A police report at the time noted that Jensen's techniques had improved — he first bought an expensive sports car, but realised this would attract attention, so bought old-model Holdens, which he changed every month or so.

Just over two years into his sentence Jensen escaped from Geelong Jail. In Melbourne he met up with several associates, including long-time friend Peter McEvoy. With a fellow escapee, Jensen took $9000 from the National Bank in Essendon at gunpoint, before fleeing to Sydney. While driving back to Melbourne in a hire car, Jensen was arrested. In October 1981 he was sentenced to nine years jail, with no minimum sentence. Five-and-a-half years later, in mid-1987, Jensen was released on parole.

A man who shared a cell with Jensen for 15 months in Bendigo Prison said Jensen was 'personable, sincere, a staunch friend and a man who inspired strong friendships'. He is the cell-mate to whom Jensen's words at the opening of this chapter were told. On their release, the men agreed that Jensen would not call or visit if he was 'hot', that is engaged in criminal activity. After a few dinners, meetings and catch-up calls, Jensen went silent. His old cell-mate believes Jensen was honoring their understanding about life on the outside.

Jensen's return to society was not easy. He was in a serious traffic accident in August 1987 and spent several weeks in hospital. According to Sandra Faure, Jensen suffered a broken pelvis and broken arm. She told police: 'I saw him about four weeks after the accident . . . He was like a little old man in appearance. I also saw him before Christmas 1987 and he walked with a walking stick and his arm was still in a sling . . .'

As Jensen's health improved, he renewed and strengthened his friendships. He frequently visited Victor Peirce's Chestnut Street home and often talked with Peter McEvoy. Jedd Houghton became another close friend, with whom Jensen made several trips to the country to go shooting.

He was well respected and loved by associates and friends, who cherished his good humor and approach to life. But Jensen had one dark secret he kept from Victor Peirce, who by all accounts was his closest friend — Jensen was having an affair with Peirce's wife, Wendy. Sandra Faure was also ignorant of the affair, which began before he moved in with her at Narre Warren and continued afterwards.

Sandra Faure also appeared ignorant of Jensen's criminal activities in 1988. Police now believe he took part in a number of armed robberies, including one in which a blast was fired from the same shotgun used to kill the two policemen in Walsh Street.

Jensen may have realised police were watching him. He had certainly heard of Lindsay Rountree's arrest, and about the rumors that police were planning to kill Victor Peirce. According to Sandra Faure, Jensen mentioned on Friday 8 October that he thought he was under surveillance and being followed; she assumed this to be police surveillance. It appears nothing more was said about the matter because Tuesday 11 October began fairly typically, with no hint of the drama about to unfold.

Sandra Faure woke about 7.30 am, made breakfast for her two children and drove them to school, oblivious of the police cars discreetly watching the journey. Later that morning she took Jensen breakfast in bed; he watched the midday movie while she did jobs around the house, including cleaning the inside of her blue Commodore stationwagon. She made lunch, after which Jensen showered.

Jensen then said he was going to get a spark plug for the couple's lawn mower. He collected his wallet, car keys, gave Sandra Faure a hug, walked to the car and drove off.

It was about 3.20 pm when Jensen pulled into a shopping centre in Webb Street and walked into a hardware store. It was the first time police had seen a man leave the house and Detective Butts ordered a surveillance officer to follow him into the store, in an attempt to positively identify him as Jensen. The officer did so and Butts ordered police move in and make an arrest.

But as three armed robbery squad cars moved to intercept the wanted man, Jensen got into his vehicle and started the engine.

What happened next is the subject of a coronial inquiry by Victoria's Coroner, Hal Hallenstein. However, in evidence given at Hallenstein's inquiry, police said they tried to cut off Jensen's route of escape by blocking his path with a car, but Jensen evaded the cars and produced a gun as he drove away at speed. Two detectives, fearing for their lives, shot at Jensen; one was armed with a police-issue .38 revolver, the other a shotgun. One shotgun blast shattered the back window of the Commodore and at least two pellets struck Jensen, killing him instantly. Jensen's car crashed into a telegraph pole and his body slumped in the driver's seat. A detective ran to the car and opened the door to move the gun from Jensen's reach and check his condition, but Jensen was dead.

The existence of the gun, a sawn-off bolt-action .22 rifle, was disputed by legal representation for Jensen's family who, like his associates, claimed it was planted by police. The legal counsel also challenged many aspects of the police version of events. The fact that the sawn-off rifle was moved before any forensic tests could be made or photographs taken, made it impossible to say whether it actually had been in the car at the time of the shooting, Hallenstein's inquiry was told. Indeed Sandra Faure was later to tell investigators: 'I know Graeme wasn't carrying a gun because he gave me a cuddle before he left and I would have felt it if he had one on him.'

News of the shooting was broken to Faure by her son, who saw the police activity on his way home from school. In her statement, made two weeks later, Sandra Faure told police that she knew something was wrong. Soon afterwards 'some men in suits' arrived. Armed with a search warrant to look for firearms, the detectives systematically searched the house — as Faure said, 'they took things apart' — and found a packet of bullets in a disused clothes dryer.

'As the time was getting on and Graeme had not returned I asked the police where Graeme was. One of them said a police officer would be here shortly. At about that time my sister rang me and told me that she'd heard on the radio that somebody had been fatally shot at Narre Warren. I hung up and went outside and spoke to the policeman who I thought was in charge. I said to him "Graeme's dead, isn't he?" He said a police officer would be there shortly. At about that time a uniformed police car arrived and a uniformed inspector told me they believed the person in the car that had been killed was named Jensen.'

Faure was driven to Webb Street, the scene of Jensen's death, by a neighbor. At the scene she was put into a police car. Mrs Faure said a policewoman in the car turned to her and said: 'Are you Wendy?' The policewoman's account was that she asked Mrs Faure: 'Do you know Wendy?', a reference to another woman living in Moray Court. Mrs

Faure's statement to police differs. 'She said it in a way as if I was actually named Wendy. I thought the Wendy reference was a reference to me being Wendy Peirce, as she is the only Wendy I know. This Wendy reference led me to believe it was Victor Peirce the police wanted and not Graeme.'

Sandra Faure was not the only person in Melbourne who thought Victor Peirce was the intended victim. Across the other side of town the same belief was about to be voiced.

6
Word Spreads

Rumour doth double, like the voice and echo
The numbers of the feared

Shakespeare, *2 Henry IV*

News of the police shooting in Narre Warren spread quickly.

Peter McEvoy, one of the four men later to be acquitted of the Walsh Street murders, was one of the first to hear, picking up a newsflash on his car radio as he drove between North Melbourne and Brunswick. The newsflash did not mention Jensen's name: just that a man had been shot dead in Narre Warren by police. According to court evidence McEvoy made a mistake in passing on the initial details — he thought Victor Peirce was the victim.

The mistake was perhaps a natural assumption. Peirce was scared police were about to kill him, having received such a message from Penny Rountree. McEvoy was aware of this, and knew Peirce feared being arrested for The Summer Hold-Up: after all, Rountree and 'Smith' had already been grabbed. McEvoy also believed Peirce was meeting Jensen that afternoon in Narre Warren: the facts seemed to fit his surmise that the police had just shot his friend Victor.

At the time of the shooting, McEvoy was spending most nights at a flat in Davies Street, Brunswick, the home of Peirce's only sister, Vicki Brooks. McEvoy was a lodger, having moved in only weeks earlier. He first met Brooks more than a decade earlier and, after moving out of a flat in Albert Park in September 1988, asked Brooks if he could stay at her flat for a few weeks. McEvoy offered to pay board, and she agreed.

Within an hour of Jensen's shooting, according to evidence given in court by Brooks, McEvoy burst through her back door and told her that her brother, Victor, had just been shot in Narre Warren. Brooks became hysterical and was still in a bad state when the telephone rang

15 minutes later. She picked up the receiver, heard a voice and dropped the phone in shock. It was Victor, her 'dead' brother.

'McEvoy [then] picked up the phone and spoke to Victor. He spoke for only a short time and then dropped the phone and went hysterical. He put his hands up in the air and said: "Oh no, oh no, not Graeme ..." McEvoy went over to the sink and started banging the sink very hard with his fists and crying out Graeme's name. He was crying and making weird noises like an animal. McEvoy yelled out, "The jacks will pay for this",' Brooks later told a court hearing.

Across the other side of town at Keilor, Victor Peirce, with his wife Wendy, had sought refuge with friends, still believing Lindsay Rountree's warning that Victor would be shot by police. Only minutes before telephoning his sister and speaking to McEvoy, Peirce also heard a newsflash. Wendy suspected the worst and phoned Sandra Faure who, crying at the other end of the phone, confirmed that Graeme Jensen was the victim. Wendy hung up and told Victor who, according to evidence later given by Wendy, began crying. Wendy was distraught: in her own words, she 'went berserk'. Not only was Jensen her husband's best friend, he was also her secret lover. She began screaming, she told the committal hearing, and crying out: 'Maggots, they ought to be knocked. Fucking maggots, they ought to be killed.'

Her children, who were also in the house, began to cry. Victor Peirce also began screaming. It was moments later, when he composed himself, that Peirce rang his sister's Brunswick flat to speak to McEvoy — and Vicki Brooks answered the phone to a brother she thought was dead.

Meanwhile, Brooks had telephoned her son, Jason Ryan, and told him to come home urgently. Ryan was at the Stockade Hotel in Fitzroy, playing billiards with his best friend, Anthony Farrell. At the hotel they had met up with Emmanuel Alexandridis, a 17-year-old small-time criminal and friend of Ryan's, and Brydon Shabo, a 25-year-old unemployed laborer, whom none of the three knew well. After Ryan's mother called, Ryan, with Farrell, Alexandridis and Shabo — who had been offered a smoke of marijuana by Ryan back at Brunswick — caught a taxi to Vicki Brooks' Davies Street flat.

As Ryan walked to the back door his mother met him and told him that Jensen had been shot dead by police. Said Brooks, who was later to be a key Crown witness: 'Jason just looked at me and went white. Anthony Farrell started crying.'

Not long afterwards, according to Ryan's mother, Jedd Houghton arrived. She had not met him before, although they had spoken several times on the phone, the most recent occasion being the previous night when Houghton was looking for McEvoy.

Houghton parked his motorcycle outside the flats and walked into the lounge, carrying his bike helmet in his hand. He was not aware of the shooting. 'When McEvoy told him that Graeme had been shot he started to cry. He sat holding his head in his hands and crying as if he were in shock.'

When the evening news came on the television, the anger set in. Brooks said: 'Jedd said nothing during the news but McEvoy kept calling the police "dogs". He was saying that they had loaded Graeme up [fabricated evidence] and they have just gone out and knocked him and that they're going to pay ... McEvoy was really carrying on ... He was banging his fists on everything and screaming out. He was really mental.'

Alexandridis, who spent most of the time in Jason Ryan's bedroom smoking marijuana, also noticed McEvoy's fury. In an interview with police three weeks after the killings, he said: 'Macca was saying "Why Graeme? Why did they have to shoot Graeme for?"... [He was] raving on and saying "They're going to get theirs".'

According to Jason Ryan, in evidence the Crown would rely on to establish how the plan to ambush police was hatched, McEvoy, Farrell and Houghton began talking and Ryan eavesdropped.

'I heard Macca say, "Two of our mates have died now two dogs have to die" ... I also heard them organising where they were going to meet that night. I heard them saying they would meet at Gordon Grove, South Yarra and that they would set up some police. I think it was Macca saying this to Anthony ... My uncles, Victor Peirce and Trevor Pettingill were also mentioned in the conversation. Macca said he had to go and pick up Trevor and then organise the car off Gary. They were going to meet Gary and get his car which is a silver Gemini. I know the Gary they were talking about, it was Gary Abdallah, but I don't know why they were using his car ...

'I went upstairs and a little while later Anthony came up. He told me he had to go to Gordon Grove later that night to meet Macca, Jedd, Victor and Trevor ...'

Alexandridis then went with Farrell to buy some beer from the near-by Moreland Hotel. While there, a news item came on the television about Jensen's shooting. Alexandridis later told police in a video-interview: '[Farrell said] "That's me mate Graeme". And he goes — he starts raving on about the "Cunts, coppers", and "They'll get theirs". And after a little while he said "You watch. Believe me," he said, "the cops will go". And I just, you know, didn't know what to say.' (Alexandridis, however, would later deny the accuracy of his statements to police, claiming he was repeatedly beaten while in custody.)

The news of Jensen's death continued to spread. Vicki Brooks telephoned her brother Trevor Pettingill at his home in Holden Street, North Fitzroy. Pettingill's *de facto* wife, Debbie Young, answered the phone and said he was asleep. Pettingill later said he had taken some prescription drugs — tranquillisers — and was semi-conscious or unconscious for most of the afternoon and evening. When Young woke him he said he 'didn't care' and rolled over and went back to sleep, according to a statement Pettingill gave police. He said he did not wake up until the next day, although the Crown version of events certainly disagreed with this. According to Brooks, Debbie Young later rang back her Brunswick flat and spoke for a short time with Jedd Houghton.

The phone bill at the Davies Street flat continued to mount. McEvoy phoned Sandra Faure to console her about Jensen's death. He also rang Jensen's sister, Faye Spear and, with Jedd Houghton, later visited Spear at her Flemington flat.

According to police, Sandra Faure, who visited the city morgue that night and insisted on seeing Jensen's body — she only got access after the autopsy, which finished in the early hours of Wednesday morning — also made a number of phone calls. She also visited Jensen's sister that night. So, by late on Tuesday 11 October, dozens of telephone calls had been made across Melbourne, spreading the news of Jensen's death. The Crown would allege at the trial that as Wednesday morning began, the final phase of the plan to kill police would begin — solely in revenge for the killing of Jensen.

The Crown would base its claims on the statements of Jason Ryan, who said that in the early hours of 12 October 1988 he was at a small flat in Gordon Grove, South Yarra, dubbed 'murder headquarters' by the Crown. The flat was rented by Farrell's girlfriend, Belinda Rice, and her sister Collette.

Ryan, who, with Farrell, Alexandridis and Shabo, left his mother's Brunswick flat around 8 pm and went back to the Stockade Hotel, said he and Farrell left the pub soon after midnight and were dropped at the flat by friends about 12.30 pm. Farrell opened the security door and flat door with a key and, about 10 minutes later, Peirce, Houghton, McEvoy and Pettingill arrived. This is an edited version of Jason

Ryan's account, rejected out of hand by the four accused, given in Ryan's final statement to police, of what happened once the four men arrived.

'I saw Victor and Jedd were carrying something wrapped in plastic bags. I could tell from looking at them in the green garbage bags that they were shotguns. I could also see that Macca had a pistol in his tracksuit pants, it looked like a little .25. I have seen Macca with this .25 at my Mum's place before that night as well . . .

'After they arrived, Victor and Jedd put the shotguns in the corner of the loungeroom and they all stayed in the lounge. We then made a big mix [of marijuana] and everyone had a smoke, then Victor, Trevor, Macca, Anthony and Jedd went into a bedroom just near the loungeroom.

'I heard Trevor say that he had picked up a car with Macca and he had done what he had to do. I could hear Trevor even though the bedroom door was shut because he is a loud talker. I knew they were all having a discussion because I could hear voices but not what was being said, except for the part about Trevor.

'When Trevor was saying he had picked up a car and everything was sweet, that would mean he had changed plates, the registration plates. Trevor and me have stolen cars before and then we take other plates from cars and put them on the stolen cars . . .

'Just before they came out of the room I heard Victor say he would get one of them and they would have to get the rest. Trevor then said he'd do it, but Jedd said no, it was his friend and he'd do it . . .'

Around 3.30 am, with Peirce and Houghton carrying a shotgun each, the five men — Peirce, Houghton, McEvoy, Pettingill and Farrell — walked out of the flat leaving Ryan behind. 'Victor then told me to stay at the flat and look after the place. I think he meant to make sure no one came and don't answer the phone or nothing like that. I looked at Anthony and he looked like he was worried, he wasn't the same as he was at the Stockade Hotel.'

Ryan dozed off in front of the television. He said he heard some shots, then began dozing again. 'About 10 or 20 minutes after I heard the shots, the downstairs buzzer was pressed quite a few times. I looked down and I saw Anthony there and I let him in. When Anthony came in I could see specks of blood on his pants, they stood out because of his white tracksuit pants . . .

'I said to him, "What happened?", and he said: "I shot the police twice. I took the gun off the police." I can't remember exactly what he said but he told me that he took the gun off the policeman and shot him twice. He also said the police screamed, or something like that. I asked Anthony if Victor was all right and he told me, "Yeah, he's gone".'

According to Ryan, Farrell was the only person to return to the Gordon Grove flat. This would fit with the Crown view that the other four men fled in two getaway cars, each seen by independent witnesses. Ryan said that about three hours after the shootings he and Farrell took a taxi back to his mother's Brunswick flat where both went to sleep, Ryan in his room and Farrell on the couch.

The Crown would say the killing of Jensen had prompted the execution-style shooting of two policemen 13 hours later — that it was straightforward revenge, a payback. And at the committal hearings, Victor Peirce's wife, Wendy, lent weight to this theory.

Wendy Peirce told the magistrate that her husband, after receiving the message on Sunday night from Penny Rountree, feared he was going to be killed. He left his home at 86 Chestnut Street and sought refuge with friends at Keilor: but with Jensen dead, a killing that reinforced Peirce's fears, it was decided a motel was even safer for Victor, Wendy and their three children. Peirce had also decided to give himself up to police for questioning about The Summer Hold-Up, thus avoiding any confrontation. But according to Wendy Peirce, Victor had other thoughts on his mind soon after Graeme Jensen was shot. Under cross-examination the following conversation took place:

— What did he [Victor] say?
— He said we were going to the motel and we'll be safe there because he said he'll be going out to meet McEvoy . . . he also said it in the car.
— And what did you believe he was going out to meet McEvoy for?
— To kill the police that killed Graeme . . .
— So you say that he went to the motel with you, telling you that he was going out to kill members of the armed robbery squad later?
— He didn't say armed robbery squad, he said the ones that killed Graeme.

Wendy Peirce went on to say that just before midnight her husband left the motel. He returned several hours later and told her he had been involved in the shootings in South Yarra.

7
Raids, Raids, Raids

Lord, have mercy, I think that it's the cops

Van Morrison, 'Madam George'

Detective John Noonan had been in bed less than three hours when he was woken by a telephone call and told about the shootings. A policeman of 17 years and a senior sergeant in the homicide squad, Detective Noonan had spent the previous evening and much of the night at Narre Warren inquiring into Graeme Jensen's death, taking statements, coordinating forensic, photographic, video and ballastic services and finally attending Jensen's autopsy. He was called to that shooting because his four-man team was the 'on-call' homicide crew, meaning that any job that fell between 3 pm and 8 o'clock the next morning was theirs. Jensen was shot dead about 3.20 pm. His crew was still the 'on-call' team for any murder in Victoria when Damian Eyre and Steven Tynan were gunned down at 4.47 am. Detective Noonan was telephoned at 5.27 am and was at Walsh Street an hour later. For Detective Noonan, it was the start of two-and-a-half years on the case.

One of the fundamental and most immediate tasks in any murder investigation is the examination of the crime scene, and the better its condition, the better the chance of finding clues and evidence. At Walsh Street, the crime scene was chaotic. First, the bodies had been removed — quite properly in the circumstances — but this meant it was difficult to tell where Damian Eyre and Steven Tynan were located when the shots were fired. This problem was compounded by the initial confusion at the scene: one policeman, who attended in the first minutes and knew both officers, told investigators that Constable Eyre had been removed from the front seat of the car to be treated. He was wrong: it was Constable Tynan. While this inaccuracy was cleared up once forensic and ballastic tests were completed, it took several days for investigators to build a picture of how the ambush was executed.

More serious was the fact that dozens of police had walked through the crime scene to look at the site of the killing, offer help, or attempt to coordinate the search for the culprits. Walsh Street residents woken by gunshots wandered into the street; ambulance officers spent almost 20 minutes stabilising each wounded policeman, discarding plastic wrappers for syringes and drugs as they treated their patients. The net effect was that the chance of finding any clues that the killers may have left behind — such as the footprints of someone who stepped into the road from the bushes — were diminished.

The police who initially coordinated events at the scene ordered that white plastic tape be put up around the police car and the Commodore and no one enter the area.

But whoever ambushed the police had almost certainly hidden in the bushes of leafy Walsh Street and fled on foot in the laneway alongside the block of flats at number 222. Yet a large part of this area was not isolated. Police wandered along the laneway and in Walsh Street itself, some to use telephones in nearby houses: even a media briefing took place close by. It was almost two hours after the murders before the 'outer perimeter' of the crime scene was expanded to cover most of Walsh Street and the area in which the killers fled. But when it was closely searched, the expanded area revealed little. Whether a clue would have been found if the outer perimeter had been isolated earlier is only a matter of speculation.

For investigators, one of the first tasks was to find witnesses. Dozens of residents in and around Walsh Street were woken by the shotgun blasts: some had turned over and gone back to sleep, others had heard footsteps or groans and some saw the killers flee. All needed to be interviewed. Statements were taken from residents in houses and flats in the immediate area, many from people before they left for work. The 'doorknock' was expanded to hundreds of homes over the following days. The first police on the scene were interviewed, as were the ambulance officers. Peter Ellis, the newsagency manager who rang Prahran police station to report the stolen car, was also questioned: even at that early stage it appeared Tynan and Eyre had been ambushed and detectives needed to establish whether the original call was part of the plan to lure police to the scene. Ellis was interviewed and cleared. David Wilkinson, the owner of the Commodore used to lure police into the trap, was also interviewed by detectives. He had been woken by the gunshots and the police sirens that followed. On looking on to Walsh Street he noticed police swarming around a car that looked familiar: he then realised it was his Commodore. Wilkinson went into the street and told police he was the owner.

Once dawn broke, police photographers took dozens of photographs of the scene from the police helicopter. Fingerprint experts, forensic staff, photographers and police video crews pored over the scene. Three shotgun shells were found close to the car. They were photographed and taken away for analysis. But there was no sign of the shotgun used to fire them, nor of Constable Eyre's revolver, which had been noticed as missing by the first police on the scene. Dozens of police, some with metal detectors, were assigned to search drains, front gardens and nearby parks in an attempt to find either murder weapon. Police divers were dispatched to search the Yarra River at the foot of the hill from Walsh Street: their unsuccessful search lasted days. By the end of the first day a police caravan was at Walsh Street. Manned by detectives on a 24-hour basis, its purpose was to collect information from residents or passers-by who remembered anything. Autopsies on the two dead policemen were organised and carried out about lunchtime. The autopsies, with assistance from forensic and ballistic experts, helped establish within 72 hours of the murders what sort of weapons were used to kill the police, how many shots were fired and the position of both police when the ambush was executed.

The amount of information generated on the day of the murders was enormous. Some of it would prove to be false, some deliberately so.

Within hours of the killings a witness came forward saying he saw three men running along Acland Street, each carrying guns. The man was brought to the scene by police and spent some time with investigators explaining what he saw. The inconsistencies in his story were queried by detectives until, after several hours, the man admitted he made the story up. He was later charged with making a false report to police, convicted and jailed.

On the day of the murders police command decided that the killings should be treated like any other murder in Victoria. But clearly they were not like any other murder. The attack, the first multiple murder of police in Victoria since the Kelly gang killed three officers near Mansfield in October 1878, was seen by many as a direct attack on the community. It became a question: 'If the police aren't safe, who is?'

Many police also resented the view of police command that the murders were not to get 'special' treatment. The police brotherhood, after all, is known for its powerful bonds, and when it comes to a fellow officer being murdered, those close-knit bonds come to the fore. When Constable Angela Taylor was left with fatal injuries after the March 1986 bombing of the Russell Street police station, the Victoria Police pulled out all stops to catch the killers. Detectives and uniformed officers alike wanted to contribute to the arrest of the bombers. On the day of the Walsh Street murders the feeling was the same, perhaps stronger because it was two dead police, not one. What increased the natural feeling of outrage among police was the callous nature of the killings. It was not as if they were shot arresting somebody, or during a shoot-out: they were just cut down in cold blood.

The reason for the extraordinary decision to treat the killings as an ordinary homicide may have been political sensitivity on behalf of senior police — not wanting to be seen to be giving murdered police special treatment — or perhaps a hope that the crime would be quickly and easily solved. It took several days for senior police to decide to set up a special investigation, and a full nine days after the murders before a taskforce was actually up and running.

Until that time, the main investigators, who numbered about six, worked from the homicide squad offices on the ninth floor of the St Kilda Road police building. Their space and resources were hopelessly inadequate, and matters did not improve greatly when the taskforce, named TyEyre, was established. The investigators were flooded with information, which was put into trays in order of priority. Those marked 'priority one' were in most cases handed to other detectives from the homicide squad and other squads, as well as suburban detectives who had been temporarily seconded to join the hunt.

An example of a 'priority one' case came on the first day, when a man living in The Righi told police that his Commodore had been stolen a couple of weeks earlier. Soon after that theft local police arrested the car thief, who was charged and bailed. The common denominators of the Commodore and the area near Walsh Street, although tenuous in their links with the murders, made it essential that police check the lead. A telephone call to the detectives who made the car-theft arrest established the name of the car thief and his address. He was more than a touch surprised when more than half a dozen armed detectives burst into his grandmother's house and questioned him. His possible involvement was quickly ruled out.

The investigation was initially headed by Brendon Cole, head of the homicide squad, with Detective Inspector David Sprague as his deputy, essentially in charge of administration, and Detective Noonan as the man in charge of the minute-to-minute decisions. Detectives initially wanted more information on the two getaway cars seen after the shootings and widespread publicity was given to the descriptions of the light-colored sedan and dark panel van. But despite numerous tip-offs, police were unable to find a car that could be positively identified as that used by the killers.

In the meantime, detectives from the other leading squads did not adopt the police force's public policy of viewing the murders as a 'normal' homicide. Some were convinced that the killings were in revenge for Jensen's death and many who held this belief were outraged that two junior constables had been cut down in revenge. Many detectives dropped the work they were doing and began searching for information that would help solve the case. Three days after the killings the heads of all squads were given briefings on what had taken place and were asked for any information available. It was the green light — if it hadn't already been signalled at 4.47 am on 12 October — for a series of hard and uncompromising police raids which, in intensity over the following days and months, was unprecedented in Australia.

Other information-gathering exercises were less vigorous. Detectives checked with informants whether anything had been overheard or said that might connect with the killings. The sources of information ranged widely: police from the licensing, gaming and vice squads checked sources in nightclubs, illegal gambling clubs and with prostitutes and brothel owners, while drug squad detectives quizzed drugs dealers and users. A wide net was cast in an attempt to drag up any information, boosted by the State Government's offer of a $200,000 reward for information leading to the conviction of the killers.

It was ironic that it was members of the armed robbery squad — the police who investigated Graeme Jensen's 'involvement' in the murder of Armaguard employee Dominik Hefti and the police who, in essence, were behind Jensen's death — who were the first to confront four of the five people later charged with the police murders. And all but one of those contacts came in raids aimed at locating Victor Peirce, who was still wanted for his 'role' in the Hefti murder.

About 11 am on the morning of 12 October, just over six hours after the police murders, Jason Ryan, Anthony Farrell and Peter McEvoy were at Vicki Brooks' flat in Brunswick. How long each had been there, however, was to be a point of contention at the trial.

In his later evidence, Ryan said he came home with Farrell some time before 8 am after catching a taxi in South Yarra. According to Ryan he and Farrell waited until light before leaving the Gordon Grove flat, walked down Punt Road to Toorak Road and caught a taxi on the corner, outside a Seven-Eleven store. Farrell would maintain he and Ryan arrived at Brooks' flat soon after leaving the Stockade Hotel, saying he and Emmanuel Alexandridis slept on the couch while Ryan slept in his room upstairs. McEvoy said he stayed all night at the flat and did not go out.

According to Vicki Brooks, however, McEvoy left early on the evening of the killings, then telephoned her about 11 pm to say he would not be coming home that night. She said he returned the next morning about 10.30 am looking tired and drawn, saying he had a hard night and needed some sleep. He went upstairs to the spare room for a couple of hours before leaving again.

Brooks also gave evidence that some time around 2 pm, nine hours after the police murders, Victor Peirce arrived at the flat with his wife, Wendy. McEvoy had left the flat shortly before Peirce's arrival, but Farrell and Ryan were still there. According to Brooks she was surprised to see her brother Victor — she had not seen him for more than six months after they fell out after a family quarrel. Even more surprising was the fact he was drinking rum and coke from a can. Peirce, a vegetarian, was not a drinker. Brooks said he had abstained from alcohol for six or seven years; Wendy Peirce also said her husband never drank. Brooks said her brother seemed scared.

Soon after Peirce arrived, McEvoy telephoned to find out if there were any messages for him. Brooks said no, but told him her brother was there. McEvoy spoke briefly to Peirce, then said he'd be there soon. He arrived and they talked.

After a while Wendy Peirce left the Davies Street flat to pick up her children from the Richmond swimming pool, and Farrell and Ryan went with her. After picking up the children and buying some dog meat at a butcher's in Swan Street, Richmond, all went to her Chestnut Street home to feed Victor's dobermans, which had not been fed for 24 hours. Ryan was hungry so walked to a local milk bar and bought a salad roll. He returned to the Chestnut Street house and went inside.

He had been back only minutes when those in the house heard what sounded like a small explosion at the front door: it was the door being blasted with a shotgun. Wendy Peirce was on the phone talking to Victor's solicitor and, as the front door crashed in, Ryan shouted 'Police!' Wendy told the caller that police were raiding the house and hung up. Within moments heavily armed men in black stormed into the house — the special operations group had arrived.

Ryan was pushed to the floor, his head covered with a black hood and his hands bound. He was roughly searched — testified to by photographs taken later in the day that showed bruising around his face — and left on the floor. Farrell suffered similar treatment, while Wendy Peirce clutched her young daughter and stood her ground. Wendy, Farrell and Ryan were taken to the St Kilda Road police station for questioning: Wendy's three children were taken to her mother's house in South Melbourne. During their interviews, Peirce and Farrell said little to police that was of any use. Ryan, however, talked readily: not about Walsh Street, but about his Uncle Victor's 'involvement' in the Hefti murder. It would be a statement that would cause Ryan great anguish.

Meanwhile, Victor Peirce, the intended target of the special operations group raid, was still at his sister's flat in Brunswick. Brooks realised her brother was scared that police were going to kill him — the death of Jensen and Penny Rountree's warning still weighed on his mind — so she walked to the nearby Moreland Motor Motel to book a room for him. She paid in cash and returned home.

Soon afterwards, according to evidence given by Brooks, McEvoy walked into her flat having just bought a copy of *The Herald*. The front page was dominated by the police murders and McEvoy held it up and said to her: 'Right whack. One of ours for two of theirs.' McEvoy later denied saying this.

Moments later, Peirce's solicitor, Charlie Nikakis, telephoned to pass on the message that Peirce's home had been raided. Peirce spoke to Nikakis briefly then said to Brooks: 'I'm not staying here, I have to go.' Peirce walked with his sister to the motel and, as they arrived, they saw carloads of police on their way to do a raid. There was little doubt whose home was the target. Peirce jumped a fence and fled. Brooks walked back to her flat and found her kitchen in a state of disrepair. As armed robbery squad detectives searched her flat, Peter McEvoy sat on the couch. Curiously, he was not taken back to police headquarters, although he was spoken to.

The fourth person armed robbery squad detectives came into contact with was Victor Peirce himself. After another night at a motel, Peirce went to the St Kilda Road police station on Thursday 13 October with his solicitor. He expected to be interviewed about The Summer Hold-Up, for which 'Smith' and Rountree had already been charged. Instead he was led to the homicide squad offices and, in a video-taped interview, he was asked about the murder of Dominik Hefti. Peirce declined to answer questions beyond those asking his name, age, address, date of birth and whether he understood the police caution that he was not obliged to say anything, but anything he said could be used in evidence. Victor Peirce said he understood this and, on legal advice, he would not answer any further questions. Peirce appeared stunned when detectives said he was to be charged with the murder and armed robbery of Hefti. It was little wonder: as later investigations would show, Peirce was not involved.

But at the time the evidence, although circumstantial, seemed strong. Peirce was taken to the City Watchhouse where, protesting his innocence, he was charged. He remained in custody for more than 30 months — during which time the Hefti charges were withdrawn and the Walsh Street charges laid — before being released after his acquittal on charges of killing Constables Damian Eyre and Steven Tynan.

For detectives from the TyEyre taskforce, however, the jailing of Peirce was a handicap. In late October, as more suspects were ruled out, police began installing listening devices — or bugs — in the homes of suspects and their associates. Police regarded it as a disadvantage that Peirce was not circulating among his friends and possibly being picked up on a bug.

So, within 48 hours of the murders, armed robbery squad detectives had spoken to Ryan, Farrell, McEvoy and Peirce, all of whom would eventually be charged with the Walsh Street murders. Yet to detectives actually responsible for investigating the police murders this meant little at that time. They had not conducted the interviews — they were still pulling together the physical evidence from the crime scene, interviewing witnesses and attempting to coordinate the first stages of a complicated inquiry. In the meantime funerals for the two police were held.

Damian Eyre was buried in Shepparton on Friday 14 October, two days after the shooting. The Victoria Police chief commissioner, Kel Glare, was interstate on business and did not return for the funeral, a non-appearance that caused resentment among many police. Glare did attend the funeral of Steven Tynan the following Monday.

As the days turned into a week, it became obvious that the inquiry would not be wrapped up quickly, so senior police authorised the formation of a taskforce. There were also fears of a repeat attack on police and security at most police buildings was beefed up. This fear continued for months, especially as some of the uncompromising raids by police on Walsh Street suspects and their associates inspired anonymous threats: plain packages were left outside Prahran police station, home of Constables Tynan and Eyre, in the early hours of the morning. There was a security scare at the Police Club when friends of Jedd Houghton were spotted in the carpark behind the club one night. On the streets, police changed their tactics and, instead of attending calls individually, they would not attend unless there were at least two cars. This applied to almost every assignment, including those previously seen as 'routine' such as a call to a burglary. This subsequently added a huge delay to the time police took to arrive to any call. One policeman explained the decision to *Sun* reporter John Silvester: 'People will just have to wait their turn because we will be minimising risks to our members.'

The taskforce initially numbered about 20 and took up residence in offices on the 13th floor of the St Kilda Road building, offices that had previously housed the Russell Street bombing taskforce, some two years earlier. The offices, however, were almost empty: there were hardly any desks, chairs, phones, and certainly no computer equipment. Detectives supposedly investigating the most brutal murder in Victoria's recent history were forced to temporarily abandon their inquiry to, as one officer said, 'beg, steal and borrow' equipment. Trucks were borrowed from the police transport branch so furniture could be acquired. New telephone numbers were established for callers with information. Filing cabinets were put into lifts and moved up four floors. Files were packed up, then unpacked at the new destination. In effect, days and days of manpower were lost.

It is something Detective John Noonan remains bitter about. 'The police department hadn't learned any lessons from Russell Street, they hadn't done anything since Russell Street, they hadn't improved anything since Russell Street, they hadn't modified any systems. The computer branch . . . gave us packages that were worthless.'

Problems were compounded by a lack of space on the 13th floor. On 15 December, two months after the murders, the taskforce moved offices again, this time up one level to the 14th floor. Although this offered more space, the shift again created chaos. Files had to be packed away, moved and unpacked. Phone numbers had to be changed and, two months down the track, the numbers were more important as detectives needed witnesses, informers and contacts to keep in touch with them. The move again ate away days of manpower.

Although the police department was unprepared and seemingly poorly equipped for an investigation of the size and immediacy of TyEyre, once it got going, the taskforce received a massive amount of assistance. Among other help, it received enormous assistance from the Victoria Police bureau of criminal intelligence, which dropped a long-term cocaine-importing inquiry to help on the police shootings case. In effect, the whole 130-strong bureau put itself at the disposal of TyEyre. The bureau provided investigators, technical assistance with the planting and maintenance of listening devices, and its specialist surveillance section. The drug squad provided its surveillance crews. The National Crime Authority in Victoria put its surveillance police at the disposal of the taskforce.

Even more remarkable was the use of almost all Victorian police who had ever qualified as surveillance specialists. As the enquiry entered November 1988 there were at least a dozen people who were 'targets' — either suspects or close associates of suspects — and needed watching or following on a 24-hour basis. Those police qualified at surveillance, numbering more than 100, were temporarily moved from where they were working and put at the disposal of the taskforce.

Victoria's annual anti-terrorist exercise, which allows units such as the special operations group and communications experts the opportunity to liaise with their Federal counterparts, was cancelled by senior police to give the taskforce access to all the Victoria Police resources it needed.

Added to this, 12 days after the murders, the State Government quickly and quietly proclaimed legislation allowing telephone intercepts. Up until then, the Victoria Police had not been allowed to legally tap telephones and, if it wanted phone taps, it needed to work with Federal Police, which had the power. (There is adequate anecdotal evidence and rumor, however, to suggest illegal tapping, although not widespread, was not unheard of in Victoria.) The advantage of legal telephone tapping, however, was that anything overheard could be used as evidence in court. To its credit, the Government proclaimed the act without publicity, something that must have been tempting as it was being frequently criticised by pro-police groups and the State Opposition for failing to give police 'adequate' powers. It was five months before news of the phone taps was published.

In the first weeks of the inquiry there were a number of possible motives and theories that had to be investigated. One was that Tynan and Eyre had caught a car thief red-handed and been shot. This possibilty was not unprecedented: only two years earlier, Senior Constable Maurice Moore was on duty in the rural town of Maryborough when, alone in a police car, he spotted a man trying to steal a car. When Moore confronted the man, Robert Nowell, the would-be thief grabbed the policeman's gun and shot him dead. Nowell was later convicted of the murder and jailed. This possibility seemed unlikely, however, as it became clear that the car had been abandoned in the middle of Walsh Street for about 40 minutes before Constables Tynan and Eyre arrived, meaning any car thief would not only have been surprisingly well armed, but extremely persistent.

Other early lines of investigation centred around the two victims. Detectives needed to establish whether the murders were random killings or whether Tynan or Eyre were the intended victims. The men's personal lives were probed, especially after numerous anonymous phone calls said either one or both police were involved in affairs with other men's wives. These allegations, like others that suggested the men were involved in illegal activities, proved groundless. The investigation into both men found no evidence to suggest a motive for murder — they were both honest and clean-living cops. Their policing activities were explored, especially the shooting and wounding of an armed robber by Tynan 10 days before his death. The people Tynan and Eyre had come into contact with in the previous week or more were checked. The results showed nothing. Combined with the way the shootings were carried out, it became increasingly apparent that the murder victims were chosen at random.

Detectives also obtained copies of all police logs in Melbourne for the evening of the killings. Anyone who had been stopped by police, whether it was for speeding, assault or anything else, was recorded on each log, and each name was checked to see who was out and about that night. Some of those names required further checking. People known to be anti-police were checked, especially those who had threatened police either individually or as a group and who had the ability to carry out their threats. Any escapees on the run were regarded as possible suspects, those with violent pasts more so.

Among the numerous lines of inquiry, detectives were also looking at the possibility that the killings were in revenge for the fatal shooting of Graeme Jensen, shot 13 hours before the murders. There was a vast amount of work to do and, after a couple of weeks, a whiteboard in the TyEyre offices listed the names of up to 100 people regarded as potential killers. And on the last day of October that list would be added to by the testimony of a scrawny 17-year-old youth named Jason Ryan.

8
Trouble

'I wasn't worried just because they had shotguns.'

Jason Ryan

Jason Ryan knew he was in trouble. He had told police about his Uncle Victor's 'involvement' in the Hefti murder, thus breaking underworld ethics about informing on others. Worse still, word of the statement had got out.

In the chaos that followed the police shootings, and the series of raids that took place the same day, Ryan and Farrell had been taken back to the St Kilda Road police headquarters. The police station was frenetic. People were being interviewed on different floors of the building and in different squad offices and, although the Walsh Street inquiry was under the umbrella of the homicide squad, coordination was lacking.

This meant a steady stream of police and suspects were going in and out of different offices.

Ryan was interviewed by two detectives from the armed robbery squad. He made his statement, implicating Peirce in the Hefti murder, and was released. He went to Coburg police station to sign the bail book, part of his bail conditions on drug charges, then borrowed some money from his father and went to a hotel for a drink.

Farrell meanwhile, had given his version of where he was that night, and was released. But while at the police station he was told that Ryan had made a statement. Who told Farrell was never clarified, although it had to be one of the many detectives involved in the inquiries of Day One. But for Ryan, this snippet of information was to prove damaging.

Ryan's statement was blunt. He told detectives that three months earlier, on the day before the Hefti shooting, he called around to see his Uncle Victor at 86 Chestnut Street, Richmond. Soon afterwards

Graeme Jensen arrived and Jensen and Peirce, according to Ryan, went out the front of the house and began talking about a shopping centre in the Brunswick area and stealing a car: 'They said that they had to steal it at night-time and put it in the vicinity of the place where it was to happen, but not too close because if the police find it they will know that something is going to go off in that area. It had to be fairly close but not too close ... I then heard them discussing what guns they would use. At this stage they both started whispering and I couldn't hear what they were saying.'

Ryan told detectives that Peirce and Jensen discussed bringing a scanner to monitor police radio transmissions, who would drive the car and who would grab the money. 'I heard Victor say "It's about your turn to get it now." I heard Graeme say: "All right, then." He then agreed that he would grab the money.'

The next evening, while staying at his father's house, Ryan was watching the television news when a report came on about the shooting of a security guard at the Brunswick Shopping Centre. Two days after that he again visited Peirce's house. Ryan said he saw Peirce remove five or six bundles of money from a secret compartment beneath the floorboards in a bedroom. Peirce took the money into the loungeroom and, with Jensen, began counting.

'Graeme then looked up at me and seen me watching. I think he said something to Victor, and Victor told me to come into the room. I then went and stood in the doorway, and stood there and asked them what they wanted. Victor pointed to a bundle of all $10 notes. He told me to count it. I counted it and found that there was roughly $620 there. I told Victor that and he said to me, "Well, you keep that for what I owe you." Victor owed me some money from a long time, because I was always lending him like, $10 or $20 from my pay. He gave me all that money, but he would not have owed me anywhere near that amount. When he gave it to me he also said: "Just don't tell anybody about what you seen." He then told me to go back into the dining room.'

For detectives hunting a bandit that had been wounded by a bullet from Dominik Hefti's gun, Ryan provided a tantalising clue. 'On this day when Graeme was at Victor's I seen that he [Graeme Jensen] had dried blood on the right hand. There was only a little bit of it and it was around the top of his fingers. I could not see any bandages on him. One thing that I did notice was that he was sweating a hell of a lot ... it seemed to be running down his face.' The statement was enough to seal the police case for laying charges against Peirce, charges that were laid the next day, then later withdrawn.

In the interview, Ryan realised he was treading on dangerous ground. He told detectives: 'If Victor found about about this he would kill me straight away. I have no doubt about that.' Yet he rationalised his statement thus: 'I have got to the stage where I don't want to end up like Dennis [Allen] did, I don't want to live a life like that. I want to get out of that sort of lifestyle and be like my father. He comes from a different style of life, he has a good job and I really want to be like that.'

Only hours after making his statement, Ryan went to the Stockade Hotel in Fitzroy, where he met up with, among others, Peter McEvoy and Anthony Farrell. McEvoy asked Ryan if he had said anything to police.

'I told him I said "No Comment". I told him I wouldn't tell 'em anything. He also asked me about what happened to my nose and I told him about the raid. He then said: "Are you sure you didn't say nothing?" and I said "I promise you, I didn't say nothing".' But then Anthony Farrell said something that frightened Ryan.

While he was at police headquarters, Farrell said, he was told that Jason had made a statement about an armed robbery in Brunswick, and in the statement Ryan said he had been paid $600 as part of the robbery. Farrell wanted to know if this was true. Ryan denied it, but was worried. Clearly, police had let him down. Only they knew about the $600 he was paid — and he had told detectives that only hours earlier.

Quite why Ryan volunteered information about his uncle's supposed involvement in the Hefti murder remains a mystery.

First, it is now clear that neither Peirce nor Jensen was involved in the murder and robbery. Among other evidence, their involvement has been ruled out by DNA tests. So, if Ryan was lying about the conversations he heard — a possibility considering his later track record — what was the purpose of putting police on to his uncle?

Second, Ryan had been trained by his family that the best way to approach police interviews was to admit nothing and deny everything, even if the police evidence was overwhelming. To give information about someone else's involvement in something — especially a family member — was just not done.

Ryan was later to say in court that one reason he told police about Peirce's 'involvement' in the Hefti murder was to test the police — to see if he could trust them. He had been trained by his family not to trust police; his Uncle Dennis had been involved with corrupt police officers who Jason Ryan did not like or trust — in fact he was scared of them. And now Farrell knew about his statement within hours. This attitude — of being scared of police, of testing them, of not trusting them — was to be crucial in the weeks to come.

During cross-examination, Ryan said the statement was a sort of plea for help. He said he wanted to tell police about Walsh Street on the day of the police murders, but was too scared. 'I wanted to go but I didn't, if you can understand that. I didn't want to go off to the police and I wanted to go home.' Ryan said he had wanted to be taken into police custody, but police hadn't offered that, let alone done it. And worse, someone had leaked details of his statement. He was scared, frightened and couldn't make up his mind. The answer was to 'test' the police again — and his opportunity came 10 days later.

The chance came from Peter Butts, the detective who led the Hefti murder investigation. For Detective Butts, Ryan's statement appeared a key to proving the murder charges laid against Victor Peirce for the Brunswick robbery. As the head of the inquiry, Butts wanted to talk to Ryan personally — another detective had taken the statement — and satisfy himself that Ryan was telling the truth, as well as find out if Ryan knew any more. The second concern was Ryan's safety.

Initial attempts by Detective Butts to find 17-year-old Ryan failed, so on Friday 21 October, Butts asked Coburg police to 'hold' Ryan when he came in to sign the bail book. Ryan duly arrived and was told to wait while Coburg police rang the armed robbery squad. Before long Butts arrived with another detective and personally escorted Ryan back to St Kilda Road police headquarters to interview him again about his statement. It was during the drive back to St Kilda Road that Ryan gave police their next 'test' — he said he knew something about Walsh Street.

Back at the station, Ryan was first questioned about the Hefti matter before being taken to the homicide squad offices to be interviewed. In what is best described as Ryan's 'first version', he gave detectives their strongest lead in the police murders inquiry. In a 69-minute video interview he provided names, times and a motive, yet conveniently kept himself out of any involvement in the killings. Much of what Ryan said would change over the following days and weeks, especially about what happened after midnight on the night of the murders. But some of his 'first version' would stay intact for the jury to hear more than two years later as his 'final version'.

To Ryan, it was again a question of trust. Under cross-examination, he was asked about the interview.

— Why did you speak to them about Walsh Street?
— I wanted to tell them, but I didn't know if I could trust them or not.
— But you did tell them something about Walsh Street?
— Some things, yes.

In his first version, Ryan said he arrived home on the afternoon of Tuesday 11 October to discover that Graeme Jensen had been shot dead by police. He said Peter McEvoy and Jedd Houghton were at his mother's Brunswick flat, both distraught and angry about the killing, both talking about how to exact revenge. Ryan said he spent that night at his mother's flat with Anthony Farrell (Farrell would maintain this is what happened throughout the case), while McEvoy did not come home that night. He mentioned a gun owned by McEvoy and a pistol and a pump-action shotgun owned by Victor Peirce.

Ryan also told police he was scared and, when offered police protection, he jumped at the chance. It was now early on Saturday 22 October 1988 — the video interview finished at 12.23 am — and Ryan was put into protective custody for the weekend, probably in a city hotel.

Detectives now had to determine whether Ryan's story had any element of truth. They also had to seek permission to put him into permanent police protection, a time-consuming application that requires approval from senior officers. Protection is not handed out lightly, not only because it is an expensive and manpower-intensive exercise, but police are wary of revealing their procedures and safe-houses to someone who is not certain of staying in the witness protection program. When Monday morning arrived, such permission had not come — and detectives were still unable to verify Ryan's story. The then head of the TyEyre taskforce and homicide squad chief, Detective Chief Inspector Brendon Cole, decided on an unorthodox solution that met with the approval of police command.

Detective Peter Butts was told to take Jason Ryan out of Melbourne and look after him. Butts's brief was to take two fellow armed robbery squad detectives and go to the country for a few days. He was not told where to go or what to do. The only requirement was to telephone the TyEyre taskforce office each day and check in.

Two nights were spent in Wangaratta, one in Bright and one in Mansfield. At Bright, on Wednesday 26 October, Ryan was taken in a four-wheel drive for a barbecue lunch. At the lunch site shotguns were produced and a number of tins were shot. According to police evidence and evidence given by Ryan in court, the teenager did not handle a shotgun and was not threatened at any stage. At the committal hearing, Ryan was closely questioned on the country trip, but for most answers his memory failed him and he replied: 'I can't recall'. During cross-examination, he was asked if police had threatened him on the country trip, a theme that was later pursued by his family.

— You had had a horrible experience with police in the past. You had been bashed, you have talked about it, back at Flemington [police station]?
— So?
— You had been bashed [by other police] in the past. You did not trust them, right?
— Yes.
— One of the reasons you did not trust them [police] was that they had assaulted you in the past?
— That's right.
— Hurt you in the past.
— That's right ...
— And here you are out in the middle of the bush with a couple of them who have got a couple of shotguns and you cannot even recall whether you were concerned about your own safety?
— I wasn't worried about my own safety.
— So it is better. You can recall. You were there with two police officers that you did not trust, but you were not worried about your own safety?
— No.
— Why not?
— I don't know.
— Or you did trust them? Is that not true what you said?
— I didn't trust them, but I wasn't worried about anything.
— You were not worried about it. You thought if they wanted to turn the shotguns on you, no problems, you could handle it. Is that right?
— I don't know about that, but I wasn't worried just because they had shotguns.

Yet the country trip — and especially the shooting element — prompted numerous rumors in the underworld that Ryan had been threatened and bashed senseless. There is nothing to suggest any truth in the rumors — it is also unclear where they started. Even so, the shooting of tins during the bush trip was an unwise move by police that left them open to criticsm at later court hearings and fuelled the Ryan-bashing rumors.

Such rumors certainly spread among Ryan's family and were adhered to by his grandmother, Kath Pettingill. Although she had no direct contact with him after he entered police protection, her daughter-in-law

Wendy Peirce did, although it is unclear whether she was the source of Kath Pettingill's claims. 'They took my young grandson at 17 away, they tortured him, they took him on this trip to the bush,' Kath Pettingill said on national television on the day of the Walsh Street acquittal. 'They held his head in the water and tried to drown him. I thought that only happened in Brazil and things like that, third-world countries, not in Australia.

'Those four days that were missing out of Jason's life, I can never remember what happened to him. Only their conscience knows what happened to him, to my grandson, on those four, five days they took him up the bush ... The way they tortured him. Only Jason or the police can respond ... He's like a robot. That's not my grandson Jason up there in the [witness] stand. My grandson disappeared the day he went to the bush and a new person emerged out of that. And I'm angry for what they've done to him.'

Kath Pettingill's theory was supported by her youngest son, Trevor, on the day he was acquitted of the police murders. Speaking to Channel Nine's *A Current Affair*, he urged his nephew to give his version of what happened on the country trip (although Ryan had already done so in court). 'Please come forward and tell them that they did take you up the bush and shot at you and did tell you what to say ... Just come and tell the truth to the public.'

Trevor Pettingill went on: 'If the jury didn't believe him the police would make sure he was right away so no author of a book or publication from reporters or newspapers could approach him just in case he turned around and said: "Yes, this is what really did happen. I was forced to do this".'

In a brief telephone conversation with this author, Ryan said he did not wish to discuss any matters relating to the Walsh Street case or answer any questions about his background. He said he was hoping to write his own book on his life. This was disappointing, because I had a number of questions I wanted to put to Ryan, among them the one posed by Trevor Pettingill. And one of those key questions that, to me, remains a big mystery of the Walsh Street case, is why — almost three weeks after the police murders — Jason Ryan took detectives on a guided tour around the back streets of South Yarra.

9
Lies, Lies, and Videotape

'Is what you're telling us here today true?'

Detective John Noonan to Jason Ryan

After four days in the bush with Detective Butts, Jason Ryan again met Detective John Noonan, this time at the Wangaratta police station. Ryan was again asked to go over events on the night of the police shootings, and again Ryan said he had seen Jedd Houghton and Peter McEvoy angry about Jensen's death. He maintained he and Farrell had spent the night at his mother's flat in Brunswick. A few details were modified, but the plot was essentially the same. One addition was the mention of Gary Abdallah's name in connection with a car. Beyond that, there were no changes of any significance.

On Friday 28 October 1988, the day after the meeting with Noonan, Ryan was driven back to Melbourne. While he was away, the application for Ryan to enter the witness protection program had been approved. From that day, until mid-1991, Ryan was under around-the-clock guard and was housed, fed and generally looked after by the Victorian taxpayer.

Over the next weekend, Ryan's story stayed the same. But on the Monday it made its first dramatic shift when he mentioned he had something more to tell detectives. It culminated on the Monday night with the 17-year-old Ryan leading detectives and a police videotape team around the back streets of South Yarra explaining how Constables Tynan and Eyre were executed. Ryan would later confess that this 're-enactment' was a pack of lies, but before he conceded this, some two weeks later, he gave detectives the names of two people who 'knew' about the killings: Emmanuel Alexandridis and Anthony Farrell.

According to Ryan's 'final version' of events for Tuesday 11 October, which was presented to the Walsh Street jury in 1991, he woke up around 11 am. It is necessary here to repeat some matters previously mentioned to give Ryan's 'final version' some semblance of cohesion, as the reader will see.

Ryan was staying with his mother at her flat in Davies Street Brunswick, where Peter McEvoy had become a lodger. Ryan's closest friend, Anthony Farrell, had spent the night downstairs on the couch. About lunch time, Ryan and 20-year-old Farrell went to the Stockade Hotel in Nicholson Street, Fitzroy, where they played billiards for a short time. At the hotel they met up with Emmanuel Alexandridis, a 17-year-old small-time criminal and friend of Jason Ryan's, and Brydon Shabo, a 25-year-old unemployed laborer, whom none of the three knew well. After a while Ryan's mother, Vicki Brooks, telephoned and told him to come home because something was wrong.

Ryan, with Farrell, Alexandridis and Shabo caught a taxi to Brunswick where they discovered that Graeme Jensen had been killed. The atmosphere was angry and bitter, with aggression directed towards police, especially by Peter McEvoy. The four stayed at the flat for a couple of hours, drinking beer and smoking marijuana. Farrell and Alexandridis went to the nearby Moreland Hotel and bought more beer, before returning to the flat. After a while, the four young men caught a taxi back to the Stockade Hotel, arriving some time around 8 pm. Soon afterwards Shabo went home. Most of this account was corroborated by others.

But what happened next remained a point of contention at the trial.

Anthony Farrell's version was that he, Ryan and Alexandridis left the hotel after 11 pm and went back to the Brunswick flat, where the three of them spent the night. Alexandridis gave the same story to police on 28 October. But six days later Emmanuel Alexandridis changed his story, saying he left the Stockade Hotel by himself and went back to his own flat in Holden Street, North Fitzroy.

In his first interview on 21 October, before he went with police to the bush, Ryan said he left with Alexandridis and Farrell, and both spent the night on the couch at his mother's flat. But his story changed on Monday 31 October, and he implicated Alexandridis and Farrell. His video interview that Monday night would be enough to have Farrell charged with murder the next day. Alexandridis was pestered in the following weeks by detectives to tell them what he knew.

Some might say that the video taken that Monday night — 20 days after Graeme Jensen's shooting — showed Jason Ryan to be quick thinking and inventive. Others might say it showed him to be an untrustworthy, deceitful liar. Perhaps both are true.

The video began in The Righi, only a few hundred metres from the scene of the police shootings. Ryan was asked by Detective John Noonan about the events that night — and a litany of lies unfolded. Ryan said that after three hours waiting at a flat in nearby Gordon Grove, where Farrell's girlfriend, Belinda Rice, lived, five people set off for Walsh Street: himself, Farrell, Jedd Houghton, Peter McEvoy and Victor Peirce. Ryan led police into Walsh Street to near the site of the shootings and was asked what happened next.

— We just seen a car roughly around this sort of thing.
— So it was in this area here was it?
— Yes.
— Do you know exactly where?
— No.
— Do you know which side of the road it was parked on.
— Um ... [pause] I'm not too sure.
— Have you got any thoughts on where it was?
— I'm pretty sure it was on this side, but I'm not 100 per cent sure.
— What type of car was it you saw?
— It was a white Commodore.
— And what did you do?
— I opened the door with a piece of strip [a plastic binding strap used to bind cardboard boxes].
— How did you get hold of the strip?
— Macca handed it to me.
— Where was that done?
— That was done as we were coming around here, in about this sort of vicinity. And he handed me the screwdriver and I got into the door with a bit of strip, the lock popped up and I went into the door. As I was getting in the door Jedd came and broke the back window with a little screwdriver and I pulled the plastic down and pulled the ignition and started it ...
— Pulled the plastic down on what?
— Underneath the steering column. I pulled that down and put the screwdriver in there and pulled it back and the red lights came on and it started up.
— Were you given any instructions on how to do this?
— No. I already knew previous to this.

Ryan said McEvoy stood near the corner of Acland Street, a police scanner in his pocket wired to an earpiece. Victor Peirce produced a shotgun that he held by his leg. Farrell stood nearby as a lookout. Asked Noonan:

— Why is it you can't remember which side of the road the car was on?

— Because I was all nervous and stuff like that.

— Would you remember if you had to walk across the road or whether you just had to go here to get to the car?

— I'm not too sure.

— You can't remember if you had to walk across the road or not.

— No, because we were all talking and I was all nervous.

— What happened after you started the car?

— I started the car and Jedd jumped into the driver's seat. He flicked the button up and he opened the [other] door and I stood across the road, the opposite from the car, and he drove it into the middle . . .

— Do you know which side of the road you stood on?

— This side, I'm pretty sure.

— Right.

— And they put the car into the middle of the road.

— Who did?

— Jedd.

— Do you know exactly where they put the car? Do you want to walk out into the road and have a look and see if that helps you at all.

— I think we were up a bit further. I'm pretty sure.

— All right. Where would you like to go?

— Up past that street sort of thing.

— You reckon it was up past that street?

— Yes.

— Is there anything that makes you think that?

— Because we were closer to Domain Road sort of thing.

— Would you like to walk up and indicate where.

— [After walking] Between here and here.

— All right. Now you said Jedd put the car in the middle of the road. Did he just drive it straight into the middle of the road, or did he have to turn it round, or what did he do with it?

— Um. I think he just pulled it into the middle of the road sort of thing.

— Were you watching what he was doing?

— No.

— Where were you?

— I was standing on the footpath . . .

— Wouldn't you have noticed what he was doing?

— No, because I was talking to Victor.

— You stated Victor was on that [the opposite] side of the road.

— Yes. But then he come across . . .

The more Ryan talked, the more holes opened up in his story. First, the stolen Commodore had been facing south in Walsh Street, so Ryan could not have stood on the side of the road he claimed when it was moved. Second, it had to be turned around before the trap was set. Third, Ryan clearly had no idea where the killing site was — he was standing only a couple of metres away when he directed police up Walsh Street. But his story was not finished.

About 15 minutes after the car was moved, Ryan said he became scared and fled Walsh Street, running back to the Gordon Grove flat where his friend, Emmanuel Alexandridis was waiting under orders not to answer the phone or let anyone in. After a while Ryan said he heard three shots, one loud one then two softer ones: a remarkably low count considering most Walsh Street residents clearly heard all six shots.

Ryan's times were also awry. He said that about 15 minutes after he fled, and after he heard the shots, Farrell arrived at the flat. But he also said he was back at the flat for half an hour before he heard the shots. Detective Noonan, a muscular and imposing man, showed great patience with Ryan, who was clearly unsure about his story. For some questions, Ryan's answers were quick, his voice strong. For others there were long pauses and answers that sounded slightly hopeful. The inconsistencies prompted Detective Noonan to ask a question that would become a regular feature of Ryan's interviews — was he telling the truth?

— Is what you're telling us here today true?
— Yes. That's correct.
— And why are you telling us about these events?
— Because I was in fear and I just wanted to get it off my chest.
— You were in fear from what?
— From my family.
— Do you think your family might harm you in some way?
— Yes. I thought they'd kill me.
— Are you making up anything that you've told the police here tonight?
— No.

But Ryan was lying, and would maintain for more than two weeks that he was at the scene in Walsh Street. Three days later he went through a lengthy interview at St Kilda Road police headquarters and even conducted a second video 're-enactment', four days after the original, in which he expanded on the original story.

Watching the second 're-enactment', which was filmed in heavy rain, Ryan appeared to have a better knowledge of what happened on the night of the shootings. This time he took police straight to the ambush scene (instead of walking past it and up the hill) and offered other, accurate details. But for investigators there were still nagging doubts, especially as Ryan had the theft of the car — which he was meant to have done — carried out on the wrong side of the street. His detailed memory of how the theft took place jarred with his fogged memory of everything else that happened. Ryan also claimed to have hidden near a doorway while waiting for police to arrive, but the doorway was the one through which newsagency manager Peter Ellis emerged with his bicycle, supposedly as Ryan hid there. Other details were wrong or missing.

What should be said here is that no one had stopped Ryan from reading newspapers, watching television or talking about the Walsh Street case to the police who were guarding him. It appears certain he picked up snippets of information that 'improved' the accuracy of his story.

It took almost two more weeks for Ryan to decide he was not at Walsh Street. Instead, he said he waited at the flat with Emmanuel Alexandridis while five men went out — this time Trevor Pettingill instead of himself, and Farrell, Houghton, McEvoy and Peirce — in search of police to kill.

But on the last day of October 1988, police only had Ryan's first version, and they acted quickly. The first step was to charge Ryan with the police murders. There was no other choice for police, despite Ryan being their best chance at that stage to solve the crime. Ryan had confessed to being at the scene, to assisting in the commission of the crime by starting the Commodore and, during the video recording, he admitted to knowledge of the plot. Noonan asked Ryan:

— At this stage you were well aware of what the plan was?
— Yes.
— And what did you believe the plan to be when they parked the car in the middle of the road?
— It was for the police to come to the car and then they were going to sneak up behind them.
— And?
— And shoot them.

Legally, Ryan was a murderer and was thus charged. Under what is loosely known as the 'aid-and-abet rule', Ryan had both aided and abetted the murder: he was at the scene, he helped steal the car, and he knew the plan. It is the same as a getaway driver being equally as guilty of armed robbery as his partner who enters a bank with a shotgun, because he is knowingly helping in the commission of the crime.

In an unorthodox move, Ryan was taken to the Supreme Court

where, shortly before midnight on 31 October 1988, he was charged with the murders of Constables Damian Eyre and Steven Tynan. In murder cases in Victoria, bail can only be granted by a Supreme Court judge, and it was Mr Justice O'Brien, before whom Ryan appeared, who immediately bailed Ryan into the care of the police protective security group.

For Anthony Farrell, the consequences were almost as immediate. For Emmanuel Alexandridis, who knew nothing of the events at Gordon Grove and no more than any other Melburnian about the police murders, an unhappy journey was about to begin.

10
A Word of Advice

'They want you to be the one that cracks and gives everybody up. We're stronger than that.'

Andrew Fraser, solicitor, to client, Anthony Farrell

Andrew Fraser is a good, tough criminal solicitor. It isn't an easy job. In the mid-1980s, one of his better-known clients was Dennis Allen, the sort of client that can involve a lawyer in a lot of extra work. Fraser helped set up 'Mr D Investments' for Allen, a company that supposedly made its money buying and selling property and renovating houses. He also made himself available to Allen at all hours if legal advice was necessary — such as during early morning police raids, and there were plenty of those. Fraser also knew Peter Allen, Dennis's brother. Fraser set up a trust account for Peter while Peter amassed money to buy a Templestowe property, on which Fraser did the conveyancing. Months later, Peter Allen was arrested for large-scale heroin trafficking and the property confiscated under seizure of assets legislation.

Through the 1980s, Fraser gained more experience and skill. His knowledge of how police operated, with clients like Dennis and Peter, was as good as Melbourne offered. He also knew what legal advice to give his clients in what circumstances.

So, on the morning of 3 November 1988, as Anthony Farrell, a frightened 20-year-old, sat in a cell of the City Watchhouse facing charges of murdering two policemen, Fraser gave him valuable advice.

Unknown to Farrell or Fraser, their conversation was being tape-recorded by police. Detectives from the TyEyre taskforce had, with the authority of a Supreme Court warrant — which is necessary before police can legally plant a listening device — organised for a bug to be hidden in an interview room at the City Watchhouse. Detectives listened as Fraser told his client that police had no evidence against him and that Farrell should not say anything — that is, absolutely *nothing* — and should not consent to anything. It was not what the eavesdropping detectives wanted to hear.

In some ways, Fraser's legal advice was perfect. His view that detectives had next to nothing on Farrell was correct — they just had the word of Jason Ryan, whose story was patchy at best. Farrell was also under no legal obligation to say anything to police. The only aspect of Fraser's advice that was imperfect, at least in the view of Supreme Court Judge Mr Justice O'Bryan, was Fraser's colorful language, which Mr Justice O'Bryan later described as 'most inappropriate and unbecoming in a professional person'.

For detectives, however, the solicitor's advice was a blow. They had hoped Farrell would 'roll' and give an insight into the killings. According to investigators, after Farrell had been charged with the murders he indicated that he was willing to talk to police, but wanted to take legal advice first.

Farrell had already shown a preparedness to talk. Twelve days after the police murders Farrell told homicide squad detective Jim Conomy about McEvoy's fury on the afternoon of Graeme Jensen's death. The interview with Farrell followed Jason Ryan's first statement to police, on 21 October, in which Jason said he was with Farrell on the afternoon of Jensen's death, then spent the night with Farrell at Vicki Brooks' Brunswick flat. The day Farrell was interviewed, Jason Ryan set off on his four-day trip to the bush with Detective Butts.

Farrell told police that he had, indeed, visited Brooks' flat on the afternoon of Graeme Jensen's death and seen Peter McEvoy's fury at the shooting, which corroborated Ryan's account of the afternoon. He said he went back to the flat that night with Ryan and spent the night on the couch, again confirming the events given in Ryan's first version.

But on 31 October, when Ryan made his first video 're-enactment', police had fresh cause to speak to Farrell. Ryan said Farrell had been at the scene in Walsh Street; had left the flat with Ryan and three others; and had come back to the flat after the shootings.

Detectives wanted to speak to Farrell, believing that if he played a part in the shootings it was probably — like Jason's 'role' in his video confession — a minor part. In other words, detectives did not believe Farrell had pulled a trigger.

On the morning of 1 November 1988 — hours after Ryan had been secretly charged with the murders at the Supreme Court — police visited a number of houses looking for Farrell. They couldn't find him, but nevertheless, word reached Farrell that police were looking for him. Farrell telephoned the TyEyre taskforce at St Kilda Road and asked police what they wanted. Detective John Noonan said police wanted to ask Farrell a few more questions. Farrell, according to police, was reluctant, but eventually agreed and arranged to meet Detective Noonan outside a fish-and-chip shop in Clarendon Street, South Melbourne. According to evidence given by Detective Noonan, he walked up to Farrell and said:

Noonan: Tony, I just want to go over some of the matters that were covered in your statement.
Farrell: Yeah, what about?
Noonan: Well, I'd rather do it back at the office than here in the main street of South Melbourne. Do you mind coming back to the office?
Farrell: How long am I going to be? I didn't have anything to do with it, told you what I know about anything.
Noonan: As I said, I just want some matters clarified that have come up since then about your whereabouts on the night of Graeme Jensen's death.
Farrell: Yeah, all right.
Noonan: I'll warn you that you don't have to say anything unless you wish to but anything you say may be given in evidence. Do you understand that?
Farrell: Yeah.

As Farrell got into the police car, he had no idea that his last taste of freedom for more than two years had just passed; by nightfall he would be in a single cell at the City Watchhouse. At the police station he was asked about his earlier conversation with Detective Conomy. Farrell was clearly willing to tell police about some matters:

Police: Is what you told [Detective] Conomy in that statement true? In that statement you have said that Macca has said things like, "They're gonna get their right whack, they're gonna pay, the dogs." Is all that true?
Farrell: Yeah. That's all right, he was right off, fucking raving mad. But he can't find out I have said this. I am as good as dead if he finds out.

This would be the last time Farrell helped detectives. Although there was little evidence against Farrell, Detective Noonan decided there was enough to charge him with the police murders. Detectives hoped that once charged, Farrell would open up and talk about the murders. Police also believed Farrell's life was in danger if he was released from custody. The 20-year-old had expressed his fears about Peter McEvoy and detectives believed this was only part of the threat. As Detective Noonan said after the trial: 'If he got killed and we believed he was involved in it and had enough to charge him and let him go, we'd obviously get criticised if something happened to him.' About 7.30 pm on Tuesday 1 November 1988 Farrell was driven from the St Kilda Road police building to the City Watchhouse. He thought police were pulling a trick on him, trying to pressure him into saying something. He was disbelieving as he was charged with the murders and led into a cell.

The following day the story was front-page news. The charge guaranteed a huge crowd of police and reporters at the Melbourne Magistrate's Court that Wednesday morning. Farrell's mother, Sue Parkinson, a woman with a string of convictions for thefts and assaults, was also at the court. It was, as *The Age* reported, a tense and emotional court hearing as Farrell stood in the dock weeping. Said *The Age* story in part:

Mr Farrell's mother, standing in the doorway of the court, began to cry as the hearing opened. More than 20 plain-clothes and uniformed police were in the court room. Suddenly, she ran across the room towards her son, calling out: 'Don't cry, sweetheart.' She was stopped just behind the prosecutor, only metres from her son. Mr Farrell's mother turned to walk to the back of the room, but eventually sat behind her son's counsel, Mr Charles Nikakis, where she apologised for her behavior and said repeatedly to her son: 'I know you didn't do it.' Mr Dugan [the magistrate] said: 'I can understand you are distressed, but it is not going to interrupt these proceedings.' A member of the homicide squad applied for an extension of the six-hour questioning limit. Asked if he understood what the application meant, Mr Farrell said, 'Yes', then 'No', then 'Sort of'. After Mr Dugan explained the application, Mr Farrell, who had stopped crying, refused to consent to it. At the end of the hearing Mr Farrell looked at his mother and said, 'See you Mum', to which she replied: 'I'm coming to see you sweetheart.'

That afternoon Parkinson visited her son at the Watchhouse. Their conversation, like that between Farrell and his solicitor, Andrew Fraser, was secretly taped by police. In one excerpt, Farrell's mother said: 'They know it wasn't you [who did the shooting] ... but they know you were there.' Farrell replied: 'I was there but.' The Crown later said this was an admission by Farrell. However Farrell, on the day of his acquittal, said that it was not a statement of admission on his part; it was an incredulous question. Either way, the two sentences were not enough to prove anything. Farrell also said after his acquittal that the taped conversation in fact proved his innocence. He said that if he *had* committed the murders, he would have told his mother about it in the

Watchhouse; instead he protested to her that he had no involvement.

But the magistrate who oversaw the committal hearing, Hugh Adams, said the tape recordings of Farrell in the Watchhouse were consistent with both guilt and innocence. When he sent Anthony Farrell to stand trial on the murders he said it was up to a jury to decide.

What the conversation did show, however, was the pressure police were placing on Farrell to 'tell' his side of the story. And the story police expected to hear was one that bore similarities to Jason Ryan's version of events from the first video 're-enactment' — and however you look at it, Farrell knew Ryan's version was wrong.

Farrell told his mother several times that he spent the night of the shootings sleeping on the couch at Vicki Brooks' flat. He said Jason Ryan was there; Emmanuel Alexandridis would back up his story because he also slept there; Vicki had seen him arrive that night; and he could not have been at the Gordon Grove flat because his girlfriend Belinda was there. But Farrell's apparent alibis had all fallen through. Jason Ryan said Farrell took part in the murders; Brooks said Farrell and her son Jason did not come back to her flat that night; Alexandridis said he himself went home drunk and alone, and would not know what Farrell's movements were; and Belinda Rice said she was in Bendigo with her parents.

'I just can't accept fucking none of this,' Farrell told his mother. Of Jason Ryan, he said: 'The little fucking turd . . . He just made up some big bullshit story.' Farrell's mother agreed: 'I told you — remember the first time you bought him around — he was trouble. And all he ever talked about was fucking police informers and dogs [police informers].'

Farrell was worried about what would happen to him next. Although he had been in trouble with police numerous times, mostly for theft, burglary and driving before being old enough to have a licence, murder was an altogether new arena for him. In the past he had been given bonds, fines and ordered to do community service. This time he was locked up in a cell — with only one hour a day exercise — and there was no immediate prospect of his being released. He faced going to Pentridge for what would be his first time in jail. He had hardly eaten or slept during his first day in custody and had been vomiting constantly. With his mother he talked about the sort of sentence he could expect for the police murders. He expected 30 years. 'Best I start me sentence now, because all this time I'm doing now, if I end up getting sentenced, the time comes off.'

But he still couldn't work out why he had been arrested. When his mother suggested that police put him in custody because someone was going to kill him, Farrell said: 'That's frog shit.'

Farrell believed detectives were exploiting his weak state of mind hoping he would 'confess'. 'They come here at 3 o'clock this morning, three detectives, woke me up wanting to know everything again. They woke me up again at fucking nine o'clock this morning and had me at the front desk. I don't think they've got enough evidence, just on what Jason said, but that's not enough.' Farrell pursued this theme: 'They can't convict me though, they know that . . . if they thought they had me they wouldn't be going through all this shit.'

'They [the police] are waiting, see, for me to work out a deal . . . They want to work a deal or something. Do you reckon I should?' His mother didn't offer an opinion, but later in the conversation, they discussed the offer of police protection. Farrell said he was told by police that Jason Ryan was in Queensland relaxing [in fact he was still in Melbourne] and that Farrell, too, if he started talking, could also have protection. 'I don't believe that for one minute,' said Farrell. His mother agreed.

The consistence with guilt *and* innocence, as magistrate Hugh Adams identified, were readily obvious. If innocent, why would Farrell be prepared to do a deal? Why was he prepared to start his sentence? If guilty, why did he say: 'If the truth comes out I can walk', and later: 'If I could tell them something I'd fucking tell them, just to get out of here.'

Yet if Farrell was contemplating 'talking' to police, his mind was made up for him the following morning. It was about 11.30 am on Thursday 3 September 1988, 40 hours after Farrell had been charged with the double murders, that Andrew Fraser visited him in the City Watchhouse. Fraser opened the conversation.

Solicitor: Anthony, how are you mate?
Farrell: Not bad.
Solicitor: Bit of a silly question isn't it?
Farrell: Yeah.
Solicitor: Mate, you've said nothing, have you?
Farrell: No. Just told them where I was when . . .
Solicitor: That's good. All right then, I reckon the way to do it, Charlie [Nikakis, another solicitor] and I have had a yarn about it, is just whack an application into the Supreme Court fucking straight away. Because these cunts have got nothing on you.
Farrell: Yeah, I know. I know that, Andrew.

Solicitor: Yeah, well they know they've got nothing on you. So if we whomp a Supreme Court bail application fucking straight in, we'll flush the cunts out.

Farrell: Yeah.

Solicitor: They'll have to come up with it and they've got no fucking evidence.

Farrell: Yeah, because Jason . . . Apparently they said . . .

Solicitor: I don't give a fuck what they say about Jason either. Because if Jason's turned fucking dog . . .

Farrell: Yeah that's right. Victor would have been pinched by now.

Solicitor: Sssh. All right. We won't talk here all right. I'm just here to let you know we're all working on it, not just Charlie, because I know your dad wants me in on it too because I've known the family for a long while. And we're going to get you the best, mate. We're going to blow these cunts out of the water on this.

Farrell: I hope so.

Solicitor: And all you've got to do is fucking keep your trap shut. That means you're in custody now, you don't have to talk to any police, you understand that?

Farrell: Yeah.

Solicitor: So say fucking nothing. And don't consent to anything.

Farrell: I haven't.

Solicitor: If they come into your cell they'll be wired up.

Farrell: Oh yeah, I know that.

Solicitor: So you just keep your trap shut, mate. This is the rest of your life here. Because don't worry, if you go down on this you're going to get a fucking monster, and we all know that, right.

Farrell: What? Never to be released?

Solicitor: I reckon that'd just about be it, wouldn't it. It'd have to be, wouldn't it?

Farrell: Hmm.

Solicitor: But listen, just keep calm son, all right? We've put the word out that you've said nothing . . . because they were concerned you might have said something.

Farrell: I don't know nothing.

Solicitor: I know that, but you know what jail talk's like.

Farrell: Yeah.

Solicitor: Leave it to us. We'll have you up for bail in a couple of weeks time, all right. Vincent's coming in . . .

Farrell: Who's Vincent?

Solicitor: Justice Vincent into the Supreme Court for bail. Probably . . . about the best judge you could get.

Farrell: Yeah.

Solicitor: We'll get you about the best fucking barristers around, mate, and we'll be there. All right?

Farrell: You reckon you could buy me a packet of smokes Andrew?

Solicitor: Yeah, sure. No problem.

Farrell: Hey, do I have to stay in me cell, because they won't let me out.

Solicitor: Yeah. It's for your own fucking protection, mate. Now what do you smoke? Anything?

Farrell: Viscount. No, get me a packet of Peter Jackson 30s.

Solicitor: Right ho. OK. All right, so that's all I wanted to let you know, that we're all working on it.

Farrell: Yeah, but when am I going to Pentridge?

Solicitor: When there's room there.

Farrell: So I could have to stay in that cell for a month?

Solicitor: Well, you could be there for a couple of weeks.

Farrell: What! In the cell?

Solicitor: Yeah. Well, they've got to let you out for exercise, but only when there are no other blokes there.

Farrell: They haven't even being doing that.

Solicitor: Yeah, I know that. Mate. They're concerned about your safety, right?

Farrell: Yeah.

Solicitor: So just leave all that to us. If it means you've got to fucking put up with it, you've got to put up with it. Right?

Farrell: Yeah.

Solicitor: If you stop and think about it, it's about the worst murder that's ever been committed in this state. And you're fucking it for the time being. Now what we've got to do is blow their case out of the fucking water, right? I'll tell you what they've done.

Farrell: Yeah.

Solicitor: They've fucking nailed you because they reckon you're the weak link in the chain. They're putting fucking enormous pressure on you in what they're doing. They want you to be the one that cracks and gives everybody up. We're stronger than that.

Farrell: Yeah, I know that.

Solicitor: So if you sit there and be strong, we'll get you out of it. All right? I'll get you some smokes mate, I've got to fly, but I just wanted to drop in and let you know that we're all in on the rort for you.

Farrell: All right. So how long do you reckon 'till I go to the Supreme Court?

Solicitor: Couple of weeks, mate.

Farrell: Couple of *weeks*!

Solicitor: Well, it takes 10 days at the best of times mate. It'll be the week after next because Vincent's on and we want Vincent. All right.

Farrell: Yeah.

Solicitor: He's the man we want. OK.

Farrell: All right.

Solicitor: Good on you, mate.

Farrell: Thanks a lot.

Solicitor: No worries.

Farrell took Andrew Fraser's advice and said nothing more to police. The legal counsel could be interpreted as a significant development in the Walsh Street story. Although Farrell denied any involvement in the killings to his mother, police and in court, detectives were convinced he could tell them something — or in police language 'he would roll'. Thus for police, to charge him was a gamble — and *if* Farrell did know something, the gamble failed.

In early 1991, not long after the four men charged with the Walsh Street murders were acquitted, Andrew Fraser took out a Supreme Court injunction to prevent the recording of his conversation with Anthony Farrell being broadcast or published. He lost. The injunction had been taken out against broadcaster Derryn Hinch, who had obtained a copy of the tape and planned to use it on his nightly national television program. Quite where Hinch got the tape is not clear, although there were a lot of copies in existence, testified to by the fact that Hinch's rival program, Channel Nine's *A Current Affair*, also had a copy and broadcast it the same night as the Hinch program — and half an hour earlier. Both programs made much of the colorful language used by Fraser, with extensive use of bleeps to delete various swearwords.

Mr Justice O'Bryan said there were no grounds on which an injunction to prevent the broadcasts could be justified. He said Fraser's legal counsel had argued that the conversation contained material that would be 'frightfully embarrassing' to Fraser if released. Said the judge: 'No doubt this will be so. Hopefully, it might also be a lesson to him to moderate his language when engaged in a professional capacity ... In my opinion the language used by the plaintiff whilst taking instruction from and tendering advice to Farrell was most inappropriate and unbecoming in a professional person.'

In a television interview after the four men were acquitted of the Walsh Street murders, Trevor Pettingill made a curious comment about Farrell's legal guidance. Pettingill was asked if he blamed Jason Ryan for the charges: 'No, because of what they [the police] did to him. Anthony was sort of in the same boat. He was only young. He knew what the truth was, right? Anthony was in two minds about what to do because of his age and he was frightened, whereas Jason was held without any legal aid approaching him ... Anthony was given legal advice, right? So, therefore he took that legal advice. Anthony's explained to me the poor kid [Jason] has been denied that and that's why he didn't have the chance to say either way.'

The decision to charge Farrell on the basis of Jason Ryan's first 're-enactment' is still the subject of debate inside and outside the police force. Certainly Farrell needed to be interviewed again after Jason Ryan's story suddenly changed, this time putting Farrell in Walsh Street about the time of the murders rather than asleep on Vicki Brooks' couch. Some detectives felt, however, that rather than charge Farrell straight away, it would be better to release him and see where he went and what he said, using surveillance, listening devices and phone taps. Their belief that he was charged too early was reinforced as Jason Ryan again changed his story.

The version detectives put to Farrell — based on Ryan's first video — changed slightly the day after Farrell talked with solicitor Andrew Fraser. Jason Ryan now suggested that Farrell, rather than being a bit-player, was one of those who actually pulled the trigger — Farrell however, was no longer willing or available to be questioned about this new development. But worse still, almost two weeks later, on 16 November 1988, Ryan's story made another shift, this one more dramatic. This time Ryan said *he stayed behind* at the flat while the four other men he had already named — Victor Peirce, Jedd Houghton, Peter McEvoy and Anthony Farrell — plus his Uncle Trevor, went out to shoot the police. A further big change came in early January 1989 when Ryan said he was alone in the flat — up until then he had maintained that Emmanuel Alexandridis was with him. So, the version police presented to Anthony Farrell on 1 November 1988 was a far cry from what it was some 10 weeks later, after Ryan made numerous changes.

But whether having the 'correct' story would have made any difference in the questioning of Anthony Farrell is hypothetical. What happened was that Farrell took Andrew Fraser's legal advice and said nothing to police. It was the start of almost 29 months in custody that ended with his acquittal on 26 March 1991.

Meanwhile, Emmanuel Alexandridis, the 17-year-old friend of Farrell and Ryan, who Ryan claimed was at the Gordon Grove flat on the night of the murders, was giving police little information about what happened that night. It was little wonder. Alexandridis had not been at the flat. But Ryan did not change that aspect of his story until early January 1989.

Detectives only had Ryan's information to work from and, although it was shaky, they believed it contained a strong element of truth. Ryan told police that Alexandridis was only a bit player — he was not privy to the planning at the Gordon Grove flat, but had seen the alleged killers walk into the night and Ryan and Farrell come back.

To Alexandridis the police attention was no doubt something of a mystery. He was certainly at Vicki Brooks' flat on the afternoon of Jensen's death and witnessed McEvoy's outbursts about the killing. But it appears that on the night of the police murders, Alexandridis left the Stockade Hotel very drunk and went home to bed: at least this was the version Alexandridis gave to police on 2 November 1988, amending a statement several days earlier that provided an alibi for Anthony Farrell. At the committal hearing he reverted to his original story, saying he spent the night at Vicki Brooks' flat with Farrell: but this claim was contradicted by the evidence of Ryan — who said Farrell was with him at Gordon Grove — and Brooks, who said neither Jason nor Anthony Farrell came back to the flat that night. Alexandridis was not called as a Crown witness at the trial because he was, by then, regarded as hostile to the Crown case. He was not called as a defence witness either.

But in early November the pressure was on and, after his first interview with police two weeks after the Walsh Street murders, he was repeatedly questioned and taken to the St Kilda Road police station a number of times. Detectives from the TyEyre taskforce wanted to know about the flat but, try as he might, Alexandridis was unable to convince them that he was telling all he knew.

On one occassion at the St Kilda Road police station, Alexandridis was put into a room with Jason Ryan. Police say this was, in part, to allay any fears Alexandridis might have had of police. At the time rumors were running around Melbourne that Ryan had been kidnapped by detectives, bashed within an inch of his life and forced to 'confess'. Such rumors were given credence by the broadcast of a photograph of Ryan on Channel Seven showing Ryan's bruised and puffed face — the picture was taken after the special operations group raid on Victor Peirce's home on the day of the police murders.

At first Alexandridis was happy to see Ryan. He told the commital hearing: 'I didn't really know what was going on and he was just saying "Tell them". I didn't really know what he was going on about and he was saying: "Tell them, tell them." I was saying, "Tell them what?" And he goes, "Tell them what's going on and all that . . . Tell them the truth". I said, "I don't know what the truth is". I said "You tell me", and I knocked on the door saying, "I don't want to hear this crap no more".'

Police were still convinced Alexandridis could tell them something about the night of 12 October. The 17-year-old was put into protection for several days and even taken out of Melbourne for a couple of days by police. But he wasn't providing police with what they wanted.

In early December Alexandridis spoke to *Sun* journalist Graeme Walker. On 7 December an article appeared on the front page under the headline:

I'M SCARED:
Youth in fear over Walsh Street.

In the story Alexandridis complained of police harassment, saying he had been bashed by police on several occasions — claims he repeated at the committal hearing. For the detectives who had been unable to get Alexandridis to tell them what happened at Gordon Grove that night, the explanation came on 10 January 1989 when Ryan told police that Alexandridis was not at the South Yarra flat. For Alexandridis it was the end of a nightmare, a nightmare that Farrell's barrister at the committal hearing, David Ross, said could have been worse. 'It's fortunate perhaps, fortunate for [Emmanuel] Alexandridis, that Jason Ryan didn't attribute to him a leading part. If he had, the police would have gone off, no doubt, half-cocked with him and charged him like they charged Anthony Farrell ... based on a lying account given by Jason Ryan.'

This new change to Ryan's story in early January 1989 added greatly to police frustration with their star witness. It also meant hundreds of hours of work had been wasted. And Ryan's explanation for including Alexandridis in his story? 'I thought it would be better for me if he was there.'

Left: Dennis Allen in his prime. He constantly wore gold jewelery around his neck, wrist and fingers, perhaps $250,000 worth.

Below left: Dennis Allen, enfeebled, confined to a wheelchair, 15 kilograms lighter, is escorted from St Vincent's Hospital to the Melbourne Magistrate's Court to face a murder charge relating to Wayne Stanhope's disappearance. Allen died five weeks later.

Below: Wayne Stanhope, disappeared 1984

Above: Dennis Allen playfully points a pistol at the head of his mother, Kath Pettingill, at a party in one of Dennis's houses.

Below: Family night out. *From left:* Victor Peirce, Trevor Pettingill, Lex Peirce, Kath Pettingill and Dennis Allen.

Top: Kath Pettingill and one of the men acquitted of the Walsh Street murders, Peter McEvoy.

Four of Pettingill's sons:

Top left: Dennis Allen

Top right: Peter Allen

Bottom left: Jamie Pettingill

Bottom right: Lex Peirce

Her other two sons were charged with the Walsh Street killings.

Victims of Dennis Allen:

Top left: Victor Gouroff disappeared in 1983.

Above: Helga Wagnegg was given a 'hot shot' in 1984.

Below: Anton Kenny was shot dead in 1985; his body was found in a 44-gallon drum (*left*) in the Yarra River in 1986, the legs cut off with a chainsaw.

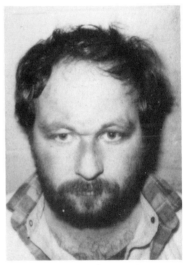

The hit.

Top left: In 1984 Dennis Allen commissioned two men to kill this man, Alan Williams, a Melbourne heroin dealer, now in jail in NSW.

Top right: But the hitman mistakenly shot this man, Lindsay Simpson, Williams's brother-in-law, who was visting Williams's house.

Bottom left: Roy Pollitt, convicted of being the man who pulled the trigger at the Simpson killing.

Bottom right: Garry Jones confessed to being the getaway driver for Pollitt.

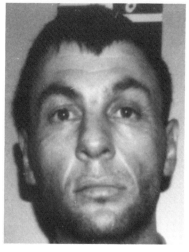
Victor Peirce

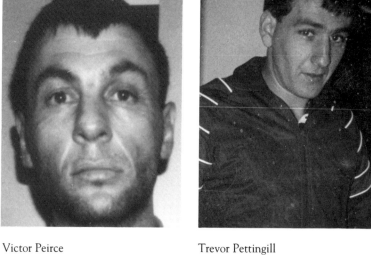
Trevor Pettingill

The four men acquitted of the Walsh Street killings

Peter McEvoy

Anthony Farrell

Victims of police shootings:

Top: Frank Valastro, cocaine dealer and armed-robbery suspect, was shot in June 1987. His death allegedly sparked the idea of making a revenge pact to kill police whenever criminal associates were shot by police.

Below left: Jedd Houghton, a key suspect for the Walsh Street murders, was shot dead in a Bendigo caravan park in November 1988.

Below: Gary Abdallah, photographed at an interview with detectives from the TyEyre taskforce, in February 1989. Less than seven weeks later he had been shot by other police.

March 1988: State Bank of Victoria security cameras at Oak Park show hold-up in progress. A shotgun blast and sledgehammer attempt failed to open a door to the banking chamber. Forensic tests nine months later established that the same shotgun was used in the Walsh Street slayings. The bandits were identified as Jedd Houghton (*with gun*) and Graeme Jensen (*hammer*).

September 1988: Police surveillance photographs show Graeme Jensen followed by Victor Peirce and Jedd Houghton (the man with his eyes masked is a passer-by) at Boronia Shopping Centre, allegedly 'casing' banks.

Below: At a later meeting police photographed Jensen (*left*) and Peirce. Less than a month later Jensen was shot dead by police.

Graeme Jensen, convicted armed robber.

Below: July 1988: Armaguard employee Dominik Hefti was carrying $33,000 in takings through this stockroom behind a Brunswick supermarket when he was confronted by a gunman. Shots were exchanged and Hefti fell here, fatally wounded; the gunman, bleeding, escaped through the supermarket and commandeered a car from a woman at gunpoint.

11 October 1988: Graeme Jensen lies slumped in his stationwagon in a Narre Warren street after being shot dead by the armed robbery squad. Police suspected Jensen of the Hefti shooting; detectives later established he was not involved.

Right: Police say they fired when they saw Jensen holding this .22 sawn-off rifle. His family and friends say it was planted.

Constable
Steven
Tynan

Constable
Damian
Eyre

12 October 1988: This aerial photograph shows the white Holden (*doors open*) where the police were shot. The killers fled along the driveway directly behind the Holden, scaled a fence and dropped into The Righi. Residents, woken by the shots, only saw two men running at the same time. The Crown alleged there were five at the scene.

Below: Street-level at the scene. Constables Eyre and Tynan arrived shortly after 4.40 a.m. to find this car left in the middle of Walsh Street.

Above: Police demolished Victor Peirce's house at 86 Chestnut Street, once owned by Dennis Allen, and dug up the site in a search for evidence. They found two pistols (*right, right below*) and this cache of ammunition (*below*). The two shotgun shells at the top right of the picture are the same brand and type as those used in Walsh Street.

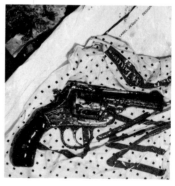

The three shells found in Walsh Street. They contained SG shot, nine lead balls, each slightly smaller than a .38 bullet.

The area of the Royal Park Golf Course near the fifth tee where a gardener found the murder weapon.

Japanese KTG shotgun, its barrel and stock sawn-off. The rusted shotgun was tested and matched the weapon used in Walsh Street and the Oak Park robbery.

Wendy Peirce and *de facto* husband Victor attend a friend's wedding. She went into witness protection, gave damning evidence against her husband at his committal hearing but retracted before the trial.

Jason Ryan with his uncle, Victor Peirce. Ryan was the Crown's key witness at the trial, giving evidence of how the murders were allegedly planned.

11
Bendigo

A man who goes out to seek revenge should first dig two graves

Chinese proverb

Jedd Houghton was sitting at a dining room table just outside Bendigo watching a friend eat breakfast as dawn broke. Houghton, a quiet man of medium height and dark hair, was about to go rabbit shooting with Paul Widdicombe, a 27-year-old mechanic and panel beater — hence the early breakfast.

It was five weeks since the Walsh Street murders and Houghton was, in effect, on the run. He knew he was wanted for the murders.

There is little doubt Houghton was one of the Walsh Street killers. Houghton was identified as a masked bandit who fired a shotgun blast during a Melbourne bank robbery in March 1988, using the same shotgun used at Walsh Street. He was known to have been supplied with a getaway car for another bank robbery in which the shotgun was used again. And he confessed his involvement to friends. Hugh Adams, the magistrate who oversaw the Walsh Street committal, said at the end of the hearing: 'There is no doubt in my mind that [Houghton] was an active participant in the Walsh Street murders.'

Houghton was also wary. Along with a scanner, Houghton had a bug detector, several handguns and a set of walkie-talkies, all tools of a professional and careful criminal. At the breakfast table, Houghton sat and played with the scanner, a device used to monitor police frequencies. A scanner can also be programmed into other radio frequencies and can, for example, pick up air traffic control towers and car telephone conversations. What frequency Houghton programmed into the machine that morning will never be known — but the effect was startling.

As he sat with Paul Widdicombe, the sound of birds came through the scanner; then, as dogs outside began barking, their barks came through the speaker. Houghton stood up and told Widdicombe that he was going outside; if Widdicombe heard anything over the scanner he should call out. Widdicombe suggested Houghton sing a song, but he instead rambled off sentences at random. Houghton walked around the outside of the house and, as he neared the window, Widdicombe suddenly heard Houghton's voice coming over the scanner. Said Widdicombe later: 'I went to the window and he was there, and there was a wire. I said I hadn't seen it there before, or placed it there, and told him to see what was connected to the other end of it. And that's when we discovered the bug. As soon as he pulled it out he said: "Now I've got you you rotten mongrels . . ." He leaned over and disconnected it. He undid one of the positive or negative terminals on the battery and unhooked the wire off it. He came inside and I was as white as a ghost having just discovered that, just outside the window. He said if they come now they'll get him for sure. From there he went out to the shed and produced all these pistols.'

At the start of November 1988, detectives were still working on the basis of Jason Ryan's video 're-enactments', which named five people at the murder scene — Ryan himself, Victor Peirce, Jedd Houghton, Peter McEvoy and Anthony Farrell. Within three weeks of the murders, three of them were in custody: Farrell for the Walsh Street murders, Peirce for the murder of Dominik Hefti and Ryan charged over Walsh Street and in police protection. Emmanuel Alexandridis was still being questioned about his 'role', which Ryan had said was staying behind at Gordon Grove.

This left two men to find, Jedd Houghton and Peter McEvoy — and the hunt was on. Not that detectives necessarily wanted to arrest either man, but they certainly wanted to locate them. From there they could plant bugs and tap telephones to gather information and, hopefully, evidence on the killings.

Detectives had been given Houghton's name within days of the police murders. At least three callers said he was involved: one person who rang said he'd overheard Houghton's name being mentioned among a group of 'heavy' criminals at a Flemington hotel. But at that stage dozens of people were being nominated for their 'involvement' and detectives were sorting through the list of names. At first, Houghton appeared an unlikely candidate. His criminal record showed nothing to suggest his involvement in Walsh Street: he had no convictions for assault, firearms, drugs or armed robbery, and he had spent only a few days in custody for non-payment of fines. His first court appearance came when he was 17, for stealing a car. He was caught red-handed by police after smashing the back window of a car and driving it from Port Melbourne to Flemington. He was put on probation.

Ten months later Houghton readily confessed to police when accused of stealing another car. He told police he found the Budget rent-a-car in a side street with its engine running. He picked up some friends and went for a joy-ride, which came to an end when the car slid round a corner and smashed into two front fences: Houghton and his friends then ran off.

He was caught again for stealing cars and police noted that he had fallen in with 'most of the undesirable elements of Flemington, Kensington and Ascot Vale'. Several police reports noted that Houghton did not appear to be violent. He was charged infrequently by police and never for anything serious.

In the early days of the inquiry Houghton wasn't regarded as a prime suspect: more of a young tearaway from Flemington. But when Jason Ryan said Houghton was at Vicki Brooks' flat with Peter McEvoy and, like McEvoy, was upset and angry about Jensen's death, the likelihood of Houghton's involvement increased. When surveillance photographs were passed on to investigators from the armed robbery squad showing Houghton, Jensen and Victor Peirce, also regarded as a prime suspect, 'casing' banks at Boronia Shopping Centre only weeks before the police murders, doubts about Houghton being a small-time criminal from Flemington disappeared.

So detectives began the search for McEvoy and Houghton — and both proved elusive. It was later established that McEvoy left Melbourne in late October and drove a hire car to New South Wales, where he spent several weeks in a caravan with a friend. McEvoy came back to Melbourne around 22 November.

Houghton was easier to find. At one point in early November police thought they had found him; a man on a motorcycle followed to several places including Vicki Brooks' Brunswick flat. But it turned out to be the wrong man.

Part of the problem in finding Houghton was police had no up-to-date pictures of him. Since the shootings, according to friends, his hair had been cut short, changing his appearance. The breakthrough came as a result of surveillance and a tip-off from an informer. As a result police heard Houghton in phone conversations: and he was calling from Paul Widdicombe's house in Bendigo.

On 8 November a detective from Flemington, who knew Houghton by sight, was driven to Bendigo. He joined a surveillance crew following a motorcycle and told investigators they were following the right man: it was Houghton. With the identity confirmed, the cavalry was summoned. Dozens of police headed north and, by Friday 11 November, Bendigo — or to be more precise, a farmlet on the outskirts of town — was swarming with police. What complicated matters slightly was that, unknown to TyEyre investigators at first, the drug squad from Melbourne was running a drug operation in the town, using undercover operatives to make drug buys. The drug operation had no impact on the TyEyre inquiry: what can be said, however, was that in November 1988, the central Victorian town of Bendigo was well policed.

The focus of TyEyre's attention was a house in Sparrowhawk Road, Long Gully, the home of Paul Widdicombe. Detectives were uncertain how Widdicombe and Houghton knew each other and who either man's associates in the area were. Within days a listening device was planted in Widdicombe's house. Surveillance crews followed Widdicombe, his wife, Houghton and other visitors to the house in an attempt to build a profile of who knew who.

What police later discovered was that Widdicombe was introduced to Houghton by Graeme Jensen. In turn, Widdicombe met Jensen through a man named Joe, who knew Jensen from prison. Jensen and Widdicombe probably first met in mid-1987, soon after Jensen's release from jail.

Widdicombe was later to tell police how his association with Jensen and Houghton evolved, and how Houghton sought refuge at Widdicombe's Bendigo home after the Walsh Street murders. Widdicombe's version of events, which is the basis of much of what follows, also provides an insight into the friendship between Jensen and Houghton, a bond that was strong enough to provoke Houghton to help kill two police in revenge for Graeme Jensen's death.

Some months after Jensen and Widdicombe met, around Christmas 1987, Jensen telephoned Widdicombe and later arrived in a car with two other men. One was Jedd Houghton. Houghton wanted to do a deal: swapping an ounce of amphetamines for some marijuana. But Widdicombe was unable to lay his hands on any marijuana, so the deal did not take place. During the visit, guns were discussed. 'I was keen to have a go at a pistol,' Widdicombe said later. 'I encouraged them to come back and have a shot.'

Houghton phoned Widdicombe several months later and asked if he could come around. 'At that stage I didn't realise it was going to be for a few days, but when he got there it didn't take long to work out,' said Widdicombe. During that visit Houghton showed Widdicombe two guns: a Colt .25 pistol and snub-nose .38. About three weeks later, Houghton telephoned and asked Widdicombe to buy some ammunition for the two guns. Widdicombe agreed and purchased several packets of bullets from a Bendigo gunshop.

Three days later, Jensen and Houghton arrived at the Bendigo house and, with Widdicombe, set off for a nearby property to go shooting. Said Widdicombe: 'I walked up the hills for rabbits and I got a few, but while I was walking through the hills I heard a couple of bullets ricochet and go over the top of me . . . The way they were letting the shots off down below I was a bit worried how mature they were with guns.'

Jensen had a .25 pistol and Houghton two guns: the snub-nose .38 and the Colt .25 pistol. 'They were like kids with new toys. They were shooting at everything. It took them no time at all to go through the bullets I'd purchased for them.'

Some weeks later Jensen and Houghton arrived again. Widdicombe had bought more ammunition and they set off for a different property, where there was less danger of ricochets. 'They played shooting games . . . they had tin cans and milk cartons and old bullet packs set up around the place and they just fired at them.'

As well as supplying ammunition, Widdicombe showed both men the difference between shotgun cartridges in a dramatic demonstration. Using a steel barbecue plate, which was about one centimetre thick, he fired two shotgun blasts using four-shot, a cartridge holding dozens of small lead pellets. 'It put hundreds of little dints in the barbecue plate. And I shot it twice with SGs [each SG cartridge contains nine pellets, each slightly smaller than a .38 bullet] and there would have been anywhere between 15 and 18 decent wallops in it and three of them penetrated.'

The demonstration surprised Jensen and Houghton — and they learned from it. Houghton later asked Widdicombe to buy him some SG cartridges, which Houghton picked up less than two weeks before the police murders. At Walsh Street, Constables Steven Tynan and Damian Eyre were both blasted with SG shot. The cartridge cases found on the street were of the same make and type bought by

Widdicombe at the Bendigo gunshop, one of only four retail outlets in Victoria that stocked the unusual brand.

Widdicombe did not hear from Houghton again until 11 October 1988, when Houghton rang to say Jensen had been shot dead by police. Widdicombe was stunned. Houghton, however, asked a favor. Could Widdicombe visit Houghton's father, who lived nearby, and pass on the news? 'I didn't go up there but I rang his father and told him about Graeme. And his father more or less said to me that Jedd was likely to do anything. Stay out of his way if he went silly ... He said he was virtually uncontrollable once he blew his top.'

The next day Houghton rang again. Said Widdicombe: 'It had already been on the news up here about the two police in Melbourne, and all he said was, "Did you catch the news this morning?" And I said: "Yes." And he made mention of the two policemen who had been shot and killed.'

A week later Houghton rang again and said he was going to bring his girlfriend, Kim Cameron, to Bendigo. Soon afterwards he arrived. It was late at night and Houghton had a friend with him named Darren. The car in which they arrived was loaded with clothes and other belongings. Darren and Houghton unloaded it into the spare room and went straight back to Melbourne. Two days later Houghton arrived with his girlfriend. He was riding a motorbike. He stayed about four days then rode back to Melbourne, leaving Kim Cameron behind.

Houghton's relationship with Kim Cameron had been brief. They began going out in early September 1988 — a month before the Walsh Street murders — and, within a week, Houghton had moved into her parents' home in Bulleen. Kim's parents accepted Houghton living with their daughter because she told them he didn't have any money or a place to stay. Kim's father, Bill Cameron, also found Houghton to be 'a likeable bloke'. Kim, however, knew little about her boyfriend. She told the inquest into Houghton's death that she did not even know his surname until after he had been shot dead by police. 'I did not ask, and he didn't tell me. I never heard his last name. I was just his girlfriend.'

A few days after leaving Kim Cameron with the Widdicombes, Houghton rang. He had left his scanner at Bendigo and asked Paul Widdicombe to bring it to Melbourne for him. Widdicombe drove down and reached a telephone box near Whittlesea where he waited, as instructed, for a call. He was then given directions about how to get to the house owned by Kim's parents. '[But] he said everything he had planned wasn't going to happen and he followed me back to Bendigo.'

Quite what Houghton had planned is not known, although TyEyre detectives later established to their own satisfaction that about one week after the Walsh Street murders Houghton was involved in an unsuccessful attempt to snatch a payroll from a Brambles security van as it made a delivery to a Target store in the outer northern Melbourne suburb of Reservoir. Although the bandit failed to get any cash, he escaped with one of the security guard's revolvers. That gun was one of four that Houghton had with him when the bug was discovered at Paul Widdicombe's house.

When Widdicombe and Houghton returned from Melbourne, Widdicombe told Houghton that he was far from impressed with his houseguest, Kim Cameron. 'I said to him the first time he got back from Melbourne that Kim had a very loose mouth, and I said we had two or three people here that she'd never met before, and she talked away like she'd known them for years ... [she] more or less said that they were on the run and wanted — I don't think she really knew what was going on herself. Jedd just used to tell her that that was how it had to be and she'd accept it.'

Houghton then made what amounted to a confession of his involvement in the police murders, aluding to the $200,000 reward posted for the arrest and conviction of the killers. Said Widdicombe: 'Whilst talking to him about Kim he said to me ... there was two hundred thousand reasons why the Melbourne police wanted to get their hands on him. Now that was the first time that I had any inclination that he was involved in that shooting.'

It was also about this time that police tracked Houghton to Bendigo. In the first days of the police operation at Bendigo, telephone intercepts and the bug in Widdicombe's house provided a certain amount of information. But surveillance of Houghton, Widdicombe and others proved difficult. Widdicombe's house was on a corner and could not be watched from a car — it would have stood out like a sore thumb. Likewise, surveillance along country roads was, at best, risky, because of the low volume of traffic and open nature of the roads.

The telephone taps and the bug made the job easier. Police would listen to travel plans — where Houghton was going or what route he intended to take — which made the job of following him much easier. The result was that surveillance was especially cautious and intermittent. After all, if the suspects realised they were being followed, police would lose the advantage. Houghton made regular trips to Melbourne on his motorcycle and, as a result, he was sometimes followed part of the way and other times he was let go, with the hope of picking him up once he arrived in Melbourne.

On one Melbourne trip, two days before his death, Houghton visited his girlfriend's father in Bulleen. Bill Cameron later told police that Houghton was not his normal self.

'I parked the car in the driveway and light rain was falling. Jedd seemed depressed and emotional. It was very unusual for Jedd as he was always a happy-go-lucky person. To me he seemed like an "iron man". He had spoken to Lynette [Cameron's wife] earlier in the evening about aspects of his life and his involvement with the police. He said that he hadn't wished to bring any problems on to my family. Jedd was leaning against the bonnet of the car. He was sort of sentimental and started to speak about Graeme Jensen who had been shot in Narre Warren. I can't remember the exact words, but he sort of said that he loved him. There were tears in his eyes when he was speaking. He went on and admitted to me that he had done the shooting at Walsh Street. He had put his arm around me. I had come to have my suspicions that he may have been involved, but I hadn't known. He wasn't the sort of bloke you would ask about that type of thing. He was usually quiet and didn't really say much. It was completely out of character for him. To me, it appeared that Jedd had come to the end of his tether, so to speak.'

On his return to Bendigo, Houghton rented a cabin at the Ascot Lodge caravan park at White Cliffs. Police, however, were still watching. According to evidence given at Houghton's inquest, police inspected the inside of the cabin in the early evening of 16 November 1988, using a key borrowed from the site manager. Houghton and his girlfriend were out and still being watched, so police took advantage of their absence and looked for a place to plant a bug. They also drew plans of the inside of the cabin in case a raid took place.

That night Houghton and Kim Cameron returned to the cabin and apparently found nothing amiss. Police continued to watch the cabin. There was little movement until Houghton climbed on his motorcycle shortly before dawn on 17 November and set off for Paul Widdicombe's house to go shooting.

It was less than an hour later when Houghton found the police listening device planted in a window sill at Widdicombe's house. Houghton was furious, Widdicombe was scared and police, who listened to Houghton's fury before the bug stopped transmitting, were worried. They had taken a great deal of care not to alert Houghton to their presence. Now it was blown.

Detectives feared that once Houghton discovered he was being watched he would disappear from sight, and possibly move interstate. Such a theory was, in part, supported by Kim Cameron, who later said Houghton had discussed moving to Queensland because he was in trouble with police.

Widdicombe later said that when Houghton discovered the bug he was carrying two handguns. Houghton promptly walked to Widdicombe's shed, fetched a bag and produced two more guns — one a .38 revolver, the other a massive .357 calibre revolver. He checked all were loaded; the ammunition in one gun was replaced with bullets Widdicombe had recently purchased.

'He was a walking armory,' Widdicombe recalled. 'I wouldn't have him back in the house like that . . . He was no longer thinking of myself, Donna or the kids . . . After he found that thing [the listening device] he just had to have weapons. All he wanted to do was have loaded guns . . . he said, "They're not going to do what they did to Graeme to me without me putting up a fight".'

The men had planned to go shooting, but abandoned the idea. Houghton, however, did not want to stay at the house in case the police came. It appears he wanted time to think, to consider his next move, and the answer was to go with Widdicombe, in Widdicombe's car, for a drive around the local countryside. Houghton took his scanner and tuned it to the local police frequency. It was about 7 am. 'There wasn't much at all going over the scanner, and he said that didn't seem right because it was a change of shift. He said there would be a lot more talk if he was getting everything . . . We heard something about someone on a motorbike and he was sure it was him they were talking about.'

Houghton instructed Widdicombe to pull over at a telephone box and telephone his wife, Donna. He woke her up, which reassured both men: police had obviously not raided the Long Gully house. 'We presumed it was safe to come back into Bendigo. He went to the caravan park.'

Meanwhile, TyEyre detectives decided Houghton had to be arrested. Detectives requested the use of the special operations group, but it appears police command initially refused to authorise its use. Four detectives from the taskforce began preparing plans to raid Widdicombe's house — then they were told Houghton had returned to the Ascot Lodge caravan park. They revised their plans, collected bulletproof vests and shotguns, and walked from the farmhouse to a police car. As they reached the car they were called back. Authorisation for the special operations group had been given; the SOG was flying up on a police plane and would arrive within the hour.

According to evidence given at Houghton's inquest, police considered several options in trying to arrest Houghton. They included using tear gas, calling him out of the cabin, or conducting a 'mobile' intercept. Tear gas was ruled out because it didn't always have an instant effect; attempting to call him out could have created a siege, with Houghton using Kim Cameron as a hostage; and the interception of a motorcycle was almost impossible, police explained to the hearing. The raid was to be directly on the cabin, with the door broken down and police rushing in. It took place about 12.10 pm. Once inside the cabin, according to evidence given at the inquest, the members of the special operations group saw Houghton pointing a handgun at them. They ordered Houghton to put the gun down; he continued to point it at police, who fired. Houghton was hit twice with shotgun blasts, once in the chest and once in the left arm. He died instantly.

Police had lost their chance to speak to a key suspect. Detective John Noonan told Houghton's inquest that it was not certain that Houghton would have been charged with the Walsh Street killings if he had been successfully arrested; that would have depended on what Houghton said during any interview.

Houghton's death did have one effect in the underworld: it prompted rumors that Houghton had been deliberately killed by police in revenge for the Walsh Street murders. Melbourne's underworld buzzed with the story that police had simply 'blown Jedd Houghton away' in a tit-for-tat exchange. One result this had on the Walsh Street investigation was that Gary Abdallah — mentioned by Jason Ryan for possibly providing a car on the night of the murders — went to ground, fearing police would 'get' him too.

News of Houghton's death raced around Victoria's prison system. One inmate, John Martin, a man in his late fifties with convictions on more than 400 charges dating back to 1950, was among those to hear. A veteran con-man, Martin was awaiting trial on one count of armed robbery and, while in Pentridge talked to Victor Peirce, whom he claimed he had known for years.

About three months after Houghton's death Martin had an exercise-yard conversation with Peirce about the shootings, Martin later told the Walsh Street hearings. (Peirce denied talking to or even knowing Martin.) According to Martin, however, Peirce said he was worried about what Jason Ryan had told police. Peirce went on: 'The only good thing to come out of all this is that by Houghton getting shot, [it] saved me the job of doing it myself. Because I don't think I would have went to trial with Houghton because he would have been the one to give me up under pressure. Because his information would have been first hand. I'm better off with him dead.'

12
Kidnap

'Why would crooks take him for a ride and let him come back?'

Kath Pettingill

On 16 November 1988 Jason Ryan struck again, making another leap worthy of a circus acrobat. For the 17 days following his first video 're-enactment' with police, Ryan had maintained that on the night of the police murders he walked through the back streets of South Yarra to Walsh Street with four other men.

Then, on the day before Jedd Houghton was shot dead by police, Ryan changed his story, creating another headache for police. Not only did Ryan decide that he did not leave the flat at Gordon Grove, he named an additional person who went out to kill police: his uncle, Trevor Pettingill.

It was Ryan's sixth video interview, and Detective John Noonan was forced to ask the old familiar question: 'Are you telling me the truth?' Again Ryan said he was. The interview began with Noonan asking Ryan about the earlier interviews.

Noonan: Why have you told me false stories in the past?
Ryan: [Long pause] I was scared.
Noonan: Is there someone you didn't want to implicate in this murder?
Ryan: Yes.
Noonan: And who is that person?
Ryan: Trevor ... Trevor Pettingill ...
Noonan: Now, as I've already told you, this is a very serious offence that has been committed and we have to know the full truth about it. We don't want you to say anything that's not true or make up anything. I want you to go through with me exactly what happened, to your knowledge, on the night prior to the killing and the morning of the killing. Now, are you prepared to do that?
Ryan: Yes.

To the continuing despair and frustration of investigators, however, the 100-minute interview was to contain more lies, lies that Ryan admitted to about eight weeks later. But this interview would, for the first time, name Trevor Pettingill as one of the men who left Gordon Grove for Walsh Street in the early hours of 12 October, an allegation that Ryan retained in his 'final' version presented to the Walsh Street jury.

Ryan said his reticence to name his Uncle Trevor was based on fear. He said that he saw his uncle several days after the shootings, and that Trevor told him: 'If you tell anyone you're off. Believe me, it doesn't matter where you go or where you hide, you're off.'

During the interview, the detectives took a break for a few minutes. Ryan sat alone in the interview room after asking police to keep the door ajar. He looked petrified and began crying. When Detective Noonan returned he found Ryan was distraught. Ryan said he was worried about the safety of his father, John Brooks.

Noonan: What else is worrying you?
Ryan: [Sobbing] I think someone's going to get me.
Noonan: Why is that?
Ryan: I think Trevor's going to get me.
Noonan: Why? Because of what you've said?
Ryan: I think he's going to find out.
Noonan: Well, you know you're under guard at the moment, all right?
Ryan: I know, but still . . .
Noonan: Well, obviously you're always going to have that fear there. All we can say is that we're obviously going to protect you to the best of our abilities.
Ryan: They haven't got me dad?
Noonan: No. We have been in touch with your father, so there's no problem.

Before the interview with Ryan, detectives had regarded Trevor Pettingill as a possible suspect: he was not necessarily seen as being involved in the killings, but certainly knew some of the prime suspects. As a result of Ryan's statement he fell under deep suspicion and an investigation began into his activities. One component of that inquiry was surveillance.

However Trevor, the youngest of Kath Pettingill's seven children, was an experienced criminal. In early 1988 he was released from prison after being jailed for seven months for the possession of heroin. The charge was the result of a raid by police from Operation Cyclops, and the raid came after several days of surveillance from a nearby rooftop; police had watched as thermos flasks containing the heroin were buried in the backyard of 35 Stephenson Street, Richmond. Soon after his release Trevor was caught dealing drugs, again as a result of surveillance, and later sentenced to eight months jail. On top of his experience with Dennis Allen's empire, which was badly damaged by police surveillance operations, and the jailing of his brother Peter Allen after a surveillance operation that incorporated the extensive use of listening devices, Pettingill was well aware of how police worked.

According to police, Pettingill was under surveillance one day in late November 1988 when he walked from his home to the Woolpack Hotel in Carlton. The walk took more than half an hour and Pettingill was watched the whole way. On his arrival at the hotel he went to a public telephone and called the police internal investigations department to complain he was being followed and harrassed. He listed the makes and models of six cars he said were following him and gave six registration numbers. On the first count he got six out of six, which was the complete surveillance team, and on the second, he got one number plate slightly wrong. Police learned from the exercise that following Trevor was useless. The mobile surveillance was withdrawn.

Thus police were not watching Pettingill's flat in North Fitzroy's Holden Street in the early hours of 29 November 1988, almost two weeks after Ryan had said his Uncle Trevor was involved in the Walsh Street killings.

Pettingill, it appears, received a telephone call about 12.30 am saying police were about to raid his house. He acted quickly on the tip-off. His *defacto* wife Debbie was six months pregnant and Pettingill did not want her to be caught up in a raid, so decided to take her to her mother's home. Pettingill put on a coat and walked outside with Debbie — straight into an ambush.

The basic facts of what happened next have not been disputed by anyone. Pettingill was kidnapped by at least four masked men, driven to an unknown location and savagely bashed. He was then released. What has been disputed, however, is who was behind the kidnapping and bashing. It is something that will most likely never be resolved. No one has been charged in connection with the abduction or the assault.

According to Pettingill, the treatment he received was brutal. Certainly there was no mistaking the severity of the injuries that were treated after he was admitted to the Preston and Northcote Community Hospital later that day.

The ambush was quick. Four or five men emerged from bushes, pointed a shotgun at Pettingill and taped his hands and eyes. At first he thought it was the police, that the telephone tip-off only minutes earlier about a raid had come too late. 'I said to my missus that it's all right, it's the police. They're taking me to St Kilda Road complex, just ring the barrister ... Eventually I was thrown through a hole in the fence and put in the back of a Commodore on the floor. My head was kicked up between the passenger's seat belt and the passenger side seat, and my head was stuck in there.' Debbie Young was left behind, uninjured.

When Pettingill felt the car driving along open road he realised he wasn't going to St Kilda Road, which was only a short drive across the City from North Fitzroy. What followed left him in hospital for about two weeks. 'They worked on me, took me up the bush, sledgehammered me, my knees, my ankles, my toes, my hands, my shoulders, my elbows. They stabbed me in the buttocks four times, once in the arm, my finger was mangulated ... They said to me: "Go to the police. Tell them the truth." But they didn't stipulate for what crime, whether Walsh Street or other matters. All they wanted me to do was go to the police and tell them the truth.'

Pettingill was dumped at the side of the road near a service station in Glenroy, a northern suburb that borders Broadmeadows and Tullamarine. He staggered to the service station, where an attendant called the police and an ambulance.

The story made front-page news. And Trevor's mother, Kath Pettingill, left little doubt about who she thought was responsible. 'I believe they were police,' she told *Sun* reporter Graeme Walker. 'It was too well done, too commando-style for it to have been crooks ... Why would crooks take him for a ride and let him come back?'

No individual police were named, although Kath Pettingill and other family members had their suspicions. But the police they believed were responsible, some of whom were members of the TyEyre taskforce, were in Bendigo, where they were taking part in drug squad raids to see if there were any connections to the Walsh Street murders. Police later pointed out the law of defamation to family members, lest they name specific police publicly.

The police deputy commissioner, John Frame, ordered an investigation into the kidnapping. The investigation was supervised by the assistant commissioner for internal investigations, Carl Mengler. It found no evidence against any police.

But three months after the kidnapping, Kath Pettingill changed her mind. She declared police were not responsible for kidnapping her son and apologised to members of the TyEyre taskforce for having said so.

Her new opinion came after another bashing that occured only days before the apology to police. This time, an 18-year-old man returned to

the Carlton flat he was sharing with Trevor Pettingill and was confronted by three men carrying guns. They bashed the youth and demanded
to know where Trevor was. Several days after the second attack Kath
Pettingill said she now knew who was responsible for that bashing *and*
for kidnapping her son. According to police, in telephone calls
monitored by taskforce detectives, she named the attackers as four
criminals from Melbourne. In a newspaper interview, Kath Pettingill
gave the attackers a cryptic warning: 'They're not in a situation to
bargain with my family.'

More curious still, Kath Pettingill later reverted to her original
theory that police were responsible. After the Walsh Street acquittals,
she said police kidnapped and bashed her son. Trevor Pettingill was not
so sure. In an interview on the day he was acquitted, he said it could
have been the same people who carried out the murders of Damian
Eyre and Steven Tynan. It could also have been the police, he said. 'If I
accuse the police, maybe I'm wrong. But in my honest belief, I do think
it's them. But I've got no proof of it.'

The kidnapping is but one aspect of the Walsh Street saga that seems
destined to remain a mystery. Some police believe criminals kidnapped
Trevor Pettingill and told him to confess because the pressure exerted
by police on Melbourne's underworld in the wake of the shootings
virtually brought criminal business to a halt. Another theory is that it
was related to drug deals or other unrelated events in Pettingill's past.
The possibility that police were behind the kidnapping cannot be ruled
out. There was a great deal of anger in police ranks in the weeks and
months that followed the police murders, and hundreds of police would
have known that Trevor Pettingill was a suspect in one form or another.
But as several police pointed out privately, if officers were seeking
revenge, why kidnap Pettingill and let him go? Why not kill him?

The bashing limited Pettingill's mobility for months as he recuperated.
As he began to recover, police from the TyEyre taskforce interviewed
him. The interview took place on 20 April 1989, more than six months
after the police shootings, and five months after Jason Ryan said his
uncle was involved.

The seven-page statement gave some background on Trevor Pettingill's life. After facing a string of charges in his teens, Pettingill was sent
to Pentridge in 1982. 'At this time Victor Peirce was in B Division and
my brother Jamie was in D Division doing number plates. When I went
out there I was only young and on my own and Jamie told them to look
after me because I was his brother . . . I was in Pentridge about four

months. I was serving the remainder of a sentence that I had been given to Turana [youth training centre]. The reason that I was sent to Pentridge was because I kept escaping from Turana.'

Pettingill went on to say how he lived with his mother in Richmond during the time Dennis Allen was active; how he had faced a series of charges, including the possession of heroin for which he was sentenced to seven months jail and his mother eight months.

He said he had known Peter McEvoy and Graeme Jensen for almost six years. He knew Anthony Farrell and had met Jedd Houghton and Gary Abdallah a number of times in 1988. But on the afternoon of Graeme Jensen's death and the night of the police murders, Pettingill said he was at his home in Holden Street, North Fitzroy. He had met a friend that afternoon who gave him some prescription drugs and he took several tablets, became drowsy and spent the night asleep with Debbie Young, his *de facto* wife. Pettingill would stick by this story when he faced the Walsh Street murder charges.

In early October 1989, almost a year after the murders, Pettingill appeared in the Melbourne Magistrate's Court to face one count of armed robbery. The charge related to a hold-up in Richmond and Jason Ryan was to be a key witness for the prosecution. But Ryan did not appear. Detectives from the TyEyre taskforce had decided that they would not 'expose' their 'star witness' to cross-examination before the committal hearing on the Walsh Street murders. The decision meant the prosecution had to withdraw Ryan's statement from the prosecution's brief of evidence, a move that led the magistrate, Mr Hugh Adams, to dismiss the charges because there was 'not enough evidence to commit him for trial'. A similar result happened with heroin charges that Pettingill was facing.

A month after the armed robbery charges were dismissed, the committal hearing on the Walsh Street murder charges began against Victor Peirce, Peter McEvoy and Anthony Farrell. At the time, Trevor Pettingill had not been charged with the murders, although his name was mentioned several times during the hearing. He was named, with the three accused and Jedd Houghton, as one of the five men who left the Gordon Grove flat for Walsh Street early on the morning of 12 October.

When the hearing finished, magistrate Hugh Adams said there was some evidence against Pettingill, but not enough for him to direct police to lay charges. 'The director of public prosecutions may address his mind to that matter,' Adams said.

A decision was not made for months. On 6 July 1990 Trevor Pettingill appeared in the County Court for sentence on a charge of drug trafficking. The charge related to the police surveillance operation in Richmond in early 1988 when detectives saw marijuana plants arriving in a car at Stephenson Street. Pettingill was found guilty and sentenced to eight months jail and sent to Pentridge. Three days later he was served with a direct presentment to face trial on the Walsh Street murders.

The move was unusual and meant Pettingill would not have a committal hearing: he would be directly sent to trial at the Supreme Court. He was however, allowed to hold a limited hearing at the Melbourne Magistrate's Court to 'test' the evidence directly related to him. And, apart from Jason Ryan's testimony, the key piece of evidence against Pettingill was from Shane Richards, a 25-year-old friend of Pettingill, who had since gone into police protective custody. Richards said Pettingill had confessed to the police murders at a Richmond hotel. Pettingill denied having the conversation.

The hearing lasted a week and made no difference to Pettingill. He would go to the jury with the others.

13
Gary

'For Jedd to work with Jason Ryan, it's just not on. Something's mixed up.'

Gary Abdallah

Before dawn broke on 6 December 1988, the TyEyre taskforce mounted its biggest series of coordinated raids. More than 100 detectives and an unknown number of uniformed men and women took part, using sledgehammers to smash down doors across Melbourne's suburbs before charging into the homes of drug dealers, gambling figures, dealers in stolen goods, suspected armed robbers and those in some way 'connected' to the Walsh Street case. For those on the receiving end, some of the raids were bruising and frightening; in police terms they were relatively successful. Almost all uncovered guns, drugs, stolen material, or led to charges being laid. Part of the purpose of the raids was simply to stir up Melbourne's underworld. This fitted with the aim of attempting to solicit any information that may be connected with the killings from those who knew, or may have been told or overheard something. The raids were also part of the hunt for evidence and suspects. Among those raided that morning were friends and associates of a 24-year-old father of one, Gary Abdallah.

Detectives had wanted to speak to Abdallah since Jason Ryan told them that on the afternoon of the Walsh Street murders, while at his mother's Brunswick flat, 'Macca said he had to go and pick Trevor up to then organise the car off Gary ... Gary from the Carlton [housing commission] flats.' On the first day Ryan mentioned this — at Mansfield police station during his trip to the bush in late October 1988 — police suspected that 'Gary' was Gary Abdallah: Detective Noonan's notes taken that day had a question mark next to the surname.

Indeed Abdallah would have been interviewed on 6 December if police could have found him — but they couldn't, and it would be nearly three months before detectives sat down to a conversation with Abdallah.

The father of a six-year-old boy to a long-time girlfriend, the good-looking and personable Abdallah was known as a ladies' man. He was also an experienced criminal, with a number of convictions for car theft, as well as convictions for robbery, assault and burglary. He had done time in youth training centres then prison. He was not a drug user and was regarded by police as an up-and-coming criminal, having learnt from his mistakes. Police also believe he had graduated to armed robbery. And while detectives could not find him, his friends became the subject of intense police activity.

On the morning of the raids, a flat in Carlton was hit by a team of detectives. The flat was home to Jill Angwin and her husband Bill. Their sole link to the Walsh Street investigation was that the couple's then 23-year-old daughter, Christine, was a close friend of Abdallah.

Mrs Angwin told *Herald* reporter Michael Doyle that the police raid was the first of three raids on her flat in six weeks. On each occasion the front door had to be repaired.

During the first raid, she said, her husband was jumped on and was later taken to hospital suffering from internal bleeding. 'It was like Clint Eastwood,' she told the *Herald*. 'I like Clint Eastwood but this was bloody ridiculous. Are we going to have to go through this all the time just because they think she [her daughter] knows something about Walsh Street? She doesn't know a bloody thing. She's a nervous wreck. Do ordinary people have to put up with this just because the police want to bash down a door?'

But police certainly did believe Christine Angwin could help them — she could lead them to Gary Abdallah. And in order to do that, a listening device was hidden in Christine Angwin's flat and her telephone tapped.

According to evidence later given at an inquest, police said Christine Angwin's diaries showed she met Abdallah several times while he was 'in hiding'. Bill Cameron, the father of Jedd Houghton's girlfriend, also visited Abdallah. Yet the police surveillance put on Christine Angwin was constantly detected. Surveillance proved almost impossible in and around the housing commission flats in Carlton where Angwin spent some of her time: police cars — even unmarked ones containing officers in plain clothes — just stood out like sore thumbs. But despite strenuous efforts by police, Abdallah, who was renting a flat in Drummond Street, North Carlton, was not traced.

Police continued to raid houses, talk to, and interview people in the hope of finding Abdallah. A telex sent to all police stations in December 1988 said Abdallah was 'an offender wanted for the Walsh Street shootings'. Detective John Noonan was later to concede in court that this telex was 'poorly worded'.

Abdallah, however, had good reason to stay out of sight. Rumors circulated among his friends and associates that police were planning to kill him, and that like his long-time friend Jedd Houghton, he would be shot dead. Abdallah was also wanted by arson squad detectives for his role in a $300,000 fire at Simon's Disco in Northcote, a northern Melbourne suburb.

These rumors were enhanced by a general feeling among many victims of police raids that police were seeking vengance for the murder of Constables Damian Eyre and Steven Tynan. Leo Musgrave, a Melbourne justice of the peace, was also anxious about the atmosphere. As well as knowing many of Melbourne's detectives, Musgrave knew many of the young criminals who grew up in the Flemington area, among them Houghton and Abdallah. According to evidence given at an inquest, Musgrave said he saw Abdallah's name on police station bulletin boards in relation to Walsh Street and feared there was 'a great potential for conflict'. According to Mrs Roma Carew, the mother of Stephen Carew, a close friend of Abdallah, Musgrave warned her in December 1988 that if police got to Abdallah first, 'the bastards will kill him'. Stephen Carew said Musgrave approached him twice and urged that Abdallah give himself up to police, with Musgrave saying he would ensure Abdallah got into the police station safely.

The fear was compounded by stories that spread quickly. Debbie Stewart, Abdallah's long-time girlfriend, said at an inquest that during raids on houses and hotels, police left messages that Abdallah 'would be going in the body bag'. Stewart said: 'The people [who were raided] were telling us police were leaving messages that when they got Gary Abdallah they would kill him.'

Throughout December and January, Abdallah managed to avoid being tracked by police. Detectives from the TyEyre taskforce left messages with Abdallah's friends and family for him to contact them, seemingly at odds with the messages Stewart said other police were leaving. Finally, on 22 February 1989, Abdallah and TyEyre detectives came face to face. Still fearing for his safety, Abdallah had arranged for solicitor Bruno Kiernan to make an appointment at St Kilda Road police station to see Detective John Noonan. When the day came, Kiernan accompanied his client to the meeting.

Noonan told Abdallah he was not wanted for the shootings. His name had been mentioned — or at least a 'Gary from the Carlton flats' — in relation to supplying a car and Noonan wanted to find out if Abdallah knew anything about this. Said Noonan: 'We don't believe you've got any part in it. We don't believe you took any part in the Walsh Street matter at all. That's why we couldn't understand why you wouldn't come in.'

Abdallah said he didn't come in 'because people were telling me I was going to be knocked.'

Noonan said this was just a rumor. 'It's like anything. A rumor starts and away it goes ... [and] it looks like it's a pack of bloody animals that's running the joint. It just gets out of hand ... You're not even a suspect in any way for it — unless you say "I was there".' Abdallah said he had no involvement.

Noonan asked whether Abdallah received a telephone call on the afternoon of Graeme Jensen's death from Trevor Pettingill, Peter McEvoy or anyone else about arranging a car. Abdallah said no. For a start, he said, he did not use telephones to talk to people, 'so that's just shit straight away'. The car that he supposedly supplied, a light-colored Gemini similar to the getaway car seen on 12 October in Airlie Street, had been sold before the shootings. (The new owner of the vehicle was traced and the Gemini seized for forensic tests. The tests proved nothing.) Abdallah could not remember where he was on the night of the police murders, but he did remember how he heard of the shooting of Graeme Jensen. 'I didn't hear about it ... until I read the paper the next day.'

What puzzled Abdallah was Jedd Houghton's involvement in the murders. He said there was no possibility that his friend of eight years would have committed the murders with Jason Ryan, who even before Walsh Street was known as untrustworthy and unreliable. 'I honestly can't believe he [Jedd] did it, because Jason Ryan, he hated his guts ... That's why I can't believe it ... He [Ryan] was give-up, a loudmouth ... and Jedd just hated him. For Jedd to work with Jason Ryan, it's just not on. Something's mixed up. It's just not on. I know Jedd too well.'

Abdallah also told Detective Noonan that Houghton planned to surrender himself to police, but abandoned the idea when tipped-off that police were out to kill him. 'He was going to give himself up until he got the message that he was going to be killed. That's when he took off.' Abdallah said he later got the same message. When Detective

Noonan said these were just rumors, Abdallah made the obvious point: 'It'd get you worried.'

After the interview Abdallah was taken to the arson squad office, also in the St Kilda Road police building, and charged in relation to the fire at Simon's Disco in Northcote. He was released on bail.

The TyEyre taskforce continued its interest in Abdallah, notwithstanding Detective Noonan's assertions during the interview that Abdallah was not a suspect. That interest began the moment Abdallah left the St Kilda Road building, when a team of surveillance police was put on his tail. Within minutes, they lost him.

But as a result of Abdallah's visit police established that Abdallah was renting a flat in Drummond Street, North Carlton. Detectives installed a listening device at the flat and set up a permanent surveillance position in a building opposite to watch comings and goings at the flat. In terms of manpower, time, energy and cost, this was a major commitment, not the sort of treatment one would expect for someone who police thought didn't take 'any part in the Walsh Street matter at all'.

Less than two weeks after the interview, Abdallah was allegedly involved in an incident that would prove a turning point. According to police, he used his mother's car to run over a 24-year-old man outside a King Street nightclub after an argument. The badly injured man was the son of a high-ranking detective in Melbourne's western suburbs. Detectives from City West police station — whose area covers the King Street strip of discos and nightclubs in Melbourne's central business district — wanted to interview Abdallah about the incident but were asked to wait until the TyEyre taskforce finished investigating Abdallah's activities. The City West detectives agreed.

The surveillance and eavesdropping continued. In an interview with me, Detective Noonan said the listening device provided nothing to implicate Abdallah in the Walsh Street murders 'in any way', although there was 'certainly a lot of information about him being involved in other crime'.

In early April 1988 Abdallah began moving out of his flat. The lease was due to expire on Sunday 9 April and the TyEyre investigators had found nothing of use to their inquiry. They planned to shut down the surveillance position that Sunday having 'finished' their investigation into Abdallah. The City West detectives were contacted and asked whether they wanted to use the lookout to wait for Abdallah to return to his flat and pick up his remaining goods. The City West police, effectively given the green light to question Abdallah about the King Street incident, took up the offer.

That Sunday Abdallah arrived. He left the flat soon after 4.30 pm and got into a Sigma sedan. It was followed by two detectives, Cliff Lockwood and Dermot Avon, who pulled over Abdallah's car, searched him, and then took him back to the Drummond Street flat. Once there, police say Abdallah produced an imitation pistol and pointed it at the detectives; Lockwood fired seven shots at Abdallah, including one from his partner's gun after he had used all the bullets in his own police-issue revolver. Abdallah was critically wounded and spent 40 days in a coma in hospital before he died.

The shooting of Abdallah, like the deaths of Graeme Jensen and Jedd Houghton, are the subject of an extensive review by the Victorian Coroner, Hal Hallenstein. Hallenstein's findings are expected in the first half of 1992.

His inquiry essentially stemmed from the shooting of Abdallah. Until then, the Victorian Government had expressed great confidence in the police and rejected repeated calls for inquiries into police tactics and police shootings. When Arthur Nelson, a 29-year-old escapee from a Canberra remand centre was shot dead by police in St Kilda in mid-1988 after allegedly lunging at a policeman with the bottom half of a beach umbrella, the then Victorian Police Minister, Steve Crabb, rejected calls for an inquiry into the training and use of firearms by police. Crabb's stand was supported the next day by then-Premier John Cain, who said he had confidence in the way police carried out their job.

The shooting of Gary Abdallah 10 months later — on top of the shootings of Joshua Yap (by Constable Steven Tynan), Graeme Jensen and Jedd Houghton — galvanised those groups demanding an inquiry into police shootings. Lobbying by the Victorian Council for Civil Liberties and the Federation of Community Legal Centres, combined with calls for an inquiry by members of Gary Abdallah's family — assisted by solicitor Bruno Kiernan — changed the political temperature. News conferences were held by Kiernan and members of Abdallah's family, letters written to newspapers and public meetings held. Statistics from the Canberra-based Institute of Criminology concluded that Victoria had a disproportinately high number of shootings by police: in 1987 and 1988 alone, 10 people were shot dead. Premier Cain said he was concerned about what appeared to be a high level of shootings. The result was an announcement that the Coroner would hold extensive inquests into the deaths and re-examine earlier shootings by police.

As well, Abdallah's family asked the deputy ombudsman, Dr Barry Perry, to investigate the Abdallah shooting. With a brief that includes examining complaints against police, Dr Perry agreed. His 329-page report was completed shortly before Christmas 1989 and said, in part, that in shooting Abdallah, 'the evidence seems to provide some basis for believing that there may have been criminal conduct'.

During the inquest, allegations were more blunt. The lawyer for Abdallah's family, Dyson Hore-Lacy, said the pistol was a plant and that Abdallah was on his knees, his hands behind his head, when he was 'shot like a dog on a short leash'. Abdallah was executed because police were frustrated by their inability to connect him with the Walsh Street murders, Hore-Lacy said. He said the killing was carried out 'with the authority and the concurence and at the direction of Detective Inspector John Noonan'.

While the findings of the Coroner will be read with interest, they are unlikely to establish what, if any, role Gary Abdallah played in the Walsh Street murders. Indeed, no one except those who shot dead Damian Eyre and Steven Tynan know for certain.

Detective Noonan had wanted to speak to Abdallah after City West detectives interviewed him 'in case there was some lever there and he'd want to talk to us because of that'. But the interview never happened because Abdallah was shot, and Noonan got no closer to finding out Abdallah's 'role' in Walsh Street. Noonan said there were a host of possibilities: 'He may have been a driver. He may have been the supplier of a car. He may have been the innocent supplier of a car. Or he might have had no involvement at all . . . All there was, was a mention by Jason that McEvoy was going to pick up Trevor and was going to go round to the Carlton flats and they were going to get a car off Gary. Now it may have been another Gary in the Carlton flats. There's nothing to say it was Gary Abdallah from the Carlton flats and there's nothing to say they did go and get the car off Gary. There's nothing to say Gary even knew they were coming round to pick a car up. They may have gone round there and Gary Abdallah wasn't home. There were that many possibilities that make it just so incidental.'

And what makes any assessment of Abdallah's 'role' more problematical is evidence given in court by Victor Peirce's wife, Wendy. She said that on a contact visit to her husband at Pentridge she asked him quietly, who actually did the shootings. Wendy said her husband whispered in her ear that it was himself, Houghton and Abdallah.

14
Forensic

Science is always simple and always profound. It is only the half-truths that are dangerous.

George Bernard Shaw, *The Doctor's Dilemma*

In the firearms section of the Victorian Forensic Science Laboratory, hundreds of bullets, shells and shotgun cartridges are stored in drawers and filing cabinets. Each is in a plastic bag, each tagged with details of when it was found and how it was used. None has been matched with a weapon and, for the Victoria Police firearms experts, it is known as the 'unsolved crime file'. Forensic experts hope that one day a weapon, or another shell, bullet or cartridge, will be found to match the exhibit and lead detectives a step closer to solving a crime.

In the Walsh Street case there was no weapon. But police knew two weapons were fired: a shotgun and Constable Eyre's own police-issue revolver, which was still missing. Three shotgun cartridges found at the scene had been bagged on 12 October 1988 and sent to the Forensic Science Laboratory in Macleod, in Melbourne's north-eastern suburbs. Walsh Street residents heard four 'blasts' and two 'reports'. With a high degree of certainty police had all three of the ejected shotgun shells (one left in the breech) and the killers had taken the revolver with its two spent bullets still in the chamber.

The shells made their way through a series of tests. The fingerprint department looked for prints, biology for blood samples, applied chemists assessed whether the shells came from any particular batch. There were no prints, no blood samples and no batch identifications that sheeted it home to any particular point of supply. After a while the shells ended up at the firearms section, where they were handed to Senior Constable Alan Pringle.

A long-standing police expert on firearms, Pringle went to the 'unsolved crimes file' and checked for other 12-gauge shotgun shells previously discovered by police. He found at least 16 files, some linked to murders, some to 'criminal damage' — a police term that would apply if a window of a house was blasted out and no one hurt — and began checking each, using a microscope, to see if the marks on the shells used at Walsh Street matched any shells in the 'unsolved crime file'. This involved looking at the 'hammer-mark' impression made at the end of the shell when it was fired and scrapings on the plastic casings of the shells made by the chamber of the shotgun.

Pringle worked through the shells in chronological order starting with the oldest — and so the last exhibit he came to was the most recent. It was a bag containing three Winchester brand cartridges fired during a bank robbery six months before the police murders. Pringle discovered that the microscopic scrapings on the plastic casings, most characteristically the marks left by the shell being *ejected* from the shotgun, matched the Walsh Street shells. The impressions left by the firing pin matched. Painstaking checks showed all other marks matched too. There was no doubt. The shells were fired by the same gun.

Matching those cartridges was the biggest forensic breakthrough in the Walsh Street case. It led to the inescapable conclusion — and the only existing *fact* in relation to who killed Steven Tynan and Damian Eyre — that the gun was used by a gang of armed robbers.

At the State Bank in Oak Park on 31 March 1988, three masked bandits were greeted almost immediately by security screens slamming down, separating the customers — and the bandits — from the staff and the money. But the robbers came prepared and, using a sledge-hammer, one tried to smash open a door into the banking chamber. But the door proved more robust than anticipated so a second bandit fired three shots into it, but it still failed to budge. After a second unsuc-cessful try with the sledgehammer, the robbers fled empty handed.

TyEyre detectives needed to establish how firm the link was between those robbers and the police killers. It could be that all, or only one of the robbers, were the Walsh Street killers; it could be one gang member lent the gun to a third party who carried out the killings; it could be the gun was sold or stolen after the hold-up. There were dozens of new questions that needed answering and thus the taskforce's inquiries were focused on this new evidence. And some questions needed quick answers. For example, what type of gun was the murder weapon? Where was it? Who were the bank robbers? Did they rob more than one bank?

The opening task was to look at dozens of unsolved bank robberies going back two or three years to establish whether the Oak Park gang committed other hold-ups. Detectives were looking for, primarily, the same single-barrel sawn-off shotgun appearing in bank security photographs. They were also looking for other similarities: if any bandits wore the same clothing used at Oak Park; if the same style of hold-up took place inside the bank with one bandit covering customers while two others tried to get cash. Other common threads were explored: the times of day, the type of target, the number of bandits, the type of getaway cars used, and where those cars were stolen from.

After a few days the number of bank jobs was narrowed to seven, later to four. All the robberies were unsolved. Detectives from the armed robbery squad who originally investigated the robberies had collated statements, interviews and photographs and packed them in boxes marked The Flemington Crew. While the identities of the bandits were not known, it was assumed the same people were involved.

The Flemington Crew files were pulled apart by the TyEyre taskforce, with four hold-ups re-investigated in an attempt to find a new lead. Complete rolls of all photographs taken during the bank robberies were obtained rather than just those held in The Flemington Crew files.

Of particular interest was the shotgun: each set of pictures showed the same weapon that was used at Oak Park — and the same weapon that killed Damian Eyre and Steven Tynan. Yet the model was hard to identify because its wooden stock had been largely cut away and fashioned into a hand-grip and the barrel sawn off to make it shorter. Shotguns are often cut down by criminals because this makes them easier to carry and conceal. A shortened barrel also ensures the shot spreads more widely when the gun is fired, making the weapon more likely to hit something at close range, and ideal for confined areas such as in a bank. When Peter Signorotto, a gun enthusiast and armed robbery squad detective attached to the taskforce, looked at the photographs, he realised he had seen that type of shotgun before. Yet despite racking his brain, he was unable to remember where.

At a conference with taskforce members, Alan Pringle told detectives that the shotgun left heavy impressions on the plastic shells when they were ejected. He said this was consistent with certain types of guns and the weapon was possibly one of two types, one of Italian manufacture. Detective Signorotto, familiar with the Italian weapon, said the shotgun in the picture was not the Italian brand. He researched the second possibility and established it was not a match either.

Several days after the gun was first linked to the robberies, Signorotto took a day off work — one of the rare breaks enjoyed by those on the taskforce. In his private library of gun manuals, books and magazines, he spent hours trying to find the model used in the bank robberies, certain that he had once read something about it. His reference books drew a blank and it took a tedious search through about 200 gun magazines before he found what he was after. An article on KTG shotguns.

Back at the office, the bank photographs picturing the shotgun were blown up and compared with two articles on KTG shotguns that Signorotto found in gun magazines. The weapons matched. The murder weapon was a Japanese slide-action shotgun used primarily for shooting pigs, and known as a KTG shotgun after the Japanese company, KTG Kogyo Co. Ltd, that manufactured it.

What followed showed the rewards of both persistent detective work and the thoroughness with which legal gun importations are recorded. In short, police established that only 42 KTG pump-action shotguns of the model pictured in the bank robbery were imported into Australia. All arrived in Sydney from Yokohama in three consignments in late 1985 and early 1986 and were distributed to gun shops in New South Wales, Victoria, Queensland and South Australia. It was not until August 1990 that detectives established the location of the last of those imported guns. Some were still at gunshops — indeed TyEyre detectives purchased one in Melbourne to use for forensic tests. Those that had been sold needed to be traced across the country and the process took months. Of the 42, 40 were seen by police across the country, the guns having turned up in every state except Tasmania. Each had no alteration to the barrel and only one was missing its stock. The owner of the last gun located, which was found in Darwin, said the stock had been eaten by termites. This left two KTG shotguns, with serial numbers JSA-53095 and JSA-53108. Both were sent from Japan in February 1986, the last of the three shipments. On 27 October 1986, both guns were sent by the importers to Bob Reid's Sports Store, a gun-and-fishing-tackle shop in Mt Alexander Road, Moonee Ponds. They arrived soon afterwards and stayed at the shop, with an asking price of $550 apiece, until a robbery almost eight months later.

About 4 am on Wednesday 8 July 1987, the front window of the gun store was smashed with a metal pipe. At least one intruder clambered through the broken window and, using a hammer and jemmy, broke a padlock that held a metal security bar across a rack of shotguns. The thief grabbed four shotguns and fled. No one was charged with the robbery. Stolen were the two KTG shotguns and two other shotguns that were bought by the gunshop as trade-ins. Neither trade-in has been located.

The first of the two stolen KTG shotguns was found four months later in the possession of Michael Hall, a career criminal with numerous convictions for theft and burglary. At 25, Hall had spent several stretches in youth training centres, been put on probation with the condition that he attend a heroin rehabilitation program at Odyssey House and then completed several prison terms in Pentridge. He had convictions on more than 100 charges.

In the early hours of Monday 9 November 1987, Hall visited a house in Ida Street, North Fitzroy, to buy some marijuana. But the seller wasn't keen and an argument developed. Hall walked to his car (which turned out to be stolen), produced a sawn-off shotgun and pointed it at the reluctant seller, who fled. Hall walked to his car and drove off, but before travelling far he was involved in an accident with another vehicle. Hall picked up the shotgun and pointed it at the driver of the other car — then ran off. Police were called and within an hour Hall was arrested at a house in nearby Nicholson Street, North Fitzroy, where police found the sawn-off shotgun, along with stolen watches, bankcards and jewellery, as well as drugs. Hall's story of how he acquired the gun and the other goods later pointed TyEyre taskforce detectives in the direction of what was, to them, a familiar name: Gary Abdallah.

Two days before his arrest Hall visited a flat rented by Christine Angwin in May Street, North Fitzroy. He had been there a number of times and on one occasion saw Trevor Pettingill and Jason Ryan.

According to Christine Angwin's flatmate, Jedd Houghton and Gary Abdallah were regular visitors. She said Abdallah was Angwin's boyfriend but was 'a bit strange, like he was suspicious of everybody. He'd never come into the flat if there were other people there. He flatly refused to mix with other people.' She said that Abdallah and Angwin never talked in front of her. If Abdallah was there he would go into Angwin's bedroom and shut the door.

It was after midnight when Hall visited Angwin's flat. He knocked on the front door, but got no answer. Angwin and her flatmate were out: it was a Saturday night and they were at a nightclub. Hall walked to the back of the flats, jumped a fence and spied an open window. Instinct took over and Hall climbed through the window looking for money.

His haul was substantial: $2000 in cash from Angwin's purse, assorted jewellery, leather jackets, bankcards, a cassette player, a color television and, for good measure, a bag of marijuana. But it was topped off by the discovery under Angwin's bed of two items: a sawn-off shotgun and a white ANZ Bank bag. On opening the bag Hall found $8000 in bundles of mostly $100 notes. Police believe the money and the gun belonged to Gary Abdallah and that it was no coincidence that the ANZ Bank at the Royal Children's Hospital in Parkville was robbed five weeks earlier by a bandit carrying a sawn-off shotgun later identified by Detective Signorotto as a KTG. Police also suspect that Abdallah and Houghton may have been involved in the smash-grab at Bob Reid's Sports Store in which the two KTGs were stolen. There is no proof of this, only that one of the guns was found in Angwin's flat and the other was used in the Walsh Street killings.

Hall made off with his booty, only to be arrested 48 hours later at Nicholson Street. By then much of the jewellery and all the cash had disappeared. He still had the KTG bearing the serial number JSA-53095, which was used as evidence against Hall when his case came to court in March 1988. After the case it was sent to the Forensic Science Laboratory and destroyed.

In effect this left JSA-53108 as the only KTG shotgun in Australia unaccounted for. And about the same time the KTG stolen by Michael Hall was being destroyed after months in police custody, the other KTG stolen from the Moonee Ponds gunshop was used to unleash three shots at the State Bank robbery at Oak Park.

So, in early 1989 — while TyEyre detectives were a long way from tracing all the KTG shotguns imported into Australia — they quickly found out that one sawn-off KTG had been found by police and destroyed, and this gun was linked to Michael Hall, Gary Abdallah and Bob Reid's Sports Store. As a result of Alan Pringle's forensic discovery, the TyEyre investigation was rapidly expanding.

Almost four months after Pringle matched the murder weapon to a gang of armed robbers, the missing KTG shotgun was found. Wrapped in a plastic garbage bag, it was dug up by a gardener weeding in a bushy area around the fifth tee at the Royal Park Golf Course. The outside of the gun was badly rusted, but inside its breech face was as good as new, indicating the weapon had been regularly oiled and well maintained before being dumped.

The weapon was identified as that used at Oak Park and at Walsh Street. Its discovery, however, only served to confirm what detectives already knew. The KTG carried no fingerprints or other clues to the owner's identity. The disappointment was that it was not found at somebody's house, thus linking them with the Walsh Street killers.

And it still left detectives with the job of finding all the other KTG shotguns in Australia. Once they were all located with their barrels and stocks intact — which they were by August 1990 — it would be safe to conclude that this was the only KTG that could have been used by The Flemington Crew at the other bank robberies being investigated.

The shotgun, however, was not the only lead. The robberies by The Flemington Crew had another common denominator: the stolen get-away cars. Most were automatic V8 Holden Commodores, predominantly stolen at night in Melbourne's southern inner-city suburbs only hours before the armed robberies.

One of two stolen getaway cars used by The Flemington Crew at the Oak Park robbery was a brown and gold Commodore. Stolen from an outdoor used-car display at Booran Motors in Glenhuntly Road, Glenhuntly, the car's door was opened by drilling a small hole underneath the driver's side handle. The mechanism was then manipulated and the door opened. Once inside the car the thief broke the steering lock and used a screwdriver to start the engine. Like the cars stolen for the other robberies, it appeared a one-off crime. But the re-investigation of the Oak Park robbery revealed that the same night the Commodore was taken, another Commodore, this one yellow, was also stolen from the same place, Booran Motors, in the same way. It was not found for some weeks and, when recovered, it bore different registration plates. Two people were charged with the theft of the second car, one a self-confessed car thief, Theo Albanis.

The two Commodores were stolen within about two hours of each other. Whoever broke the chain barrier to get access to the caryard stole a car at the front — the yellow Commodore. The car directly behind it, the two-tone Commodore used in the bank job, also disappeared. Both vehicles had drill marks under the driver's door handle and both were started in an identical fashion.

When detectives made the discovery, the obvious common link, Theo Albanis, was in Pentridge serving a jail term for car theft. They visited Albanis, but he denied stealing the two-tone Commodore. The yellow Commodore he knew about, but he flatly denied any knowledge of the other car. Detectives were disbelieving. After numerous visits to Pentridge over a number of weeks, with each visit resulting in Albanis telling detectives a new story that was subsequently checked and found to be false, Albanis finally relented and admitted to stealing both cars. The trail leading to The Flemington Crew was now hotting up.

Albanis was born in Greece and moved to Australia while young. He grew up in the Footscray area, leaving school in 1984 to take a job as an apprentice panel beater and spray painter. His fascination with cars grew and he spent more and more time driving, repairing and rebuilding cars. And driving often meant taking other people's cars, without permission, for joy rides, especially on weekends.

Before long Albanis was caught by police and subsequently ended up in a youth training centre. On his release he continued to steal cars for joy-rides. But by 1987 Albanis, then 19, had discovered there was a lucrative side to car theft and he joined the ranks of the professionals. His function was steal-to-order.

Demand was high, supply plentiful and the work well paid. Someone would approach him and ask him to obtain a certain make, model and color of car. Albanis would find a vehicle to fit the order, steal it and deliver it to the customer. Payment ranged from $700 to $1000, depending on how difficult the car was to locate. Most of Albanis's customers would strip the vehicles for spare parts or convert them into 'legitimate' vehicles, often using a scam that involved buying a wrecked vehicle for a few hundred dollars and transferring the identity plates from the wreck to the stolen car. Add the wreck's number plates, restamp the engine numbers, and it took an experienced policeman to tell the stolen car was a fake.

Among his peers, Albanis was considered a very good car thief. He developed his own system for breaking into cars, using a cordless electric drill to make a hole under the lock to allow easy entry. Inside the car he usually used a shifting spanner to manipulate the ignition. Often it took him only 10 seconds to break into and start a car.

Some time in 1987 Albanis was introduced to a Maltese man, Stephen Saliba, a stolen-car dealer from the western Melbourne suburb of St Albans. In his early thirties, Saliba had convictions for receiving stolen cars and was known to the stolen motor vehicles squad. He immediately commissioned Albanis to steal cars for him and Albanis brought about 20 cars, mostly Holden Commodore and Calais models to the St Albans address, according to evidence given in court. For each order Albanis was paid $1000, but as the jobs grew in number he cut his price to $700.

According to evidence given in court by Albanis, Saliba picked him up from his parents' home in November 1987 and the men drove around Toorak, Collingwood, Clifton Hill and North Fitzroy looking for a suitable V8 Commodore SLE. The car was an 'order-job' and the right vehicle needed to be stolen. It took three hours to find one, which they came across in Falconer Street, North Fitzroy. Albanis broke into the car and started it, before following Saliba — who was driving his own car — back to St Albans. The stolen red Commodore was used as a getaway car the next morning at a Flemington bank robbery by The Flemington Crew.

In March 1988 Albanis met a request by Stephen Saliba to supply another Commodore. This was the theft from Booran Motors that led to the unmasking of Albanis. The two-tone Commodore taken that night was delivered to Saliba's house in St Albans. Saliba asked Albanis to park the vehicle just round the corner from his house. The next morning it was a getaway car at the Oak Park bank hold-up where the KTG shotgun was fired.

Albanis told police about a third car theft that involved a Commodore linked to The Flemington Crew. The order was for a V8: the color was not important. Albanis was picked up by Saliba and again they drove to the South Yarra area to begin the search for a suitable vehicle. Again finding the right car proved difficult. Eventually a green V8 Commodore was found in Stanhope Street, Malvern.

Albanis used a screwdriver to break into the car, started the engine, then followed Saliba's car as the men headed north. Before long Saliba stopped at a telephone box and made a call. The men then drove to Kiama Street, Lalor, and waited. Less than 10 minutes later another vehicle arrived with two men. One came over and Albanis introduced himself. Albanis explained what to do if the car stalled, then the visitor spoke privately with Saliba and handed over $1000. The two buyers of the stolen vehicle then left, each driving a car. Saliba and Alabanis left in Saliba's car.

Later that morning the green Commodore was used as a getaway car by The Flemington Crew at a Cheltenham bank.

It took numerous interviews for TyEyre detectives to encourage Albanis to tell his story. Each case needed checking out and Albanis was temporarily released from Pentridge to show detectives where the cars were stolen from and corroborate other aspects of his story. It seemed correct.

The next step was to find Stephen Saliba. The man who took the theft orders and apparently had the telephone number of one of the gang members appeared to be the key to the identity of The Flemington

Crew. But there was a problem: Saliba was in Malta.

One member of The Flemington Crew was Jedd Houghton. He appears to have been the man that picked up the green getaway car in Lalor, spoke to Theo Albanis and handed $1000 to Stephen Saliba. The description Albanis gave of the man he spoke to that night matches that of Houghton; when shown pictures of 12 men, Albanis picked out a photo of Houghton.

After Houghton was shot dead by police on 17 November 1988, newspaper articles and television reports said police thought Houghton was involved in the Walsh Street murders and probably fired the fatal shotgun blasts.

Whether it was a coincidence or not, five days after Houghton was shot, Saliba applied for an Australian passport. Eight weeks later, on 15 January 1989, his home in Concord Circuit, St Albans was put up for sale at $125,000. Four days later a contract note was signed for $115,000. The purchaser later told police he was surprised at how quickly and readily Saliba accepted the offer. Saliba told the purchaser he wanted to leave Australia quickly and pushed for an early settlement. The final purchase monies were paid in the unusually quick time of 25 days. In the meantime, a shipping company agreed to pack and ship Saliba's belongings after it was telephoned by someone saying they represented the Waterside Workers Union. The shipment was completed quickly and at a cut rate. On 15 February Saliba, with his wife Antoinette, flew out of Melbourne to Los Angeles. They flew on to New York, London, then Valetta, the capital of Malta, arriving on 25 February. One week after the couple arrived in Malta, Theo Albanis admitted stealing cars used by The Flemington Crew.

Had Albanis's confessions come when he was first spoken to by police, detectives would have had the opportunity to question Saliba before he left Australia. And, if Albanis's story was true, Saliba held the key to the identities of the bank robbers and he had to be pursued, making the decision to send detectives to Malta a foregone conclusion.

On 31 May 1989, Detective Inspector David Sprague and Detective Senior Constable Col McLaren arrived in Malta. Both men had been attached to the TyEyre taskforce from its first days, Detective Sprague as the second-in-command, his boss being homicide squad chief Brendon Cole. But Cole had since left the taskforce and returned to running homicide, while Detective John Noonan, junior in rank to Sprague at the time of the shootings, had since been promoted to detective inspector, the same rank as Sprague.

This left the question of who had ultimate control of the taskforce a matter of uncertainty, and certainly Noonan and Sprague had different views on the matter. The trip to Malta was to signal the start of a difference in views between the two detectives that plagued the task-force for the rest of its existence. The disputes that followed were extraordinary and could not have been forseen by Sprague and McLaren as they stepped from their Air Malta flight at Valetta Airport early on a Wednesday afternoon.

The following day, the first day of the northern hemisphere summer, the detectives went to the Maltese police headquarters and were told Saliba was waiting to speak to them in a nearby office. This was their first surprise. The TyEyre taskforce had asked Maltese authorities not to forewarn Saliba of their arrival, yet he was waiting in a police superintendent's office. (This was later explained to Sprague by Saliba: 'I have relatives in the police force here and I know you haven't brought papers to extradite me ... I've got good contacts, I told you, it only costs a few Maltese pounds.' Saliba then correctly named the hotel Sprague was staying at and the fact the Melbourne detectives had just passed through Greece.)

In an account of the police interviews in Malta, which were given as evidence in the Melbourne Magistrate's Court in 1990, Saliba was asked about the car thefts. In turn, his first answer was a question. 'If I tell you what you want to know, what's in it for me?' During the interview and in a subsequent seven-page statement, Saliba denied being a dealer in stolen cars. He said Theo Albanis organised the car thefts and that he received only $100 for his role. Being unemployed and on a pension, he used the money to help pay bills and bank repayments, Saliba said. He also named another person 'involved' in the car thefts: we will call him 'John'.

Two days later, Detectives Sprague and McLaren again saw Saliba. They told him the information about 'John's' involvement had been checked in Melbourne and was false. 'I knew this would happen,' Saliba replied. 'I'm in deep shit now.' Later in the interview Jedd Houghton's name was mentioned and Saliba became worried:

'I can't help you. The people in Melbourne are very heavy and I can't help you.'

'Who are you afraid of?' said Detective Sprague.

'I can't say. If I say anthing they'll get me,' replied Saliba. Sprague asked what Saliba needed to tell the truth.

'I want an indemnity. I'll tell you everything if you give me a piece of paper telling me I won't be charged. Do this and I'll tell you the other names.'

Sprague said it was not in his power to grant indemnities. That was a matter for the Director of Public Prosecutions.

Later that afternoon Saliba allowed the Melbourne detectives to visit his home. At the house Sprague found two cordless electric drills. When he asked Saliba about them, he became agitated. When Sprague asked who was involved in the armed robberies, Saliba effectively ended the interview.

'Put them back. The interview is over. It's over. No more. You don't understand, I can't tell you. You can't protect me from them.'

Saliba told the Maltese police superintendent who was also at the house that he wanted the interview to finish. The superintendent told Sprague and McLaren to leave the house. The Melbourne detectives repeatedly asked for the cordless drills, which Saliba said were given to him by Theo Albanis, to be seized. The Maltese policeman refused to do so.

It was the last time Victorian police spoke to Stephen Saliba, the man who promised so much but delivered so little.

But the legacy of Malta was profound in an unexpected way. When Detectives Sprague and McLaren returned to Melbourne, other members of the taskforce viewed the results of their trip dimly and bitter comments were passed. Sprague, in turn, expressed a belief that information was leaking from the taskforce, a view that did little to boost morale within TyEyre. It is true that there had already been friction among some members of the taskforce, but in the wake of the trip to Malta a chasm was opening up.

15
Macca

'Who'd be fucking stupid enough to do a job with Jason or Anthony? They're only fucking kids.'

Peter McEvoy

Two weeks before Detectives Sprague and McLaren left for Malta — and seven months after Constables Eyre and Tynan were gunned down in Walsh Street — Peter McEvoy was charged with the police murders. McEvoy's name had been linked to the killing within hours of the murders because of his past friendship with Graeme Jensen. They had known each other for more than a decade and after Jensen's release from jail in 1987 their friendship firmed. At Jensen's funeral McEvoy was one of the pall bearers. So when Jason Ryan told police less than three weeks after the killings that McEvoy left the Gordon Grove flat shortly before the murders, police suspicions firmed.

But police had little to link McEvoy to the killings. There was certainly Jason Ryan's testimony and accounts of McEvoy's anger on hearing about Graeme Jensen's death, but little else, and certainly no forensic or confessional material. So detectives 'let McEvoy run', essentially police terminology for hoping he would say or do something to implicate himself, or lead police to some evidence. Although McEvoy disappeared from Melbourne in late October 1988 for several weeks after taking a hire car to New South Wales, his return attracted plenty of police attention.

In the time McEvoy spent in New South Wales, police made a series of video recordings with Jason Ryan (including those implicating McEvoy and Trevor Pettingill), Ryan and Farrell were charged with the police murders and Jedd Houghton was shot dead. As Victor Peirce was in jail, this left police with only two of the five people named by Ryan as the 'killers' still walking free: McEvoy and Pettingill.

Taskforce detectives spent a lot of energy in the early part of 1989 finding Gary Abdallah and investigating the robberies of The Flemington Crew, but plenty of attention was focused on McEvoy. But, like Pettingill, McEvoy was wary and experienced, and mobile surveillance proved useless as it was continually detected.

McEvoy had moved out of Vicki Brooks' flat within days of the police shootings, partly because of a row over a telephone bill that led to Brooks' phone being cut off. After leaving Brunswick, McEvoy spent time at several addresses, travelled to New South Wales, then on his return to Melbourne finally settled in a flat in Bentleigh. There, police bugged McEvoy's accommodation, placing their fourth bug on McEvoy since the investigation began. His telephone was also tapped but picked up nothing that was used in court. Police affixed a 'tracker' to McEvoy's car to overcome the restrictions of mobile surveillance. A 'tracker' is a device that gives off a signal letting those following at a discreet distance know where a vehicle is. But McEvoy was no fool. The mechanical devices failed to produce any evidence that was used against him. And in the months leading up to his arrest, McEvoy found two listening devices and one tracker. The listening devices, worth up to $2000 each, and the tracker, the value of which is not known, were not returned to police.

In February, then again in April 1989, Detective Noonan spoke to McEvoy in what Noonan has described as 'prods', with the dual purpose of 'making sure we knew what McEvoy still looked like'.

Detective Noonan's accounts of these conversations came from notes taken at the time by another detective. Neither conversation was tape-recorded. Detective Noonan's statement to the committal said that on 14 February 1989 he went to the Brighton police station after getting a message that McEvoy was there and wanted to talk with him. McEvoy has not disputed the content of the conversation.

Noonan: I believe you wanted to see us.
McEvoy: No, I didn't want to see you.
Noonan: All right, I'll see you later then.
McEvoy: Just a minute, Mr Noonan. If there's something you want to know, just ask me. I've got nothing to hide.
Noonan: I'd like to ask you a couple of things actually, but not under these conditions. I'll see you when I need to, no doubt.
McEvoy: I don't need that shit, Mr Noonan, because I had nothing to do with Walsh Street and I'm not worried about it. I know I can tell you to get fucked and say nothing, but I'm talking to you because I didn't fucking do it.

Noonan: Well, we are in possession of certain information that suggests otherwise but, as I said, I will discuss this with you at another time.

McEvoy: That's bullshit Mr Noonan. I know what the stories are that are going around. And who'd be fucking stupid enough to do a job with Jason or Anthony? They're only fucking kids.

Noonan: That may be the case. Have you discussed the Walsh Street incident at all with Victor Peirce?

McEvoy: No, I haven't, but I can tell you he's cold [innocent] on that Armaguard job where the guard got shot.

Noonan: What do you mean, he's cold on it?

McEvoy: He didn't do that job. I was with him that night and we saw it on the TV, it was on the news.

Noonan: Well, that's got nothing to do with us, that's the armed robbery squad that's handling that. But now you have mentioned it, where were you when you watched the news with Victor?

McEvoy: I can't remember, Mr Noonan.

Noonan: Well, when did you see Victor that day?

McEvoy: I was with him all day.

Noonan: Where were you all this day?

McEvoy: I can't remember, Mr Noonan.

Noonan: Do you remember where you were on the afternoon of Graeme Jensen's death?

McEvoy: At Vicki's [Brooks] place.

Noonan: Did you speak to Victor Peirce at all that day?

McEvoy: Yes, I spoke to him on the phone.

Noonan: Was that after you had heard about Graeme's death, or before?

McEvoy: After youse killed him. I know what happened.

Noonan: What did you talk about with Victor?

McEvoy: I can't remember, Mr Noonan.

Noonan: What did you do that night, the night of Jensen's death?

McEvoy: Can't remember, Mr Noonan.

Noonan: Well, did you go out that night?

McEvoy: Can't remember, Mr Noonan.

Noonan: Do you recall where you slept that night?

McEvoy: At Vicki's place. I went to bed about midnight.

Noonan: Were you at Vicki's place all night?

McEvoy: Yes, of course I was. Why don't you ask her?

Noonan: Yes, well, I have spoken to Vicki and she says you definitely didn't stay at her place that night.

McEvoy: She's a fucking liar or you're a fucking liar, because I slept at her place that night.

Noonan: Are you certain about what you did that night?

McEvoy: I know where I slept that night, that's just fucking shit. I stayed there that night. Go back and ask her.

Noonan: What did you do the day the police were killed?

McEvoy: Well, you know what I fucking did, Mr Noonan. You raided me at Vicki's.

Noonan: Well, what time did you get up that day?

McEvoy: I can't remember, Mr Noonan.

Noonan: Where did you go that day?

McEvoy: Nowhere, Mr Noonan, because of that raid. And speaking of raids, that cunt McDonald [a detective attached to the taskforce], the fucking girl, he raided my girlfriend's place. Real fucking hero, belting up women and running around with a fucking shotgun, the fucking cunt. Jean's [Jean Campone] got nothing to do with this. And your name's been mentioned too, Mr Noonan, fucking harassing people and fucking running through houses.

Noonan: What you got told and what actually happened are probably totally different, but I'm not going into that.

McEvoy: That's what you'd like me to believe. I'll bet you wouldn't be talking to me like this if I wasn't in here, would you, Mr Noonan? No, you'd be banging me off the fucking walls, wouldn't you, Mr Noonan?

Noonan: All right. We'll speak to you again.

McEvoy: Ask me whatever you want to know now, I don't mind. I've got plenty of time.

Noonan: No. When I talk to you, I'll talk to you in a formal interview situation and I'll put certain allegations to you, not like this discussion.

McEvoy: What, put a .38 in my head, that's what you'd like to do, isn't it Mr Noonan?

Noonan: So when I want to speak to you again about Walsh Street, you'll be prepared to talk to me, is that right?

McEvoy: Yes, Mr Noonan, any fucking time you like. Ask me now. What do you want to know?

Noonan: I've already asked you some things I'd like to know the answers to and you've said you can't remember.

McEvoy: I don't give a fuck what you say. You've got nothing on me because I didn't do it.

Noonan: I'll see you again.

After a brief conversation with another policeman, Noonan said he again spoke to McEvoy.

Noonan: I believe you've got some listening devices in your possession.

McEvoy: My solicitor has got them.

Noonan: You also mentioned to the police that you know the police have been following you and you quoted car numbers. What are the numbers of the cars you think have been following you?

McEvoy: Not think, I know. But I'm not telling you what they are.

At the second meeting, on 5 April, Detective Noonan was waiting for McEvoy when he walked into the Cheltenham Police Station to report on bail.

Noonan: Peter, can I have a quick word with you.

McEvoy: Yeah, all right, what is it this time, Mr Noonan?

Noonan: You have previously told me that you stayed the night at Vicki Brooks' place, that's the night Graeme Jensen was killed. Is that right?

McEvoy: That's right, Mr Noonan.

Noonan: Is there any mistake about where you were that night because Vicki says you definitely weren't there that night.

McEvoy: I'm telling you I stayed there that night. And that's fucking that.

Noonan: Is it true that you were pretty upset at Vicki's place the day Graeme Jensen was killed?

McEvoy: When those cunts knocked him, of course I was fucking upset.

Noonan: Did you talk about killing the police at Vicki's?

McEvoy: Look, I told you I didn't do it. I might have said something because of what you cunts did to Graeme. [Noonan then showed McEvoy a bank security picture of a robbery committed by The Flemington Crew].

Noonan: Do you recognise that bloke, Peter?

McEvoy: Not me, Mr Noonan, I'm cold on that ... I've got nothing to hide, Mr Noonan.

Three weeks after this conversation, the KTG shotgun was found at the Royal Park Golf Course. With any chance gone of finding the murder weapon in the possession of a suspect, police discussed arresting McEvoy among themselves. When he appeared on the Channel Nine news on 3 May 1989 saying he feared police were about to shoot him dead because they believed he was involved in the Walsh Street killings — plus the fact nothing that could be used as evidence was being gained — detectives decided there was no value in letting McEvoy 'run' any longer.

Not surprisingly, senior police were sensitive about how McEvoy was to be arrested, especially in light of his claims that police were planning to kill him. This sensitivity essentially stemmed from the disquiet expressed as a result of the police shooting of Gary Abdallah less than a month earlier. And in the wake of this, senior police gave the unique and extraordinary instructions to the TyEyre taskforce that when McEvoy was arrested, not only were senior police to be informed beforehand of exactly when it would take place, but that it must be carried out at a police station when McEvoy reported on bail.

This was not what taskforce detectives wanted to do. They planned to arrest McEvoy at the flat where he was staying in the early hours of the morning, a style of raid often used by police because it catches people while they are half-asleep, confused and psychologically on the back foot. It would also be less dangerous if there was trouble than the public foyer of a police station. But orders were orders and, shortly after midday on 10 May 1989, McEvoy arrived at St Kilda police station and was arrested.

McEvoy said little in his subsequent interview with police, but maintained he had done nothing wrong.

For the TyEyre taskforce, this left Trevor Pettingill as the only suspect who had not been charged. But there was plenty left to investigate. The identities of The Flemington Crew still needed to be established, the robbers' links to stolen cars presented a solid lead that needed following, and there were dozens of other inquiries to be made.

But another dramatic shift in the taskforce's direction was about to take place. The split that emerged after Detectives Sprague and McLaren returned from Malta was about to be ripped right open.

16
Under Pressure

A man's best fortune, or his worst, is his wife

Thomas Fuller, 1732

It was the day before Christmas, but Wendy Peirce was not in a festive mood. In fact she was confused, angry and very drunk.

Ten weeks earlier her life had been turned upside-down. First, her husband Victor had been warned that police were about to kill him. Two days later, members of the armed robbery squad shot dead her lover Graeme Jensen. The next day, hours after the Walsh Street shootings, her home at 86 Chestnut Street was raided by members of the special operations group hunting Victor. Then the following day, Victor was charged with the murder of security guard Dominik Hefti and refused bail. This confused her greatly: she knew her husband was not involved in the Hefti robbery but, try as she might, she was unable to convince detectives of his innocence.

She was already angry at police for shooting Jensen and jailing Victor, then police shot dead Jedd Houghton, a close friend of her husband. On top of this, police kept raiding 86 Chestnut Street, each time rifling through her belongings.

One raid, on 1 November — the day Anthony Farrell was charged with murder — epitomised Wendy Peirce's state. She was drunk when police arrived and confronted Jim O'Brien, a rather large and hefty detective from the TyEyre taskforce. She told friends that O'Brien attacked her, but later admitted in court that she was 'throwing her weight around' and could not remember what happened because she was drunk. During the raid a handgun was found in the house. She was arrested and charged with possessing a pistol, assaulting police and using indecent language. She later pleaded guilty.

Peirce said there were nine raids on 86 Chestnut Street in the 10 weeks between the Walsh Street murders and Christmas. A raid on 9 November left Wendy Peirce crying and hysterical as police demolished the laundry and bungalow at the back of the property in search of weapons.

In late November, TyEyre detectives were granted a series of Federal Court warrants allowing them to seize jewellery once owned by Dennis Allen. Many of Allen's gold chains, bracelets and gem-encrusted rings had found their way to family members after Dennis's death. Yet he died owing huge back-taxes on his undeclared income as a drug trafficker and the Federal Court granted the warrants to allow the jewellery to be seized in an attempt to settle the tax debt on Allen's estate. The jewellery was identified from police affidavits on their knowledge of Allen's assets, plus numerous photographs of Allen taken while he was alive, which usually showed him wearing a splendorous array of chains and jewels.

Jewellery was seized from two pawnbrokers, in Russell Street in the City and Chapel Street, Prahran. Each pawnbroker held jewellery with a retail value of more than $50,000 against which they had lent around $7000 each. The pawnbrokers lost both the jewels and the money they lent: the family members who pawned the items lost them. The jewellery at Russell Street was pawned by Victor Peirce. (Word of the seizures spread quickly and attempts to find more jewellery failed. It had been quickly and safely hidden.)

For 31-year-old Wendy Peirce — her husband in prison, three children to look after, the police raids continuing and her house now in disrepair — Christmas seemed a bleak prospect. But she had little idea how bleak it would be.

On the day before Christmas 1988, Wendy Peirce began drinking early. By lunchtime she was very drunk — and becoming very angry. According to later testimony, she became so drunk she could remember only parts of what followed.

Certainly, Wendy Peirce was drinking at the Australia Hotel in Bridge Road, Richmond, where an argument began among a group of women. The row revolved around a statement made that Wendy and her husband were 'dogs', or police informers. Later, Wendy Peirce said: 'She was putting the family down, and I was sticking up for the family.' But at the time it was too much: Wendy Peirce cracked. According to witnesses she walked up to mother of four, Glenys Wills, said 'Have you got something to say to me?' and without waiting for an answer, Wendy Peirce attacked her, attempting to gouge out her eye with a broken glass. Wills was left badly scarred. Wendy Peirce then fled back to 86 Chestnut Street.

Back at home Wendy rang her sister-in-law, Vicki Brooks, and told her what she had done. Brooks, who had told Wendy about the 'dog' allegations and urged her to do something about them, listened intently. So too did detectives from TyEyre, who had placed a telephone tap on Brooks. But TyEyre detectives did not need to ring Richmond police to let them know what had happened. On completing the phone call with Wendy Peirce, Vicki Brooks immediately dialled Richmond police station and told them that Wendy was responsible for the attack on Glenys Wills. There was no love lost between the sisters-in-law. Before long, Wendy Peirce found herself under arrest.

At the Richmond police watchhouse, she was visited by Detective Col McLaren from TyEyre. McLaren had spoken to Wendy Peirce several times since the Walsh Street murders. He also knew her — and most of the family members — from his time as a detective at Richmond. He sat down with Wendy Peirce and told her she was being held for attempted murder. She was aghast. 'Attempted murder! They didn't tell me that before. My kids are going to spend Christmas without Victor and without their mum. I'm going to have a heart attack.'

McLaren, wearing a hidden tape-recorder, asked Wendy if she had attacked the woman with a glass; she had denied any involvement to the police who arrested her. She nodded. McLaren asked her why. 'Because she was going on, she was air-raiding [carrying on about] me, saying 'Dog, police informer' and that . . . I got the message back that she was calling Victor a police informer and I was a police informer . . . Look, this can't take [compare] to what Dennis has done.'

Wendy Peirce was refused bail and spent Christmas Day in the City Watchhouse. And if things looked bad then, they were about to get worse. On 28 December, police from the search and rescue squad joined TyEyre detectives and dug up the side and front gardens at 86 Chestnut Street. On 30 December, Victor Peirce was driven from Pentridge to the Melbourne Magistrate's Court and brought before Magistrate Harley Harber, where he was charged with the murders of Constables Damian Eyre and Steven Tynan. Before being charged, police applied to have Victor Peirce put in their custody. As Peirce was already in custody in prison, it was up to him whether he wanted to take part in an interview with police. He refused.

'I don't want to see the police,' he told the court by way of explanation. 'I don't know why I've been brought here. I've been told I've been brought here on two counts of murder. I know nothing about it. I haven't been questioned by the police. I feel safer out at Pentridge.'

Peirce was taken next door to the City Watchhouse. On his way he shouted to reporters: 'They charge innocent people with what they haven't done.' At the watchhouse Victor Peirce was charged with the Walsh Street murders. He was then returned to the court where he was formally remanded in custody. He told the magistrate: 'I deny these charges . . . Can I be taken back to Pentridge? I don't want to stay here.' Later that afternoon Peirce was returned to Pentridge.

A few days later, police began their last raid on 86 Chestnut Street. Rather than sledgehammers and shotguns, mechanical diggers were used to destroy what was left on the property — and detectives used shovels and picks to sort through the wreckage. The house was legally owned by the Australian Taxation Office, having seized it as part of Dennis Allen's estate. With electricity to the house cut off, it was systematically broken up and removed over several days in the first and second weeks of 1989. The garden surrounding the house and the soil underneath the house was dug up to a depth of two metres. 'Nothing that left the place couldn't have been held in two cupped hands,' one neighbor remarked. An assortment of bullets, shotgun shells and two handguns were found. Some of the shells were of the same brand and type as those used at Walsh Street, but this proved nothing. Like the buried guns and ammunition, ownership would always be in question. After all, the house had been lived in by Dennis Allen who not only had a habit of burying guns and ammunition, but was also seen on one occasion by police turning up the stereo in the house and firing handguns in the back garden.

The demolition and search was filmed for television news and reported and photographed in newspapers. A rock band even used a press shot of the house's destruction in a poster promoting gigs. Still in jail on the attempted murder charge, Wendy Peirce didn't need to be told what was going on at home. Her life seemed to be crumbling around her. On 4 January 1989 — shortly before her house was destroyed — she made an application for bail in the Melbourne Magistrate's Court. Despite pleas that her three children were in the care of her mother, who was unable to look after them properly because she was on medication, Magistrate Linda Dessau refused bail.

It was 10 weeks after her arrest before Wendy Peirce applied for bail in the Supreme Court. She was set free on the condition that she report daily to police.

Wendy Peirce moved to her mother's house in South Melbourne

where she again took charge of her children. While she was there, Detectives Col McLaren and Joe Noonan — John Noonan's younger brother — paid a visit, one of dozens of such visits by TyEyre detectives to the associates of those suspected of the murders. The visits were an attempt to continue putting pressure on Melbourne's underworld and make a breakthough in the case. McLaren had seen Peirce in Fairlea Women's Prison a number of times in early 1989 while she was on remand for the attempted murder of Glenys Wills. Each time it was on a trivial matter: checking something in relation to Dennis Allen's jewellery; organising the return of her children's bicycle helmets, items taken away when Chestnut Street was destroyed. It was a deliberate effort by Detective McLaren to keep in touch. He believed she knew more than she was saying — and he felt she may 'roll'. Each time he saw her, she seemed to give a little more. The visit was therefore no surprise, and the message was certainly clear. The two detectives told her they knew about the bank robberies of The Flemington Crew and suggested she come clean on Walsh Street. But Wendy Peirce said she did not know what they were talking about.

Not long after this meeting, Wendy Peirce and her three children moved into a house in Cheltenham where they stayed for about three months. But the pressure building in Wendy Peirce was reaching the point of bursting. Regular visits to her husband in Pentridge, looking after the children, the dislocation of a new house: it was beginning to be too much. She telephoned the TyEyre taskforce and asked for Detective McLaren. She wanted to meet.

McLaren arranged to meet Peirce at the New Orleans Hotel in Prahran and arrived with Geoff Calderbank, another taskforce detective: the reason for two detectives was for security — there had been a number of death threats against individual TyEyre detectives and they did not want to fall into a trap — and to ensure anything Peirce said was corroborated by another officer. Peirce was nervous and wary. She tapped down McLaren to see if he was wearing a hidden tape recorder (he wasn't) before she, herself, was searched by a policewoman to ensure she wasn't likewise 'wired'. After these preliminaries, Wendy Peirce began talking. She said she was sick of running — that she would 'think about coming good and telling the truth'.

Peirce also wanted to know if police knew anything about rumors that Victor had been unfaithful to her. There is some suggestion that police first raised the rumors with her some time earlier, although Peirce later said she had suspicions about her husband having affairs with other women, but did not believe it was true. She asked the police for proof, and was shown letters written by Victor Peirce to another woman — they were love letters.

The influence of that correspondence is hard to judge. Wendy Peirce later told a court hearing that they had no influence on her decision to enter protective custody. She had just had enough. 'I'd been in prison. I'd missed my children for 10 weeks. I had missed Victor for 10 weeks. And I was under a great deal of pressure for five years since these raids [started at]... Chestnut Street and I'd had enough. I was at breaking point. I couldn't stand it any longer. I had to come through and tell the truth.'

During cross-examination by Geoff Flatman, counsel for Victor Peirce, she was asked about the first statement she gave police — on the day the laundry and bungalow at Chestnut Street were destroyed — in which she effectively stated her husband's innocence. She told the court the statement was not true. Flatman asked why she had changed her story and talked with police.

Peirce: I knew I wouldn't win in the end and it was choosing between my children — [it] would have been better for my children to have a mother than no parents at all.
Flatman: Why do you not think you would not win in the end, Mrs Peirce?
Peirce: What was the use of going on fighting? As I explained to you, the hassles of court cases.
Flatman: Yes?
Peirce: And I had my children to think of. What would I prefer: my children to have no parents at all, or a mother?
Flatman: Why did you think that you would not win in relation to Victor's innocence, Mrs Peirce?
Peirce: Because he's guilty.
Flatman: But why did you think you would not win?
Peirce: Why?
Flatman: Yes?
Peirce: Well, I just knew what he had done. And what was the use of keep going on fighting?

During the meeting with detectives at the New Orleans Hotel, two young women walked past and saw Wendy through a window: they waved. They were the daughters of one of the solicitors known to her husband and it was not long before the solicitor — and others — became aware she was talking to police, putting further pressure on Wendy Peirce.

It took a series of telephone calls and a second meeting at a hotel before Wendy Peirce decided to enter the witness protection program. The date for Wendy and her three children to be picked up by detectives was provisionally set for the next day, Saturday 15 July 1989. The arrangement was that she would telephone about midday and make final arrangements.

That morning, Wendy Peirce began drinking heavily. Combined with medication for nervousness, it proved a bad combination. Just after midday she telephoned the TyEyre taskforce offices sounding nervous. In a cryptic conversation she said people were at the house and she could not really talk; she would try and get rid of them and call back in an hour.

By 3.30 pm police had not heard from Wendy, so telephoned the house. She answered and her voice was slurred. She mentioned that she had taken some heroin, but that she was all right. She would be ready between 6 pm and 7 pm and would call police back. But the call didn't come, so detectives rang again, but found the phone constantly engaged. Just after 9 pm they got through. Detectives said she was delirious. Her visitors were still in the house and she had just been forcibly injected with heroin.

Detectives decided that Wendy Peirce had to be taken into custody as quickly as possible as it appeared her health was deteriorating and she was under threat from being injected again with heroin. Detective David Sprague telephoned local detectives, told them who was in the house and about the heroin. The local police organised a search warrant for drugs and raided the address about midnight. Those present, including Wendy Peirce, were taken back to Cheltenham police station. Once there, she was examined by a doctor and questioned by TyEyre detectives. She then agreed to enter police protective custody.

Two weeks later, in a video interview with detectives, Wendy Peirce gave her version of what happened that day. She said that while she was on the telephone, Peter McEvoy's girlfriend, Jean Campone, who was visiting the house, overheard some of the conversation and appeared to become suspicious. Campone left while the phone call continued and, before long, returned. Soon afterwards Trevor Pettingill, his *de facto* wife Debbie Young and their baby arrived. Wendy Peirce was surprised: it was the first time Trevor had come to the Cheltenham house. The visit was unexpected.

About the same time, a convicted armed robber and heroin user who we will call 'Pete' arrived. Out of prison only a few weeks after sharing a cell with Victor Peirce at Pentridge, 'Pete' had visited Wendy a number of times in the previous weeks, but they fell out and she told him she didn't want to see him again. When he arrived she was surprised because she had 'thrown him out' about a week earlier. And while the visitors were in the house, someone took the phone off the hook. So when TyEyre detectives, unaware of what was happening, kept trying to get though to Wendy Peirce, her telephone was permanently engaged.

According to Wendy Peirce, 'Pete' went into the bathroom and came out with a syringe containing heroin, which he offered to Wendy Peirce. She was not a drug user. She told detectives she did not even smoke marijuana and had taken drugs only once before — at Dennis Allen's house in late 1983. On that occasion, Allen broke her nose in a fight in the afternoon, before Dennis's wife [Sissy Hill] injected her. 'I didn't know it was heroin. They told me it was speed,' said Peirce. She collapsed and was taken to hospital by ambulance where she stayed overnight. Wendy Peirce said she thought it was a deliberate attempt to kill her.

At Cheltenham, Wendy Peirce said she declined 'Pete's' offer of heroin, but he nevertheless injected her. She was later injected again. 'I didn't want to have heroin at all,' she told police. She said she was drunk at the time. Asked how many injections she had that night she said: 'Well, I had marks on both arms. Three or more that I recall ... I can't remember much of that day after I had the [first] injection.' The interview continued:

Police: Are you familiar with the term in the underworld called 'hot shots'?
Peirce: Yes.
Police: Can you explain what that is?
Peirce: It means to shoot you up with heroin so you die.
Police: In the incident concerning you a couple of weeks ago, have you got any opinion in that regarding a hot shot?
Peirce: Yes. I believe that they tried to do that to me.

Wendy Peirce was asked what condition she would have been in if the raid had not taken place. She replied: 'I would have been dead.'

The arrival of Wendy Peirce as a potential Crown witness was a huge breakthrough. Police were not sure what she would tell them, although she had indicated at the second hotel meeting that she would talk about armed robberies, murders and Walsh Street. But the first thing to do was check Wendy Peirce's health. She was examined by a police doctor:

he found the effects of the heroin, combined with some valium she had taken, were not too serious and she soon recovered. Detectives also needed to allay the fears of her family that she had been kidnapped by police or was being forced into making statements. Three days after going into police protection she made a brief video in response to a series of phone calls and messages, especially from her mother.

On the video, Wendy Peirce said she and the children were fine. 'You don't have to panic about anything. I'm not being bashed or tortured or anything like that. I've come here of my own free will . . . I love you all and I'll see you soon.' The video was shown to Wendy Peirce's mother, then handed back to police because, as Wendy Peirce said on the tape, she did not 'want it to get in anybody's hands'.

Instead of being put into the care of the police protective security group (PSG), the unit that usually guards witnesses, she was guarded by members of the TyEyre taskforce themselves. There were several reasons for this.

First, Wendy Peirce was in a traumatised state. Detectives felt for her to go straight into the regimented routine of the PSG could alienate her, and prompt her to leave the program straight away. There was, after all, no legal reason for detaining her; if she wanted to leave at any time, she could. There was also a feeling the PSG might not be sensitive to her delicate mental state. Certainly Jason Ryan's early days with the PSG caused him to complain to detectives. Ryan, however, was facing murder charges and his alternative to protection was prison. Having made statements concerning numerous people, this was an unrealistic alternative. Ryan, however, complained about the treatment he was given, an example being an occasion when he was taken shopping and he claimed his police protecters said: 'There's the dog food. There's your food, arsehole.' It was felt that to potentially expose Wendy Peirce, a determined woman with no great love of police, to such attitudes would prompt her instant departure from the program.

Said Detective Sprague, who organised the initial protection for Wendy Peirce: 'Detectives were the best ones to look after this type of witness, when they came in. Because they were mature people, they deal with these sort of people all the time. If you get a young person from the PSG who's been a policeman for two years and can't understand the type of person he's dealing with — and people had to put up with a lot of abuse from Wendy. She's very difficult to live with. And our people were the best people to do that.'

Police command agreed to Detective Sprague's request to house

Wendy Peirce, her children and her minders in a series of hotels and motels in Melbourne. Some were expensive, such as the exclusive Como Hotel in South Yarra. Every few days the family moved location as taskforce detectives worked 12-hour shifts, armed with shotguns and revolvers, to provide an around-the-clock guard for the family. It was an expensive exercise, but considered worth while.

Part of the reason for detectives guarding Wendy Peirce, as well as controlling her environment, was to elicit as much information as quickly as possible. Detectives wanted to cover a lot of topics before moving her into the protection of the PSG, as they would have to do eventually. And there was a need for haste. The Walsh Street murders were nine months earlier, and police were under pressure to prepare their case for a committal hearing. Added to this, detectives feared Peirce might suddenly change her mind and leave witness protection. So it was considered imperative that they get as much as possible as quickly as possible.

As a result, she was interviewed almost every day in the first six weeks — and it didn't take long for detectives to realise they had a key witness. The interviews covered a range of topics, from armed robberies to murders, shoplifting to bashings — and took in many secrets of the Pettingill family. About 20 video interviews were made in the first few weeks, some quite extraordinary.

But the enthusiasm of Detectives Sprague and McLaren regarding their new witness was not matched by all those in the taskforce. Some resented the fact they had to spend all their time guarding her. The taskforce's operations virtually came to a halt because the 24-hour guard took away almost all investigators. Most detectives had no idea what Peirce was saying in her interviews because of a security clamp. But worst of all, Peirce made allegations about taskforce detectives.

Before Wendy Peirce entered the witness program, the taskforce's operations had been marred by personality problems, the clash of egos and attitudes that were incompatible. Discontent was simmering and it came to a head on 28 July, less than two weeks after Wendy Peirce arrived, in an ugly incident that irreparably damaged the TyEyre taskforce.

17
Discord

split *v.* **6.** *to divide (persons) into different groups, factions, parties, etc, as by discord*

Macquarie Dictionary

When the Walsh Street murder investigation began on 12 October 1988, logistical problems quickly became apparent. It took only hours before detectives ran into their first hurdles and, in the days that followed, more obstacles appeared: a lack of equipment; poor coordination; detectives being forced to move offices. It all retarded the progress of the inquiry, some of it marginally, some of it not so.

Some complaints are typical of any investigation. Investigators — along with every police chief in the world — are always unhappy with their manpower and resources. Detective John Noonan remains strident in his criticism of the police department's lack of preparedness for the investigation. He says the department appeared to have learnt nothing from the Russell Street bombing more than two years earlier. There were inadequate computer facilities — and when suitable programs were found, the system crashed. On one occasion more than 300 statements were lost. Senior police were initially reluctant to form a taskforce — it took more than a week before the team of investigators was assembled. Nine days after the murders detectives moved into a new office without furniture or telephones. Detectives were forced to drop their inquiries in search of desks, chairs and other materials. The office was too small, and the taskforce moved again almost eight weeks later, again losing time in the move.

Despite the criticism — and some of it is justified — it is also clear that senior police gave unprecedented support to the inquiry. Hundreds of officers were authorised to work on the case and millions of dollars spent.

Like all big projects, some things did go wrong. But in terms of problems that nagged the taskforce throughout its existence, many stemmed from, or were exacerbated by, a conflict principally between its two senior officers, Detectives John Noonan and David Sprague. Their clashes embroiled all those involved in the case, and what followed was an extraordinary and almost unbelievable situation that both men say undoubtedly damaged the inquiry.

Police not involved in the investigation said it was inevitable that conflict would occur, especially as the Walsh Street case was so high-profile and the pressure to catch the killers was enormous. Like many confrontations, it would just be the result of working too closely, too hard, for too long. From the day of the murders the workload was enormous. For weeks, few detectives took a day off work, let alone a weekend, and days of 18 hours or more were common. When the breakthrough on the The Flemington Crew came in early, the taskforce was back to regular 18-hour days.

The ultimate fracture of the taskforce stemmed from its structure. Initially it was headed by Detective Chief Inspector Brendon Cole, the then head of the homicide squad; Detective Inspector David Sprague, then attached to homicide, was his deputy; Detective Senior Sergeant John Noonan was third in command, the leader of the four-man homicide squad team that attended Walsh Street on the day of the murders.

This provided a clear line of authority and responsibility. It was a direct transfer of ranks from homicide, where the chief inspector runs the office, the two inspectors provide advice when needed and run the administration, and the senior sergeants run the murder inquiries.

But within weeks, the TyEyre chain of command became less clear. Detective Noonan was promoted to the rank of inspector, attached to Russell Street police station, but was kept at the taskforce and given the temporary, and higher rank of detective inspector. (In the Victoria Police, unlike some other Australian forces, all detectives — except for rare exceptions — return to uniform when they take promotion. Say, for example, a detective senior constable is promoted to a sergeant. He then spends time in uniform and has to pass exams before he can take promotion to detective sergeant.)

The effect was Detectives Sprague and Noonan were now of equal rank, although Sprague was technically senior, having been promoted earlier. But there was no equal upgrading among the detectives: no senior sergeant to liaise between the officers and the non-commissioned men. And 10 weeks after the taskforce was set up there were only two sergeants — this fell to one after Easter 1989, leaving a yawning gap between detectives and officers. What confused the line of command further was the departure in about March 1989 of Brendon Cole, who returned to his post as head of homicide. He was not replaced and Sprague was not promoted to run the taskforce: there was, in effect, a vacuum at the top. There were now two chiefs and lots of indians. But the problem ran deeper.

From the first day, Detective Noonan saw the murders as 'his' investigation, something that became clear during a number of interviews I had with Detective Noonan. He said Inspector Sprague was in charge of the administration of the taskforce, not the actual investigation, and there is merit in this view. Noonan was the chief investigator at the time of the murders, and remained so throughout the two-and-a-half year case. But his promotion, and Detective Cole's departure, meant the line of command was blurred.

John Noonan is a tall, strongly-built man with a penchant for weight-training. He is a no-nonsense detective who holds firm views on how things should be done. If he disagrees with something, he lets it be known. His manner is direct — he calls a spade a spade — and he has an enormous capacity for work, prompting one investigator to describe his ability to work on and on — in awe — as 'machine-like'. Noonan does not tolerate people he considers to be lazy.

David Sprague is shorter, older and quieter, and says that during some confrontations he was intimidated by Detective Noonan's physical presence. With more experience of long-term investigations, Sprague prefers a more democratic style of decision-making, counselling the views of other detectives before going ahead. He is also more diplomatic, testified to by his reluctance to lay blame during research for this book.

Detective Noonan said some early problems stemmed from 'interference' by the then assistant commissioner for crime, Vaughan Werner who, Detective Noonan said, directed that forensic reports be sent to his office rather than to the investigators. Detective Noonan said that in the early stages he confronted and heavily criticised the assistant commissioner.

Werner, now an Australian Government police adviser in Papua New Guinea, agreed that he saw the forensic reports. 'Having ultimate responsibility for the investigation, it would have been negligent for me not to have seen them.' He said he had no recollection of any confrontation with Detective Noonan.

There was friction between the taskforce and police in other sections of the department. In some cases relations became strained or broke down altogether, according to independent police sources. These sections included the armed robbery squad, which has ultimately provided information that has led to the solution of numerous underworld murders in recent years, the drug squad, the major crime squad, and the bureau of criminal intelligence, which was responsible for following targets, as well as planting and monitoring listening devices.

And all was not rosy within the taskforce. When Anthony Farrell was charged with murder, some detectives disagreed with the decision and there was a loud argument. One detective had a stand-up row with John Noonan and, in reference to the fact that John's younger brother, Joe, had been appointed to the taskforce, asked Noonan why he hadn't also appointed his grandmother to the team. Soon afterwards, that detective, and several others, left.

These problems aside, the amount of work was huge and the dedication and commitment of the taskforce detectives nothing less than admirable. In the early stages, it appears most niggles and personality clashes that occured were minimal and readily resolved.

It is hard, especially as an outsider, to determine when the relationship between Detectives Sprague and Noonan began to deteriorate. Views on the reasons behind the clashes differ depending on who you speak to. It is put down to personalities, to politics, or a combination. The bottom line, however, was who controlled the taskforce. And some say the pressure was building long before the first identifiable problem emerged in June 1989, soon after Detectives Sprague and McLaren returned from Malta after their attempts to elicit the names of the The Flemington Crew from car-thief Stephen Saliba.

Much of the following material has come from a series of interviews with taskforce members. Some remain incredibly bitter towards others and have vowed never to work with those people again. The vehemence is, in some cases, astounding. Much of what was said has not been published here on legal advice. Suffice to say, the case has left deep feelings of bitterness.

Noonan said he was far from happy with the result of the visit to Malta. When I put this to Sprague, he was more than a little surprised. 'John has never ever said to me that that job wasn't done properly in Malta. Never ... And I would sit there and argue with him quite strongly if he ever suggested that. He's never ever raised that issue with me at all. He was told the problems we were having. We got two chops at Saliba: one where we got a statement and we got another chop when he was interviewed and we searched his home ... At one stage he [Saliba] wasn't going to talk to us at all. I thought we did bloody well to come back with a signed statement indicating involvement in two cars.'

Detective Sprague said the 'threat' by Saliba against himself and McLaren was treated seriously by Maltese police, prompting an armed guard on the hotel room of the two Melbourne officers. Detective Sprague said he submitted a full report on his return, detailing what was done during the trip. That report was sent to the chief commissioner, Kel Glare.

'Does he [Noonan] think we went for a 14-day holiday? Well he's wrong. He's totally wrong. I'm not going to get into trivialities like that.'

On his return to Melbourne, Detective Sprague felt that Stephen Saliba may have been tipped off about aspects of the visit. He also said there was a feeling that other material was being leaked from the taskforce. Whether any leak was deliberate or unintended — such as a taskforce member telling a fellow policeman and word then getting out — was not necessarily the issue. If there were leaks they had to be plugged and Sprague said he subsequently raised this at a meeting of all TyEyre detectives.

Sprague said that beforehand, he spoke privately with Noonan and said he would raise the issue. But when it came up, Sprague said Noonan unexpectedly failed to support his view.

Detective Noonan's recollection is different. 'Sprague accused members of the taskforce of ringing Saliba and telling him that they were going over there.' Detective Noonan said he disagreed with Sprague's argument and the way it was presented — and said so. 'Then we had a big fallout after that. He said I was disloyal to him by not backing him.'

Detective Sprague's recollection of the meeting is different to Detective Noonan's, although Sprague does agree that he accused Detective Noonan of not supporting him: he felt he received tacit backing for raising the subject at the earlier, private meeting. The cause, however, is not necessarily important. The effect was.

It was about this time that Detective Col McLaren's persistence with Wendy Peirce appeared to be paying off. She telephoned the taskforce, asked for him and said she wanted to meet. Noonan told McLaren that if he met Wendy Peirce he had to wear a hidden tape recorder and tape the conversation. McLaren thought this unwise. He had secretly taped Wendy Peirce at the Richmond Watchhouse soon after she stabbed

Glenys Wills with a glass. She confessed. Wendy Peirce knew about that at this point — and McLaren felt he needed to be above board with Wendy Peirce if there was a possibility she would 'roll'.

By the time the meeting was arranged, Noonan was attending a trial in Mildura, the result of an earlier and unrelated homicide squad investigation. McLaren still didn't want to wear a tape and explained the reasons to Sprague, who sought the advice of a senior officer. They agreed with McLaren and, in contravention of Noonan's instructions — but with the approval of a senior officer — McLaren talked to Wendy Peirce without taping the meeting. When Detective Noonan returned and discovered the meeting had not been taped, he was annoyed, and let his feelings be known. Relations deteriorated further.

But it was the subsequent arrival of Wendy Peirce in police protection that precipitated the split. Sprague said that Mrs Peirce named three police on the taskforce she did not want to talk to: Detective Noonan, Detective Jim O'Brien and Detective Col Ryan. Noonan had arrested Peter Allen, Wendy's brother-in-law, three years earlier for heroin trafficking and Mrs Peirce acted as his assistant at the five-month trial (Allen conducted his own defence). Allen had an intense dislike for Detective Noonan, and it appears Wendy Peirce shared this feeling. Detective O'Brien was also involved in the Peter Allen investigation: he was also a former Richmond detective who had charged several family members. Mrs Peirce had assaulted O'Brien during a raid at Chestnut Street after the police murders and was charged. Detective Ryan was another one-time Richmond detective who had charged family members. Mrs Peirce later told a court that Detective Ryan assaulted her while she was holding her daughter in the first raid after the murders.

Detective Sprague adhered to Wendy Peirce's request. He also decided that she should be guarded by taskforce detectives rather than members of the police protective security group, who are generally younger and less experienced than detectives. Because she was uptight, Sprague felt she could be better managed by taskforce detectives, who had more experience in understanding people such as Wendy Peirce. Police wanted to avoid upsetting and possibly 'losing' her. Sprague also wanted to interview Wendy Peirce about as much as possible, as quickly as possible, and with the taskforce guarding her, there was ready access to the witness.

To Detective John Noonan, however, the use of taskforce police to guard Peirce and her three children in Melbourne hotels was an extravagent waste.

'You can't differentiate between witnesses. You can't treat one better than the others. You don't house one better than the others and what I was very critical of was the fact they put her up in an expensive motel and wined her and dined her and did what they did on the pretext of obtaining evidence.

'I was particularly not happy with the fact that they used the entire taskforce to guard her and she was one cog in a wheel and they threw all the resources that I had, without any consultation with me . . . and left my investigation at a stalemate for six weeks.'

Detective Noonan said the inquiry was at a crucial stage, an assertion Detective Sprague found hard to comprehend. 'There was no crucial stage. The only crucial stage was that she came into the program.'

Sprague disagrees that Mrs Peirce was 'wined and dined'. The cost, he said, 'was approved by a deputy commissioner, not me. They obviously saw the value of that person coming into the program.'

Senior police, aware that Wendy Peirce did not want contact with three of the taskforce detectives, including John Noonan, ordered that Noonan have no contact with the new witness. They also ordered that the master tapes of all video interviews be handed on completion to the assistant commissioner for crime, Vaughan Werner, or his deputy, Chief Superintendent Kevin Holliday. The tapes were then put into the assistant commissioner's safe.

This, in effect, meant Detective Noonan was not seeing Mrs Peirce's evidence — nor could he get access to copies — a ludicrous situation considering Detective Noonan was in charge of collating all of the evidence ahead of the committal hearings. And the preparation of the brief of evidence was becoming a pressing matter.

In early June 1989, during a remand hearing in the Melbourne Magistrate's Court, the Chief Magistrate, John Dugan, urged police to provide a brief of evidence on 3 July. Police failed to meet that deadline and when Wendy Peirce entered police protection less than two weeks later, providing a stream of new evidence, police sought more time, requesting an extension to 26 October. Dugan said this was unfair to the accused and set a committal date for 18 September. There were further delays and the committal ultimately began on 31 October 1989.

But the effect of the Chief Magistrate pressing for an early start was that the task of compiling the brief became increasingly urgent. Police hoped the department of the Director of Public Prosecutions would provide legal assistance to help prepare the brief of evidence. But the DPP declined to give direct help.

This was surprising, considering the mass of evidence obtained by the taskforce in almost eight months of work, let alone the importance of the case.

Aware of the DPP's reluctance to become involved, senior police appointed Chief Inspector Allen Bowles to assist in preparing the case and, if necessary, become the prosecutor during the committal hearing. Bowles, then head of the police prosecutions department, was one of the rare breed of police who had completed a law degree. He was one of the first, completing law in 1978 and being admitted as a barrister and solicitor of the Supreme Court in 1980. He qualified in law shortly after the Chief Commissioner Kel Glare and the former Victorian commissioner, Bill Horman, and is a friend of both men. Bowles had extensive court experience, acting as a police prosecutor in Melbourne's magistrates courts for more than seven years. But the non-involvement of the DPP surprised even him.

'I think it was politics. Politics of the DPP, the fact that they thought we didn't have enough evidence and they just didn't want to run with it ... I don't think they thought it was a "winner" at that stage and they didn't want to be associated with such an important case, which they regarded as a loss. That's my interpretation.'

Bowles said the timetable imposed by Chief Magistrate Dugan to complete the brief led to a great deal of pressure on police to compile the material. 'He [Dugan] gave us an unrealistic timetable,' Bowles said.

Back at the taskforce office, Detectives Noonan, O'Brien and Ryan — the three police Wendy Peirce didn't want to talk to — were pursuing inquiries. They flew to Queensland to interview Bill Cameron, the father of Jedd Houghton's girlfriend. When Ryan returned, he stepped into a lift and talked to an armed robbery squad detective. Ryan was more than a little surprised when told that he was expected to return to the armed robbery squad. So too was O'Brien, who found a note on his desk telling him to telephone Caulfield police station about reporting for work on Monday. Both men were being transferred out.

When they asked why, they were told allegations had been made against them by Wendy Peirce. Then they were told they were being transferred soley because the taskforce was being wound down and numbers cut. (No allegation was substantiated in any way. Ryan and O'Brien returned to work on the Walsh Street case in 1990.)

The decision to move both men upset many taskforce members. Ryan and O'Brien were regarded as professional and highly competent detectives — and Ryan was seen as one of the hardest-working and most committed of the taskforce members. It was his early work that prompted Jason Ryan to open up to police. O'Brien was at the Walsh Street site within two hours of the killings and had an intimate knowledge of the crime. Both men had extensive dealings with the family and that experience was invaluable to the investigation. Yet, of the 14 members in the taskforce, they were dumped.

For weeks tension had been building and a number of other incidents took place that added to the build-up. Insiders say some police were trying to follow the evolving dispute, concentrating on that rather than the inquiry. Detectives wanted to know what was going on, but couldn't find out. Morale fell. Few people were told what Wendy Peirce was saying, exacerbated by the clamp on the videos. A number of meetings were called to clear the air and discuss the problems, but nothing was resolved. One detective said that when news of the dumping of Ryan and O'Brien came through, 'the joint exploded'. Matters came to a head on 28 July 1989.

Allen Bowles, the newcomer to the taskforce with the role of helping pull the evidence together, had little idea of the pressures that had been building, and when he walked into the taskforce offices, he found a shouting match in progress. 'I wasn't even invited,' said Bowles. 'I just wandered in because I was around there doing something. I just sat there. I thought: "Gee, this is all new. What have I let myself in for?"'

He said an argument raged for about 20 minutes. 'I didn't like the way it was done. It was so vehement. The discussions were pretty heavy.'

Accounts of that day vary, although all those I have spoken to who were present agree that discussions were heated. Said Detective Sprague: 'I've never ever abused him [Noonan] like that in front of people in that situation ... I voiced my discontent later. But unfortunately it continued with John and me.'

On that day, the taskforce divided. Sprague moved to an office on another floor while Noonan remained at the taskforce offices. Within a week senior police, who were well aware of the argument on 28 July, reduced the number of police on the case from 14 to six. Some detectives stayed on — as guards and interviewers — until the series of video-recordings with Wendy Peirce was complete.

But several investigators have told me the cutbacks were premature, because investigations were far from over. The inquiry into Trevor Pettingill was incomplete; inquiries into the bank robberies by The

Flemington Crew were unfinished; a number of Gary Abdallah's associates needed to be questioned; and other matters were far from finalised.

While Detective Noonan remained on the 14th floor at the taskforce offices, with the main objective of compiling the brief, Detective Sprague set up office on the ninth floor of the St Kilda Road building in the homicide squad. It was the start of what became known as the 'A Team' and the 'B Team' and, despite the efforts of some detectives to keep channels open, for the most part neither group talked to the other. There were now, in effect, two groups of police independently investigating the murders of Damian Eyre and Steven Tynan: one pursuing jobs from the taskforce offices and finishing the brief, the other investigating the substance of Mrs Peirce's interviews.

Allen Bowles, brought in to help prepare the brief, found a new role as mediator-cum-message-deliverer. Detectives Noonan and Sprague would come to his office if something needed to be passed on to the other.

Bowles said he regarded the decision to keep the tapes from Detective Noonan as pathetic. Bowles, however, was privy to the tapes and found a way to overcome the obstacle. 'I was a chief inspector at the time and my main task was to get the job done ... What I did was the moment I got the tapes I took them up to Noonan and said here you go ... He could use it because he had far more knowledge of the overall story ... here you've got an investigation running with not all the information coming in.' Bowles said Detective Noonan initially got the transcripts of the interviews, and much later copies of the tapes.

Detective Noonan found the ban on viewing Mrs Peirce's videos hard to comprehend. 'Why I was left out in the first place, I've got no idea. I thought she must have made allegations but I've since found that she hasn't said anything about me at all other than she didn't like me. And that's probably something in my favor,' Noonan said. 'I'm trying to put a brief together and I don't even know what she's saying. It's just ludicrous.

'But they left me running everything up to a stage where they took everyone away, so I was running really nothing in the end. All they wanted to do was use me to put the brief together.'

The material involved was phenomenal: 940 statements, 6500 information sheets, 11,700 separate conversations from telephone intercepts, 1700 listening device tapes, 900 exhibits spread across six offices, not to mention the dozens of video interviews made with numerous witnesses. With the deadline for the committal approaching, Noonan said the team needed to telephone witnesses to warn them they would be needed in court; detectives were still compiling material on Trevor Pettingill, who had not been charged; and many other inquiries were incomplete.

According to Detective Noonan, the committal was due to start on a Monday. On the Friday before, with the office crowded with photocopies as numerous copies of the brief — each copy filled four binders — were being put together, Assistant Commissioner Werner and Chief Superintendent Kevin Holliday arrived and told detectives they would have to vacate the office by Monday. Werner and Holliday disagree with Detective Noonan's recollection of events. Noonan, however, believed the taskforce faced eviction. 'All we did was change all the locks on the doors. Went and bought our own locks, changed them all and refused to give them keys.'

When Detective Noonan wanted to interview Mrs Peirce, more problems followed. After some manoeuvring and lobbying, involving numerous high-level meetings, he was allowed to interview her. The problems in the taskforce were quickly apparent to senior police, including Chief Commissioner Kel Glare, who became directly involved.

Detectives Noonan and Sprague concede that their disagreements, illustrated by some of the episodes in this chapter, damaged the inquiry into the police murders. But perhaps more importantly, it leaves one wondering how the clash between the 'A Team' and 'B Team' was allowed to go on for so long and was never resolved. When Detective Sprague officially left the taskforce in October 1989, some 12 months after the Walsh Street murders, he kept in contact with Wendy Peirce. Detective Noonan prepared the brief of evidence and successfully took the matter through the committal hearing.

But quite amazingly, it was not the end of the bitter dispute between the two detectives. Nor, according to Detective Sprague, would it be the end of the damage to the inquiry.

18
Evidence

Eyes are more accurate witnesses than ears

Heraclitus, c. 500 BC

Six months before the committal hearing began, police came close to losing one of their Crown witnesses. It was April 1989, and the witness was tucked inside a 'safe-house' guarded by heavily armed police in Melbourne's bayside suburbs. But the house was becoming the subject of local interest. Cars coming and going at odd times, lots of men moving in and out of the house. It was enough to prompt residents to call the local police who, for security reasons, had no idea that the house was being used by other police. From there, a team of police from Frankston, wearing casual clothes, mounted a drug raid on the house.

It appears that the police guards inside the house, under orders to shoot to protect their witness, recognised one of the raiding party as they came up the driveway. Instead of following orders and having a shootout, those inside the house put down their revolvers and shotguns as the raiding police came in.

The police guards were heavily reprimanded for failing to protect their witness and for allowing unauthorised people into the house: a classic case of damned if you do and damned if you don't. It must have been very close to a bloody incident. If a shot had been fired by the guards, the subsequent shootout could have left any number dead and wounded — the witness included. After the raid a new 'safe house' was found.

As the date of the committal hearings on the murder charges drew closer, Allen Bowles, the police prosecutor brought in to assist compiling the brief — the combined evidence against the accused — still hoped the Director of Public Prosecutions would take over the case and prosecute it.

Bowles said he supplied the DPP with some aspects of Wendy Peirce's statements, urging that it become involved. But the DPP didn't. Said Bowles: '[The DPP] didn't have what they considered a completed brief and they weren't prepared to give advice on an incompleted brief.' The problem was that Wendy Peirce was still doing interviews with police and her story was changing, with more and more material being given. The brief would not be complete until Wendy Peirce's story was finalised — and when that would be was not known.

In the end, Bowles was left to prosecute the case, assisted by another policeman with a law degree, Senior Sergeant Col Moffitt. 'That didn't phase me at all,' said Bowles. 'By the time we had got to court I'd analysed the evidence, spoken to all the witnesses and believed we had a very good case.'

But the Crown lost one advantage with the DPP not supplying a prosecuter for the case. Usually, if a Queen's Counsel prosecutes a committal, he also prosecutes at the trial. This means the prosecutor has built up an intimate knowledge of the evidence, some of the defence strategies and the ability of Crown witnesses to withstand cross-examination. As Bowles puts it: 'It only makes sense if you are going to have an important case. You try and get the person going to do the matter before the judge and jury to do it at the committal . . . I'm taking the people through their evidence, seeing how they are cross-examined, reacting to evidence . . . In hard copy [transcripts] you're not seeing any of the body language. You can never describe fully to another prosecutor how a witness responded in the box.'

Bowles said Jim Morrisey, the Queen's Counsel who ultimately prosecuted the case in the Supreme Court, thus 'had a very sharp learning curve to take on all that information'.

Ten weeks before the committal began, the murder charges against Jason Ryan were withdrawn. Police said this was done because his 'final' version of events revealed he was not privy to the alleged murder plot and he did not assist in the killings. In his first video 're-enactment', Ryan said he was privy to the plan and helped steal the car in Walsh Street. On that testimony — admitting knowledge of and aiding in the commission of the crime — he was charged with the murders. Once his story changed, taking him away from the scene and absolving him of knowledge of the plot, police deemed there was insufficient evidence to retain the murder charges. Once the double-murder charge was withdrawn, Ryan stayed in the witness protection program. Strictly, he did not need to. It had previously been a condition of his bail on the murder charges. He may have had his own feelings about life back on the streets, however.

The committal hearings of murder charges against Victor George Peirce, Peter David McEvoy and Anthony Leigh Farrell began on 31 October 1989. It took place under tight security. Special operations group police escorted the accused to the court, although this sometimes took the ridiculous route of taking a prisoner from the Melbourne Remand Centre, five city blocks from the courthouse, out to Pentridge Prison in Coburg, then back to the court. The reverse journey followed after the hearing. For the accused, this was undeniably unfair, turning a 10-minute trip into one-and-a-half hours of rattling around in the back of a prison van.

On the opening day, the court was packed with police, journalists, lawyers, and friends and family of the accused. Chief Inspector Allen Bowles began with the Crown's case of events. He said evidence would show that all the accused were upset when news of Graeme Jensen's fatal shooting reached them; including the late Jedd Houghton, Trevor Pettingill (who had not been charged at that stage) and Jason Ryan, six men gathered at a flat in Gordon Grove, South Yarra, and cemented the final aspects of a plan to kill police in revenge for the shooting of Jensen. 'The identity of these officers was not important, their selection was mere chance,' Bowles told the court. 'They were killed, it is alleged, in retribution for the killing of Graeme Jensen.'

Bowles said testimony by witnesses would confirm aspects of the story and support the Crown case. Some would be relatives of the accused, among them two people in protective custody, Wendy Peirce and Jason Ryan.

Three weeks into the trial Jason Ryan, entered the witness box to testify against his Uncle Victor, his friend Anthony Farrell and his mother's former lodger, Peter McEvoy. He was closely questioned on his varying versions of what happened at Walsh Street, his life with Dennis Allen and his criminal history.

Ryan's credibility was a key issue at the committal and trial, and it was pursued strongly by defence counsel. Ryan admitted numerous lies in his video interviews, especially the 're-enactments'. There were so many lies that the defence counsel asked — and got — Ryan to mark transcripts of his interviews with colored pens to show which sections were the truth and which false! Cross-examination by David Ross, QC, counsel for Anthony Farrell, illustrated the problems Ryan had.

Ross:	Mr Ryan, have you ever given a fake name?
Ryan:	Yes.
Ross:	What fake names have you given?
Ryan:	Ryan.
Ross:	Beg your pardon?
Ross:	Ryan.
Ryan:	Ryan is a fake name, is it?
Ross:	That's right.
Ryan:	What is it? What is your real name?
Ross:	Jason Brooks.

Indeed, Ryan was right. His mother, Vicki Brooks, was one of Kath Pettingill's children. Vicki married John Brooks, took his surname, but when they separated she reverted to the surname of Ryan, which she had used from childhood. Jason then adopted the surname. But the question of credibility went far beyond Jason Ryan's surname.

In his summing-up, Ross analysed the testimony of Ryan, which was the key evidence against his client, Anthony Farrell. The arguments were part of the defence for all the accused, although at the committal, because Ryan's testimony was almost the only evidence against Farrell, Ross conducted the attack during the summing-up. Ross was colorful in his conclusions about Ryan. 'A psychologist or psychiatrist could have a birthday party on such a person,' he said. 'It defies decription that there are so many lies told about so many subjects on so many occasions.'

'He is a witness who is so full of flaws as to be totally without credit and without credibility. At the age of 17 years or so he was already an experienced criminal. He was a person who was familiar with burglaries and with robberies. He was a man of violence ... and he has been charged and convicted for an offence that occured in February 1988 connected with drug running.'

Ross said Ryan 'was a liar of epic proportions'. He told the magistrate: 'We say to you that you should reject that evidence of any involvement of Gordon Grove in these crimes at all. And we submit to you that you should be firmly of the conclusion that Gordon Grove played no part in any visit that night by Jason Ryan or Anthony Farrell.'

Ross said part of this proposition was based on evidence relating to the key to the flat. Farrell said he lost the key to the front door before September 1988, although he retained a key to the downstairs security door. Police later recovered both keys, with the front door key found in the car of one of Farrell's friends. The suggestion that Farrell had lost this key was supported by evidence given by the occupants, the Rice sisters.

There was no evidence that the three accused, with Houghton, Pettingill and Ryan, had been in the flat that night, Ross said. There were no dirty coffee cups, no signs of four or more hours of occupation. 'It defies ordinary common sense that there would have been no fingerprint left by those men who were there for so long. It's just not possible. No coffee cups, no smell of habitation.' (Police raided the flat about two weeks after the murders. Fingerprints can survive for several months.) There was also no sign that the flat had been cleaned up, to remove fingerprints or other signs of use.

According to Ryan, Farrell was the only one who ran back to the flat after the shootings, yet, asked Ross, why did he not flee with the others?

Ryan said Farrell had a change of clothes at the flat, which he used after the killings. But Belinda Rice said Farrell had no clothes at her flat. Said Ross: 'If he had no clothes there at the flat then the further account Jason gives of how he [Farrell] changed and so on, and changing blood-stained clothing, is likewise in doubt.

'The next question is why did they leave the flat in broad daylight rather than leave the flat in the dark hours when one would have thought the night would have shielded their departure ... It beggars rational explanation that Anthony Farrell and Jason Ryan, in the knowledge that the crime had been committed, should walk down Punt Road, Anthony Farrell carrying a bag containing blood-stained clothing, when all reports tend to indicate that the whole area was abuzz with police.'

Ross pointed to other problems with Ryan's story. The taxi driver who supposedly picked up Ryan and Farrell that morning and then drove them to Vicki Brooks' flat in Davies Street could not be found, despite extensive police inquiries. Farrell had run out of money at the Stockade Hotel, so how could he pay for the taxi fare? And the couple who, according to the Crown case, took Farrell and Ryan to Gordon Grove from the hotel on the night of the murders could not remember doing so.

The fact that Ryan was a known police informer also presented problems, Ross said. 'Would Trevor Pettingill, whom he had lagged, have included him? Would Jedd Houghton, who certainly is said to have expressed a hatred for him, have included him? On his own story he was distrusted and mistrusted so much — this is on his present story

— that he was not let into the plan and he was not invited to participate in the main purpose of the exercise. In fact he was precluded from doing so. If that is so, why was he even there? We say he was there, on his own story, to guard a flat in which no clues have been left and to which none of the main participants was returning. That no one was coming back, and Jason was on guard. That's the Crown case. So all this non-action of Jason was to cost the participants, on one version of his story, $500 for his silence. We say the proposition about all this is quite incredible.'

Anthony Farrell, said Ross, was charged on 1 November 1988 on the basis of a video 're-enactment' that was a tissue of lies. Said Ross: 'It's fortunate perhaps, fortunate for [Emmanuel] Alexandridis, that Jason Ryan didn't attribute to him a leading part. If he had, the police would have gone off, no doubt, half-cocked with him and charged him like they charged Anthony Farrell ... based on a lying account given by Jason Ryan.'

During the committal hearing, other witnesses against the accused were closely grilled. Among them were two prison inmates who told police they overheard Victor Peirce making a number of 'confessions'. The prisoners, Michael Warner and Harold Martin, both had convictions for crimes involving dishonesty.

Warner had spent 12 years in jail, on and off, in the 19 years between 1969 and the Walsh Street shootings. At the time of the murders he was serving a four-year term for passing $3000 in valueless cheques. Warner said while he was in prison he discussed the shootings with Keith Faure and Peter Allen, Victor Peirce's brother. They told Warner that a meeting took place at 86 Chestnut Street before the murders.

Warner also said he saw Peirce two days after Anthony Farrell was charged with the murders and Peirce was worried because Farrell knew something. According to Warner, Peirce then said he was involved in the shootings.

The credibility of witnesses from within the jail system is always a problem, especially if, as in this case, both prisoners were removed from prison and put into the protection of police 'safe houses'. Both were also conmen. Their motives in making the statements was rigorously examined and their tarnished pasts reviewed to the detriment of the credibility of their evidence. The latter was especially apparent in the case of Harold Martin.

Aged 60, and with a criminal record of more than 400 convictions stretching back to 1950, Martin said he first knew Victor Pierce as a teenager. Martin said Peirce talked to him several times in prison and told him he was not worried about the Hefti murder because he had more on his plate; that he was worried about Jason Ryan; and that he was relieved Jedd Houghton was dead because he was a weak link. Martin said that soon after Wendy Peirce went into police protection, Peirce said: 'If I get my fucking hands on her, I'd rip her fucking head off and rip her up piece for piece. It'd nearly be worth getting convicted of.' Martin's credibility, however, was never strong.

During cross-examination by Victor Peirce's counsel, Geoff Flatman, Martin was asked about his convictions, most for dishonesty, and the false names he used over the years.

Flatman: Cecil Charles Cook?
Martin: That's a new one.
Flatman: You used it?
Martin: No, I don't think I did.
Flatman: You wouldn't use it ...
Martin: I think they've pulled that one out of the fire somewhere. I don't think I ever remember using it. Not Cecil. You've got to pull the line on Cecil.
Flatman: No, I can understand your reticence. H. Gordon Smith?
Martin: Jesus, I was going bad that day — Smith.
Flatman: H. Gordon Smith. Have you ever used that name?
Martin: Smith?
Flatman: Gordon Smythe, I'm sorry. Ever used the name Gordon Smythe?
Martin: You'd credit me with something better with Smith, wouldn't you? Honestly.
Flatman: Well, Smythe is pretty good.
Martin: Yes, that's a bit different, yes.
Flatman: Did you use that?
Martin: Probably, yes.

The credibility of a third witness from inside the jail appeared better, but was damaged at the trial. Lindsay Rountree, whose wife warned Victor Peirce that police were planning to kill him two days before Graeme Jensen was shot, testified that Peirce and Jensen tried to recruit him to form a pact to kill two police officers each time a criminal associate was shot.

Rountree said the plan came after the fatal shooting by police of Frank Valastro in mid-June 1987. Valastro, a short man in his mid-30s, had convictions for rape and armed robbery and, like many experienced armed robbers, had moved into the drug trade, dealing at a wholesale level in heroin and cocaine. (Indeed, his career is otherwise remarkable in that it marked the first reliable link with Colombian cocaine cartels in Australia. His story is told in *Untold Violence*.) He was also dealing in guns.

A two-pronged police investigation ended with his East Bentleigh house being raided by a four-man team from the special operations group. According to one officer, Valastro saw the police, reached into the front of his jeans, produced a pistol and aimed it at the raiders. The policeman fired one shotgun blast that hit Valastro in the shoulder. One pellet hit an artery and Valasto died of blood loss. It was later established that Valastro's gun was faulty and could not have fired a shot.

Rountree said two months after Valastro's death — when he and Peirce were not in jail — Peirce approached him and asked if he wanted to form a pact. 'This was to have been a crew and if the police were going to start killing crooks then we would kill two police for every one crook that was shot. I told Victor I did not want to be involved in this,' Rountree explained.

About six months later, in February or March 1988, Rountree said he was again approached about forming a pact, this time by Graeme Jensen. 'He asked me to form a pact with him and Victor about the same thing Victor had asked me about before. I said no. That was the last time anything was ever mentioned to me about taking two out for one.'

Rountree was arrested as a result of Operation No Name for The Summer Hold-Up several days before Graeme Jensen was shot dead. He was refused bail and was therefore in custody when Constables Damian Eyre and Steven Tynan were shot dead at Walsh Street.

Rountree said that in Pentridge he saw Peirce a number of times. On one occasion Peirce told him that Jason and Tony [Farrell] were present at Walsh Street. 'He was worried because Jason knew who had pulled the trigger, that it was Victor and Jedd. He was worried about what Jason had said to the police in regard to Walsh Street.' Rountree told police that another inmate, Keith Faure, was present when the conversation took place.

'I don't believe what they did was right. If they wanted to do something about Graeme Jensen being shot, then they should have gone after the police that actually shot him. If they had done that it may have thrown a different light on it as far as a lot of people are concerned. There are a lot of people who don't agree with just picking two out at random and letting them have it.'

Rountree denied seeking a lower sentence on the armed robbery charge he faced when he spoke to police about Peirce's 'confession'. At the trial he maintained no such discussions took place. His credibility, and motives for volunteering the Walsh Street information, were thus thrown into doubt when a tape-recording of him discussing his sentence with detectives was played to the court during the trial.

During the committal, several prosecution witnesses failed to give evidence as the prosection hoped. Emmanuel Alexandridis, who had told police he went home drunk by himself on the night of the killings, told the court he was bashed by detectives during his interviews and that he in fact spent the night with Anthony Farrell at Vicki Brooks' flat in Davies Street. Matthew Murphy, the friend of Farrell who the Crown said dropped off Farrell and Ryan at the Gordon Grove flat on the night of the killings, retreated from his statement. When he entered the witness box, Murphy said his memory of that night — and of the statement — was gone because he had suffered brain damage as a result of a car crash. His girlfriend, Tracey Graupner, who was driving Murphy's car on the night of the murders, had told police she remembered driving along Punt Road [off which Gordon Grove runs]. In the witness box, she said she remembered nothing of the evening.

Others gave evidence that corresponded with their statements to police, among them Vicki Brooks, Jason Ryan's mother, who witnessed much of the activity at her Davies Street flat on the afternoon of Graeme Jensen's death.

For the prosecution, however, Wendy Peirce was the jewel in the Crown case. In the lead-up to her appearance, police were uncertain whether she would give evidence. The prosecutor, Allen Bowles, said that before entering the witness box she was uptight and nervous. 'I was a very happy person when she started to fire up in the witness box and answer questions,' said Bowles.

And fire she did. Her cross-examination took several days and was highlighted by a series of clashes with her husband's barrister, Geoff Flatman. One such exchange followed a series of questions relating to Mrs Peirce's decision to give evidence against her husband. Flatman was mid-way through a question when prosecutor Allen Bowles, interrupted:

Bowles: Your Worship, she has answered this on numerous occasions.
Magistrate: Yes. Mr Flatman?
Flatman: Perhaps Mr Bowles would be kind enough to explain what the answer means. I do not understand it.
Peirce: Well, you're not listening clearly.

Magistrate:	Next question.
Flatman:	I will try to listen, Mrs Peirce …

There were more such exchanges during Wendy Peirce's appearance in the witness box. Her testimony covered a range of subjects: her affair with Graeme Jensen; intimate details of the Pettingill family; her motives for entering police protection; and the murders of Victor Gouroff, Helga Wagnegg, Greg Pasche, Anton Kenny and Wayne Stanhope. In the months leading up to the committal, she had twice led police to a site in a National Park where she said Stanhope's body was buried. A search failed to find Stanhope's remains, although police found a belt-buckle, part of a shoe and a piece of material similar to that of the jacket Stanhope was wearing on the night he disappeared. Park rangers told police that human remains, if only partly buried as suggested, would have been eaten and removed by animals, including the wild pigs in the park.

Mrs Peirce also told the court she had given false alibis for Victor in the past. On one occasion, when she was pregnant, her husband was seeking bail on drug trafficking charges in the Supreme Court. 'I passed urine to say the water had broken, so Kathy [Pettingill] rushed me into the hospital in a taxi and I stayed overnight and in the end Justice Gobbo gave Victor bail …'

The most damning aspects of Mrs Peirce's testimony were a 'confession' her husband made to her after the police murders, his 'ownership' of a single-barrelled sawn-off pump-action shotgun and his 'involvement' in a series of armed robberies, including some of those of The Flemington Crew.

During her interviews with police, Mrs Peirce was shown bank security photographs of the robberies committed by The Flemington Crew. She studied the pictures and named the bandits. They included, in different hold-ups, her husband Victor, Graeme Jensen, Jedd Houghton and Peter McEvoy. Asked how she recognised each particpiant, Mrs Peirce cited their clothing and shoes, their features (the bandits wore balaclavas or stocking masks) and their stance. She said she had seen her husband and Jensen wearing balaclavas at 86 Chestnut Street as a joke, so she knew what they looked like wearing one.

She also told detectives that her husband told her when he was planning robberies. She was aware when he was conducting surveillance on prospective targets. And she knew when he completed a job, because he came home with money.

She said she saw her husband with a shotgun twice, once when he was sawing off the barrel in a shed. She said she talked to Victor as the barrel was sawn off. When he finished the job he turned to her and, using her nickname, said: 'This will be a beauty, Witch.'

Mrs Peirce said on the night of the police murders, when she, Victor and the children went to a motel at Tullamarine, Victor left around 11.30 pm. 'Victor said, "Don't worry, I won't be late. I'm going to kill the jacks that knocked Graeme".' He returned about 7.30 am.

Said Mrs Peirce: 'He said to me, "They're dead." They killed two jacks. I said to him: "Who did you do it with?" He said, "Jedd and Macca." I said: "Good one." I said: "Was it the armed robbery squad?" He said, "No, two policemen in South Yarra".'

The next morning, when the Peirce family left the motel, news of the shootings came across the radio. Said Mrs Peirce: 'Victor said: "Right whack", and I laughed.'

The evidence at the committal hearing, which ended after 59 sitting days, was enough for the magistrate, Hugh Adams, to commit the three to stand trial in the Supreme Court for murder. He said it was up to the Director of Public Prosecutions to decide whether there was enough evidence to lay charges against Trevor Pettingill, named by Jason Ryan as one of the men who left the Gordon Grove flat on the night of the killings. It was nearly five months later that the DPP laid murder charges against Pettingill and directed him to stand trial without a committal hearing.

It was over to a jury to hear the evidence and make a final decision.

19
Trial by Jury

'As an uncle, I've had to put up with his lies for many years.'

Trevor Pettingill on Jason Ryan

As the Walsh Street committal continued in court number three, around the corner and up the stairs a related hearing took place. In January 1990, papers were processed authorising the extradition from Malta of car thief Stephen Saliba.

Saliba certainly offered enormous potential to investigators. In Malta six months earlier, he told police he helped steal a car used in one bank robbery by The Flemington Crew. He acknowledged that the car used at the Oak Park bank robbery, in which the KTG shotgun was fired, was parked around the corner from his house only hours before the hold-up.

Saliba had rejected Detective Sprague's overtures to return to Australia voluntarily, saying he was scared of the 'heavy' people in Melbourne; he would not name names without an indemnity. But this was impossible for Sprague to offer. In Victoria, only the Director of Public Prosecutions can grant indemnities, and will do so only on seeing the charges and the evidence. To indemnify someone before knowing what they might say is just not done.

Detectives Sprague and McLaren felt Saliba was close to 'rolling' and telling what he knew: if they brought him back there was a good chance he would talk. He could then be put into police protection. Therefore they sought the extradition, which was approved in Victoria and by the Federal Government, which authorises all overseas extraditions. All that was needed was the go-ahead to get him. It never came.

The reason why Saliba was not extradited is still not clear to me, despite many attempts to find a definitive account. It appears the decision was made by the prosecutor in the Walsh Street case, Jim Morrissey, based on advice from Detective Noonan. Despite a request for the written report that tendered the advice, Detective Noonan would not show me its contents, saying it was confidential. He said that had Saliba been extradited and given police details of The Flemington Crew, his evidence could not have been used in court for legal reasons. 'There's other things in there you obviously don't know about, and I'm not going to go into them,' Noonan told me. Morrissey would not comment on any aspect of the Walsh Street case. The only clue he offered was reported in *The Sunday Age*. Asked why Saliba was not extradited, he said: 'I'm glad of your advice that Mr Saliba was a key witness and that he was not brought back from Malta. But I have no comment to make on a thing like that except you had better check your facts, all right?'

For Detective Sprague, however, the reasons why the extradition was not pursued remain puzzling and unclear. Sprague said he was never asked for his advice on the extradition he helped prepare. Nor was he given a reason why Saliba was not brought back.

Certainly the Saliba case involved a great deal of hypothesis, not the least of which was the likelihood of him 'rolling' on his return to Melbourne. It also depended on successfully fighting the extradition in Malta, and then bringing him back before the Walsh Street trial finished. And *if* he was extradited, Saliba may well have come back and said nothing. He may have said he delivered a car to Graeme Jensen and Jedd Houghton — and with both men dead, the Crown case would have advanced no further. Had he got to court, stepped into the witness box and changed his story, he may have seriously damaged the Crown case presented to a jury. The Saliba case leaves a lot of 'ifs', although one aspect is obvious: it deepened the chasm between the 'A Team' and the 'B Team'.

On 21 January 1991, Wendy Peirce appeared in the Supreme Court in a pre-trial hearing. The judge who heard the Walsh Street case, Justice Frank Vincent, presided, with the prosecution, legal counsel for the defence and the four accused present. The hearing, known as a *voire-dire*, was to test the admissibility of evidence that Mrs Peirce was to give, to establish whether it could be used. In the witness box, she was asked to identify the people in the bank security photographs of The Flemington Crew.

She said she was unable to recognise any of them, contradicting statements she had already made to police. Her answers were enough to indicate she would not be giving the evidence the Crown expected.

Later that day Mrs Peirce signed herself out of witness protection. It dealt the Crown case a severe blow — they had just lost one of their main witnesses. The jury would never hear her testimony.

Why Mrs Peirce decided not to give evidence remains a subject of deep passion among some former members of the TyEyre taskforce. The versions of what happened to her in the months leading up to the trial — and why she declined to give evidence — are sharply different. My attempts to find out which story is accurate have failed.

The simple facts are that Mrs Peirce left a safe-house in Canberra on the weekend of 12 October 1990 — the second anniversary of the Walsh Street killings — and spent several days in Melbourne at her mother's house. She then returned to police protective custody. Once back, Detective Noonan told her she would be conducting all pre-trial preparation (a routine procedure for major witnesses, essentially recapping the evidence she would give) under his command with another detective.

Either before or after Wendy Peirce left Canberra, Detectives Sprague and McLaren — and a third detective who kept in close contact with Mrs Peirce and who conducted some of the initial video interviews — were told that Mrs Peirce would have her pre-trial preparation with other police, and not them. Several weeks earlier, these three police were also told they were not to contact another witness, Shane Richards, who would now deal exclusively with Detective Noonan and his officers.

The decision, which meant Wendy Peirce would not prepare for the trial with the detectives who did the majority of the original interviews, still rankles Detective Sprague. 'I still feel — and I know McLaren feels — that if she'd been left with us to deal with, she would have gone through with it all right.' Several other police support this view. It is rejected by other police, including Detective Noonan.

For legal reasons it is not possible to thoroughly canvass this aspect of the Walsh Street case. After the Walsh Street trial finished, Mrs Peirce gave media interviews explaining her position. She told the *Sun-Herald* that she never intended to testify against her husband. 'Why would I tell them something that wasn't true?' She told *Age* reporter Paul Conroy that police had tried to fabricate evidence against her husband. 'They were trying to make me tell lies,' she said.

For the Crown, the *voire-dire* hearing of Wendy Peirce — less than three weeks before the trial opened — meant she was now a 'hostile witness' and could not be called to the witness box as she was now, in the Crown's view of events, not a witness of truth. Although the defence could have called her, it chose not to for an obvious tactical reason. If she appeared as a defence witness — say, to provide alibi testimony for her husband — then the Crown would be able to cross-examine her and quesion her about the evidence she had earlier given police. Clearly, the defence did not want the jury to hear this material.

The non-appearance of Wendy Peirce meant the defence could focus its attack on Jason Ryan. This was done with vigor, pursuing the series of lies he told police and playing the videotapes of the two 're-enactments' to the jury.

For the jury, Jason Ryan's account of the night in South Yarra was the key to any decision. Prosecutor Morrissey described Ryan as a man who had 'come from the inside' to give his version of events. But under rules of evidence, little of Ryan's family history — stories about growing up with his Uncle Victor and Uncle Trevor and the guns, drugs, women and violence — could be used in evidence because it might prejudicially affect the fair trials of Victor Peirce and Trevor Pettingill. So Ryan's distrust and fear of police, fostered in his formative years with his Uncle Dennis, were only partially explained. The Crown could only hope that the jury could read between the lines in an attempt to understand its star witness.

Also attacked was Jason's mother, Vicki Brooks. From the first interview with police following the murders, she was remarkably candid considering the non-cooperative attitude normally adopted by her family's members. Yet it took her two years to tell detectives she was holding something back — that Peter McEvoy told her the day after the murders that he was one of those who killed Damian Eyre and Steven Tynan, saying: 'They wanted an out-and-out war, now they've got one.' Brooks said that several times in the following weeks McEvoy threatened her life.

When she made this statement Brooks had left her Brunswick flat and settled in a house in another part of Melbourne. She had found a job, new friends and had little contact with her family. Police offered her support in her new life and kept in close touch. Shortly before the trial she moved into the witness protection program. The defence seized on the big lapse in time before she mentioned the McEvoy threat. A senior solicitor with Legal Aid, Ernie Burrows, became a surprise witness for the defence. He said Vicki Brooks told him between 1988 and 1990 that she was being pressured by police to tell them that McEvoy said certain things to her about the police murders. Burrows said she told him McEvoy said nothing to her — and that she was scared of Detective John Noonan.

After hearing the evidence of Ernie Burrows, Vicki Brooks said it was untrue and that she did not speak to him about McEvoy at all. Detective Noonan later told the jury that he did not harrass Brooks, nor did he know of any police officer who put pressure on her. To say police pressured Brooks to say something incriminating against McEvoy was 'a straight-out lie', Detective Noonan said.

The two prison witnesses with convictions for dishonesty, who were strongly attacked at the committal, were further discredited at the trial to the point where prosecutor Jim Morrissey told the jury in his summing up that the Crown would not rely on their evidence. Lindsay Rountree, the convicted armed robber who was closely questioned at the committal, was again asked if he sought any favors for giving evidence. He again denied this. The defence then played a tape of him discussing his armed robbery sentence with a detective from the TyEyre taskforce and asking about a shorter jail term.

For the police who gave evidence, there was also a surprise. At the committal hearing their evidence was tested in detail and at length. Some spent days in the witness box. Before the jury, however, their appearances were brief, as if there was a defence strategy to keep the police in the witness box for as short a time as possible.

Some of the Crown's evidence also became clouded in doubt. The woman who saw two men in Punt Road shortly after the shootings, a panel van screech to a halt, pick up at least one of the men and drive away quickly, said her memory was no longer clear. It was possible, she told the jury, that one of the men was carrying not, as the Crown suggested, a weapon, but a beer bottle. They could have been coming from a party. The time of her sighting was not certain — it could have been as the ambulance arrived, she said, which was 15 minutes after the shootings. The panel van played an integral part in Crown's scenario that five men were in Walsh Street — and this testimony did not help enforce its case.

Each of the four accused chose to give unsworn evidence to the jury. In effect, this meant they were asked a series of questions by their own legal counsel, which they answered. They could not be cross-examined by the Crown.

Unsworn evidence was one of three choices each man had as part of his defence: he could give sworn evidence and thus be subject to cross-examination; he could give unsworn evidence, which still leaves the accused open to a perjury prosecution if lies are told; or he could remain silent, thus leaving the Crown to prove its case without any input from the defendant.

After the verdicts were handed down, there was strong criticism about the use of unsworn evidence. To me, this was a nonsense. While there is a good argument for abolishing its use, holding up unsworn evidence in this case as a bad example of its use, or an example of why it should be abolished, sounded like the complaints of a poor loser. The law, after all, is a game governed by rules — some things can be done, others can't. In an adversarial system, each side is trying to win. The rules are set when each side begins the battle and, in this case, like hundreds of others, police knew the ground-rules when it began. To complain afterwards about the rules in a specific case is ridiculous. What made the value of this criticism more dubious was a frequent reference by critics of the need to abolish unsworn statements. These were all but abolished in 1986 and can only be used now when a defendant does not have legal representation and so cannot give unsworn evidence because he does not have a barrister to question him. It is relevant to note that a judge is required to tell a jury before unsworn evidence is given, and again during his summing up, that the accused had three choices — silence, unsworn evidence or sworn evidence — and that unsworn evidence is not tested by cross-examination. Unsworn evidence is also liable for perjury, which carries a maximum 15-year penalty.

In their question-and-answer evidence, each man denied any participation in the Walsh Street shooting. Peter McEvoy said he saw Jedd Houghton on the night of the killings at Graeme Jensen's sister's flat. He then left alone to visit a friend in North Fitzroy, before going back to Vicki Brooks' flat in Brunswick where he slept the night. He was up early on the morning of the murders and visited his friend in North Fitzroy again. He then spent some time doing other jobs before going back to the flat later that morning. 'At the time that two police officers met their death I was asleep in Davies Street, Brunswick,' McEvoy told the jury.

Trevor Pettingill said he spent the night at his flat in North Fitzroy with his *de facto* wife and her sister. On the afternoon before the killings he obtained some tablets that he took. They made him drowsy and he spent the whole night asleep. Shane Richards, a Crown witness who gave evidence that Pettingill 'confessed' his involvement in the toilet of a hotel, was not telling the truth, Pettingill said. Richards had said Pettingill displayed stab marks on his legs that were inflicted when he was kidnapped. Pettingill, standing in the body of the court, told the jury: 'I have worn my shorts into court today and if anybody would like to look I have got no stab wounds whatsoever to any leg.' As for Jason Ryan's evidence, Pettingill said: 'As an uncle, I've had to put up with his lies for many years.'

Anthony Farrell gave the most unsworn evidence, explaining his relationship with his girlfriend Belinda Rice and events leading up to the night of the murders. He said after leaving the Stockade Hotel that night he took a taxi with Jason Ryan and Emmanuel Alexandridis to Davies Street, Brunswick, where Vicki Brooks let the three of them in. Farrell said he thought McEvoy was also at the flat. Farrell said he was stoned and drunk and fell asleep on the couch watching television.

Victor Peirce told the jury that he had not discussed any matters in relation to Walsh Street with Lindsay Rountree while he was in jail. Peirce said the two other prisoners, whose evidence the Crown later said it would not rely on, were unknown to him. He said he did not speak to them in prison and only knew them from their court appearances. 'It's common knowledge in jail that there have been cases where prisoners have come to court and given false evidence ... that people have confessed to them, when in actual fact they haven't.' Peirce said he was asleep in a Tullamarine motel room with his wife and children at the time of the murders. His wife, Wendy, was not being called on his behalf, he said, 'because she's an emotional mess'.

After seven weeks, a shorter trial than many expected — partly because Wendy Peirce had failed to appear — the jury was sent to consider its verdict. In a tactical sense, the trial had gone almost perfectly for the defence. For the Crown, things began to go wrong before the jury was sworn in, when Wendy Peirce became a hostile witness. Mr Justice Vincent's handling of the trial was regarded by all camps as exemplary and extremely fair.

The evidence against each of the accused needed to be dealt with individually, rather than seeing the four men as a group. The jury needed to establish whether the Crown proved its case beyond reasonable doubt. If such a doubt remained, the jury had to find the accused not guilty. If there was no reasonable doubt about the evidence, then it would return a guilty verdict.

The basis of the jury's decision can only be subject to speculation. Victorian law prohibits soliciting, obtaining or publishing statements about jury deliberations. Judging by the evidence, however, Jason Ryan's testimony must have been central to any decision. On the morning of Tuesday 26 March 1991, after six days considering the evidence, the all-male jury returned and said it had reached a verdict. The court was packed as the foreman rose.

20
Unanswered Questions

'It was a conspiracy to clean up the whole family.'

Victor Peirce, March 1991

As the foreman of the 12-man jury announced the four 'Not Guilty' verdicts, detectives looked on, stunned. Some held their heads in their hands. In the dock, the four accused hugged one another. In the body of the court, relatives of the four accused leapt to their feet, cheering and clapping. It was 895 days since one of the most extraordinary cases in Australia's criminal history began. It was now over.

Initial reactions were predictable. Inside the court, Victor Peirce asked the presiding judge, Frank Vincent, if he could say something. Vincent agreed. Said Peirce: 'Now that I have been proved not guilty, I would like to demand an inquiry into Mr Noonan's investigation and the way he conducted the investigation.'

'We want an inquiry,' shouted Peter McEvoy as he was taken away by prison staff. In a television interview later that day, Trevor Pettingill and Anthony Farrell also demanded an inquiry. All four men said they feared being killed by police.

Inside the corridor of the court, Kath Pettingill thanked the defence barristers for their work. She then turned and said: 'I didn't hear the press say *hip hip hooray* for the boys. You're very biased, you're very biased.'

Outside the court, Detective Noonan was confronted by a battery of television cameras and reporters as he walked from the building. As he strode across Lonsdale Street to a car, a reporter asked what he thought of the decision. 'Well, obviously I don't agree with it, but that's our legal system.' Detective Noonan continued walking.

On the courthouse steps, Constable Steven Tynan's parents and younger sister were asked about the verdict. Tynan's mother, Wendy, spoke for the family. 'It makes you feel very empty. I just hope there will be a bit of a public outcry. It's the only voice we have got left ... Everyone pays for their deeds and now time will tell. We think in a higher justice they will get what they deserved.' Damian Eyre's parents did not attend the court.

The protected Crown witnesses who had given evidence were in a secret high-security area in the Russell Street police station when the news came through. Several began crying. Across all police radio channels operators broadcast: 'Announcement all units. The verdict in the Walsh Street trial was all four not guilty, repeat not guilty. All units are warned, keep yourselves in control.'

Shortly after the verdict, while Peirce and McEvoy were sent back to Pentridge on other charges (and released on bail a few weeks later), Trevor Pettingill and Anthony Farrell were discharged from custody — released by prison officers at the courthouse. They stumbled out of the court looking dazed. Farrell's mother and Kath Pettingill led the pair through a crowd of cameramen and journalists to a waiting car, driven by *A Current Affair* journalist Martin King, and the acquitted men were whisked away. The subsequent interview at a South Yarra rental unit was buoyant. They drank wine, laughed, joked and those present — including Pettingill's *de facto* wife Debbie Young — hugged one another. The contrast to the post-trial drinks on the 14th floor of the St Kilda Road police building, a gathering that at best resembled a wake, could not have been greater.

The official police position was summed up by the chief commissioner, Kel Glare, who said: 'The jury's verdict is in, the case is closed.'

Detective Noonan took this view further in a newspaper interview hours after the verdict. 'The result was definitely one of disbelief and total disappointment ... The jury has found them not guilty. They didn't find them innocent.' On the acquitted men's calls for an inquiry, Detective Noonan said: 'That's just rubbish and any inquiry that anyone wanted to start would be welcomed by us.'

That welcome may need to be extended. An inquiry appears certain, taking the form of an inquest on the deaths of Damian Eyre and Steven Tynan by the Coroner, Hal Hallenstein. Whether it covers the problems experienced within the taskforce, Stephen Saliba's extradition, Wendy Peirce's decision not to give evidence and the accused's complaints about the inquiry, remain to be seen.

One group that was unrepresented after the trial was the jury. Unable by law to voice the reasons for their decision, jurors were left to hear the comments of upset police, and read newspaper articles and watch television reports on evidence they never heard. Jason Ryan's past was explored; the criminal history of the family was detailed; and extracts of Wendy Peirce's video interviews were published and broadcast. The inference was that the jury made a mistake.

My own conclusion is that the jury was hard done by. While police were confident of convictions shortly before the jury returned — the unsourced and clearly incorrect rumor circulating among police was that three had been found guilty and the jury was still debating on Trevor Pettingill — the 12 men picked from members of the public could only base their decisions on what they saw and heard in the Supreme Court over seven weeks. On the evidence the jury was presented with there was room for a reasonable doubt — and if a jury has a reasonable doubt about the guilt of an accused person, it must acquit them. Obviously the decision was not easy, testified to by the time it took the jury to reach it.

For some police, the jury takes the blame for the result. This is nonsense. The simple fact is the Crown case presented to the court was not strong enough to secure a conviction.

In a way this is further enforced by private conversations I have had with TyEyre detectives while researching this book. Several have expressed doubt about the accuracy of Jason Ryan's 'final version' of events on the night of the murders. And it was Ryan that probably held the key to the jury's decision. If the jury doubted his credibility *or* his story, then they needed to look elsewhere for compelling signs of proof. And the way the defence conducted its case, those signs were not strongly represented.

The doubts of police range from the belief that Ryan is still holding something back, that his role is distorted, to the feeling — by a number of police — that the version is still far from the truth. The doubts expressed are similar to those used by defence counsel, among them: Why would someone like Victor Peirce allow Ryan to become involved? Why would he guard an empty flat? Where is the taxi driver who supposedly drove him and Farrell to Brunswick? Extrapolating this view, some also question the involvement of Farrell and Pettingill. They wonder if Gary Abdallah had some involvement, especially considering that Wendy Peirce said her husband whispered in her ear in prison that the 'shooters' were himself, Jedd Houghton and Abdallah. There is also the question of why, according to statements made by

Wendy Peirce to police, her husband made no mention in numerous conversations with her about the 'involvement' of either Jason Ryan or Anthony Farrell.

It must be said too, that other TyEyre police believe Ryan's account completely. But only the acquitted men and Ryan himself know the truth, and none is going to change his story. Even though an acquitted person can never be tried again for the same offence, admitting at a later date to involvement in a crime can leave that person open for a perjury prosecution, a charge that carries a maximum 15-year jail term.

Obviously Ryan was a key to the Crown case and he needed to be shown as a credible witness to the jury. On the way this was handled, Detective Noonan said: 'I would have done it differently. But I'm not going to criticise the way the prosecutor did it. He had a good brief [of evidence] and presented a good case. But certainly it could have been presented in a different manner and probably in hindsight he may agree that he underestimated the jury. He's got an unusual way of speaking, Morrissey [Jim Morrissey, the Crown prosecutor]. He's a very clever man, but he expects other people to pick up his vibes. Him and the judge related quite well, but the judge doesn't make the decisions, it's the jury.'

So what has been learnt from the Walsh Street case? For police, there are many lessons. One is that, considering the size of the Walsh Street inquiry, it went remarkably well. It was the biggest ever conducted by the Victoria Police and, for several months, involved hundreds of police working on various aspects. The enormous resources and amounts of money that went into it strained various aspects of the department, and sometimes things went askew, yet for the most part things held together.

Some, naturally, didn't. Listening devices were readily discovered by bug-detectors — this comes down to cheap devices that can be upgraded, money willing. Phone tapping equipment did not always work. But as it was the first time the Victoria Police legally tapped telephones — and it was using borrowed, second-hand equipment for some of the time — the overall performance was good. The determination and sheer hard work of taskforce detectives and others associated with the case can only be admired.

Perhaps most importantly, police realise the need to have a balanced taskforce. The situation John Noonan and David Sprague found themselves in — the same rank with only junior ranking detectives below them and no senior sergeants and only one sergeant in between — is unlikely to repeat itself in the near future. Senior police are also more likely to look at the compatability of police who work closely together, to avoid the dramatic break-up of the TyEyre taskforce that left some detectives concentrating on the internal ructions rather than the inquiry itself.

Lessons are there to be learnt, although Detective Noonan believes the police department is not willing to listen to his experiences. In mid-1990 he prepared a 30-page report on problems the taskforce had experienced that he intended to use as the basis of a two-day debriefing for TyEyre members. But senior police blocked the plan and held a debriefing that Detective Noonan described as pointless. Late in 1991 he was preparing a more comprehensive report on his experiences at the taskforce and the need to remedy the problems he encountered.

'Like most major organisations they [the police force] don't like to think they've got people in positions of authority — positions where it counts — who are incompetent or who shouldn't be there; or that they've made so many repeated mistakes over a period of time; or that they've been running in a particular way for many, many years and taking absolutely no notice of people who try to say what they are doing is wrong, or should be enhanced or corrected in some way, which is exactly the way they have done it for so many years now. And that's all going to be pointed out to them in no uncertain terms. Hopefully they'll learn something out of it,' Detective Noonan said.

'Constructive criticism is obviously the name of the game and that's the way it will be done. Personalities aside, it will be constructive criticism. But it still won't be accepted in the light that it should be. It's there to improve things and make sure we don't make the same mistakes again.'

Detective Noonan said part of the problem was that the department needed to accept that it had a problem. 'They're not asking for ways of helping or improving. It's like they're waiting for a big cannon to be fired at them. They're not welcoming constructive criticism. They're going to put up with it if and when I supply them with this report. It's not, "We look forward to hearing from you", or, "We look forward to your ideas on how things can improve". It's never ever been looked at, never ever been asked. It is just waiting for that dreaded arsehole [himself] to give us a payout on things that happened. They're aware of most of them, 75 per cent of them, and they are embarrassed about what they've done. But at the same time they'll be saying, "Why should he do that? Why should he come and bring all that up now? It's happened, there's nothing we can do about it." What they forget is something can be done about it to ensure that it's not going to happen again.'

Perhaps it will take another incident of the magnitude of Walsh Street — and an inquiry of this size — to see whether many of these problems were unique to TyEyre, or whether they will be repeated.

Certainly senior police acknowledge that witness protection was an area that experienced difficulties and needs to improve. While the witnesses were by no means the first the Victoria Police has guarded, the number for one trial — six, excluding Wendy Peirce — was a record. Mistakes were made with witnesses, detectives broke rules of the program (visiting a witness at a safe-house, which is forbidden for security reasons), witnesses complained about their treatment, and during the Walsh Street inquiry a number 'escaped' from their minders. There was also the incident in which police raided a supposed safe-house, narrowly avoiding a bloody shootout.

And after the trial, some witness also encountered problems. Shane Richards, to whom Trevor Pettingill allegedly confessed his involvement in the police murders, found it hard to settle down. Police arranged for Richards to live in a bungalow at Noble Park, in Melbourne's south-eastern suburbs, but the former Crown witness felt isolated and threatened: he slept with knives under the bed and would only go out at night. After some weeks, police provided Richards with a bank account containing $9500, part of a package that included a birth certificate, Medicare card, picture-identification card and bank account in a new name.

Richards left the bungalow at Noble Park, despite three months rent being paid on it, and travelled to the western Victorian town of Warrnambool where he tried to get work, but failed. He lived in rented rooms and motels. Then the money began to disappear. Richards again tried for work — a cleaning job and then a house painter. Each time he used references supplied and supported by the police: both job applications failed.

Richards was into his last $1000 when he caught the *Abel Tasman* ferry from Melbourne to Tasmania. In a small town about 40 kilometres from Launceston he purchased a .22 rifle. Tasmania's gun laws do not require identification or a shooter's licence before someone can buy a firearm: guns can be freely bought over the counter.

The rifle cost $250, and Richards returned with it to Melbourne, believing the weapon offered the best protection against any threat. But his girlfriend found the gun and called police, who raided the Hawthorn boarding house where Richards was staying. Richards was charged with possession of a rifle and a silencer: he failed to attend a subsequent court hearing and a warrant was issued for his arrest.

Then the money ran out. Less than six months after the Walsh Street trial, one of the Crown's protected witnesses began sleeping at Salvation Army hostels, still searching for work. In an interview with Frank McGuire of the ABC television's *7.30 Report*, Richards said he could never recommend entering the witness protection program. 'I haven't got much of a future, really. My whole life's completely wrecked.'

Richards said police threatened him and then offered him $5000 to give evidence at the Walsh Street trial. He said without the offer of money and other promises, he would not have given evidence. The offer of money is denied by police.

The problem with police offering money is that it is an inducement to give evidence and any such testimony should be inadmissible in court. It is a delicate problem for police: witnesses must know they will be protected, relocated and generally looked after, without, in effect, being offered anything before their court appearance. Richards maintains he would not have given evidence without the promise of money. It is possible that one day soon a defence lawyer will have a protected Crown witness's evidence ruled as inadmissible because of inducements.

Richards is bitter about what he was offered, and what came through. Although he says he was first offered $5000, and after the trial it was boosted to $9500, he failed to get other promised rewards: a house in the bush, plastic surgery, a job, a passport and a tax file number.

Whether any such offers were made by police is not certain, although Richards was certainly under the impression the promises would be fulfilled. This raises another problem with witness protection; detectives may encourage a witness to talk by talking about possible rewards, but in reality, detectives have little to do with the witnesses' protection, and even less with their relocation.

What witnesses expected to receive and what they actually got was not a problem unique to Shane Richards. Jason Ryan, it is believed, expected in the vicinity of $30,000 cash for his evidence, but got about $13,000.

However, the most remarkable story about relocation packages that I have come across involves convicted armed robber Lindsay Rountree. Four days before Graeme Jensen was shot and five days before the Walsh Street murders, Lindsay Rountree was arrested for his part in The Summer Hold-Up. As a result, Rountree's wife warned Victor Peirce that police were gunning for him.

Some weeks after his arrest, Rountree began talking with detectives about alleged jailhouse conversations with Victor Peirce that dealt with Walsh Street. Rountree was eventually taken from the prison system and put into protective custody, with an around-the-clock police guard. In 1989 he pleaded guilty to his involvement in The Summer Hold-Up and was sentenced to a minimum six years jail. His driver's licence was ordered cancelled for five years.

Peirce was charged with the robbery and, in August 1991, once the Walsh Street trial had been completed, a committal hearing on The Summer Hold-Up was held. But Rountree's evidence against Peirce, who Rountree said was a fellow bandit in the raid, was never heard. As a result, the magistrate hearing the case dismissed the bank robbery charges against Victor Peirce.

And the reason Rountree didn't give evidence? According to several sources, among a number of promises made to Rountree — or promises Rountree thought were made — was that he would get a driver's licence under a new identity. Rountree considered this important in getting a job. But because of his conviction on the bank robbery charge and the court order banning him from having a licence, Rountree was told by police he would not get one. In turn, Rountree refused to help police any further or give evidence against Peirce. No licence, no evidence.

On 15 August 1991, the day The Summer Hold-Up charges were dismissed, Victor Peirce walked out of the court and told reporters: 'I knew all along I would be cleared of the charges. I have done nothing wrong.'

For some, the Walsh Street case is in the past and they are now settling down to a new life — literally. Jason Ryan, like the five other Crown witnesses, must start again with a new identity. For Ryan, he must consider himself an orphan at 20, but an orphan who knows he cannot do certain things, and must always be aware his life is in danger. There certainly is a threat to Ryan — not necessarily from those he betrayed, but from someone who may seek favors or a folk-hero status in prison by killing the 'dog' of the Pettingill family.

While he may occasionally see his mother — and that bond was not especially strong from the start — Ryan certainly has to sacrifice contact with the rest of his family. Yet whether he can resist the influence of his late Uncle Dennis is another matter. Ryan was an active criminal who has forsaken that life for three years. He is now bigger, fitter and stronger, partly due to his introduction to weight-training and fitness routines by his police minders. The change is so dramatic that he is barely recognisable as the scrawny 17-year-old who made the video 're-enactments' in Walsh Street late in 1988. His reading and writing have improved greatly as the result of correspondence courses.

But if he becomes short of money in the future, the temptation to revert to the proven methods of income — drugs and burglaries — may prove too much. My understanding is that Ryan believes he was 'shafted' by the police department when he left the witness protection program: promises he was made about setting him up in a new life fell far short of his expectations. Like the other five protected witness, how well Ryan survives, only time will tell.

The Walsh Street case may be closed, but the story is far from finished. There are more court hearings to take place on matters related to the biggest investigation ever seen in Australia. The report of the police shootings inquiry by Coroner Hal Hallenstein, covering the deaths of — among others — Graeme Jensen, Jedd Houghton and Gary Abdallah, is expected in the first half of 1992. An inquest will be held by Coroner Hallenstein into the murders of Constables Damian Eyre and Steven Tynan. Other spin-offs include an increased debate on the use of unsworn statements. Steven Tynan's mother, Wendy, has been behind a push to have juries sit behind one-way glass during trials, so they cannot be 'intimidated' by facing the accused.

For police, too, there are haunting reminders of the Walsh Street murders. One month after the trial finished, police from City West were ordered to investigate a car abandoned in the middle of Walsh Street, West Melbourne. It had been pushed into the middle of the street and one of its windows broken. It was 3.30 am. Similarities to the scene in Walsh Street, South Yarra, some two-and-a-half years before, were uncanny. No one was charged over the West Melbourne incident and there was no obvious motive or suspect. It could have been a prank, a warning or a coincidence. Like the murders of Damian Eyre and Steven Tynan, there are many unanswered questions.

. In my mind, however, there is no doubt that the two rookie policemen were killed because they were just that — police. Lured to South Yarra by an abandoned car in leafy Walsh Street, they were shot down as a payback killing by members of Melbourne's underworld for the death 13 hours earlier of Graeme Jensen. And one of the men that stood in Walsh Street waiting for police to fall into the trap was Jedd Houghton, a great friend of Jensen and a fellow armed robber. But who was with Houghton that night — and at least one more person was needed — remains unclear. Only those who were in Walsh Street that night know what happened when the two police stepped from their divisional van to examine the white Commodore. And he, she or they, are still walking free.

Index

Police Club, 66
Pollitt, Roy, 27-8
Pringle, Alan, 122-4, 127

Rice, Belinda, 80, 89, 165
Richards, Shane, 114, 174, 178, 184-5
Richardson, Jack, 25-6
Rogerson, Roger, 25
Rose, John, 14
Ross, David, 163-4
Roundtree, Lindsay, 42, 45-6, 50, 53,
    167, 176, 185-6
Roundtree, Penny, 46, 58, 65
Royal Botanic Gardens, 18
Royal Melbourne Hospital, 39
Royal Melbourne Show, 28
Russell St bombing, 62, 67
Ryan, Col, 47, 155
Ryan, Jason, 15, 28-38, 54-5, 63, 71-84,
    107-114, *passim*

Saliba, Stephen, 125-133, 172-3
Sasano, Mario, 48
7.30 Report, 185
Shabo, Brydon, 54, 79
Shepparton 10, 66
Signorotto, Peter, 124-7
Silvester, John, 67
Simon's Disco, 119
Simpson, Lindsay, 27-8
'Smith' 42-5, 53
Sprague, David, 63, 131-3, 148,
    150-160, 172, *passim*
St Vincent's Hospital, 20
Stanhope, Wayne, 31

Station Hotel, 36
Stewart, Debbie, 117
Stockade Hotel, 54, 57, 64, 73, 79, 95
Summer Hold-up, 43, 45, 46, 53, 58,
    66, 168
Sun, 96
Sun-Herald 174
Sydney 23, 25, 49

Tally Ho Boy's Home, 48
Target, 103
Taylor, Angela, 62
Tsen, Jimmy, 10
Tynan, Steven, 9-13, 66, *passim*

Valastro, Frank, 167-8
Valetta 132
Vincent, Frank, 91-2, 173, 178, 179

Wagnegg, Helga, 34
Walker, Graeme, 96
Wangaratta, 75
Ward, Vicki, 35
Warner, Michael, 166
Werner, Vaughan, 152
Wesson, Bill, 17
Widdicombe, Donna, 105
Widdicombe, Paul, 97-8, 100-105
Wilkinson, David, 11, 60-61
Williams, Alan, 22, 25-7
Wills, Glenys, 141-2, 155

Yap, Joshua, 10
Yarra River, 34, 35, 61
Young, Debbie, 56, 110, 113, 146

UNTOLD VIOLENCE
Crime in Melbourne Today
Tom Noble

'Books on Australian crime have traditionally concentrated on the organised variety . . . this one doesn't,' said one critic. Noble takes the careers of three criminals – Dennis and Peter Allen, and the strange nazi-dreamer Phillip Wilson – and looks at the main criminal industries. These include amphetamine factories, prostitution, armed robbery, car theft, burglary, gambling, the China-town rackets, and the newcomer, cocaine.

'The Bible of crime in Melbourne'
Bob Bottom

'It is a better read than most crime thrillers and has one other major bonus. It's all true.'
John Silvester, *Sun*